STORYSCAPES

PETER LANG
New York • Washington, D.C./Baltimore • Bern
Frankfurt am Main • Berlin • Brussels • Vienna • Oxford

STORYSCAPES

South African Perspectives on Literature, Space & Identity

EDITED BY
HEIN VILJOEN &
CHRIS N. VAN DER MERWE

PETER LANG
New York • Washington, D.C./Baltimore • Bern
Frankfurt am Main • Berlin • Brussels • Vienna • Oxford

Library of Congress Cataloging-in-Publication Data

Storyscapes: South African perspectives on literature,
space and identity / edited by Hein Viljoen, Chris N. van der Merwe.
p. cm.
Includes bibliographical references.
1. Afrikaans literature—History and criticism. 2. Identity
(Philosophical concept) in literature. 3. Space and time in literature.
I. Viljoen, Hendrik Marthinus. II. Van der Merwe, Chris.
PT6510.S76   839.3'609384—dc21   2003006187
ISBN 0-8204-6789-8

Bibliographic information published by Die Deutsche Bibliothek.
Die Deutsche Bibliothek lists this publication in the "Deutsche
Nationalbibliografie"; detailed bibliographic data is available
on the Internet at http://dnb.ddb.de/.

Cover design by Lisa Barfield
Cover art, *Hartland* (Heart Country, Region of your heart), by Cronjé Lemmer

The paper in this book meets the guidelines for permanence and durability
of the Committee on Production Guidelines for Book Longevity
of the Council of Library Resources.

Printed in the United States of America

Dedicated to our students through the years

Contents

Acknowledgments ix

Introduction: Learning about Space—and about Ourselves
Hein Viljoen, Minnie Lewis and Chris N. van der Merwe 1

Part I: Stories and Identities

1. Listening to the Voices: Narrative and Identity in the Work
   of Karel Schoeman
   Willie Burger 25
2. To Belong or Not to Belong
   Heilna du Plooy 39
3. External Events and Internal Reality: Fugard's Construction
   of (Afrikaner) Identity in the Plays of the Nineties
   Annette L. Combrink 55
4. The Latin American Connection: History, Memory and Stories
   in Novels by Isabel Allende and André Brink
   Marita Wenzel 71
5. Myth and Identity
   Marianne Dircksen 89

Part II: Places and Landscapes

6. Land, Space, Identity: The Literary Construction of Space
   in Three Afrikaans Farm Novels
   Hein Viljoen 107
7. When Outsiders Meet: Boerneef and A. H. M. Scholtz
   Chris N. van der Merwe 125
8. Civilization and Wilderness: Colonial Spatial Binaries and the
   Construction of Contemporary South African Identity in André
   Brink's *An Instant in the Wind* and Kirby van der Merwe's *Klapperhaar
   slaap nooit stil nie* (One Can Never Sleep Quietly on a Coir Mattress)
   Louise Viljoen 137

Part III: Cultural Identity

9. The Construction of "Colored" Space and Identity
   in Dido's *'n Stringetjie blou krale* (A String of Blue Beads)
   Minnie Lewis 157
10. The Underestimated Strength of Cultural Identity: The Search for
    Cultural Specificity between Localizing and Globalizing Tendencies
    Rien T. Segers 175

Notes on Contributors 199

Acknowledgments

This book grew out of a joint research project under the general title of Problematics of Space and Identity, undertaken in the Research Focus Area of Languages and Literature in the South African Context at the Potchefstroom University for Christian Higher Education. Academics from other universities, namely Chris van der Merwe, Minnie Lewis (both from the University of Cape Town), Willie Burger (Rand Afrikaans University), Louise Viljoen (University of Stellenbosch) and Rien T. Segers (University of Groningen), later joined the project and also wrote chapters for the book.

We would like to thank the contributors for their dedication to this project and for the spirit of cheerful cooperation in which they bore our queries and suggestions.

We would also like to thank our assistant for this project, Sonja Steyn, for her enthusiasm in doing all the formatting and helping to solve many of the queries and to find many missing bits of bibliography. Thanks also to Werner Kapp, for his help with making the corrections in the manuscript.

We also want to thank Karen Radell, for first mooting the idea of this book, and Phyllis Korper, our editor, and Sophie Appel, the production coordinator at Peter Lang, for making the idea a reality.

The project was supported by the National Research Foundation of South Africa (NRF) under GUN 2052347 and by the Focus Area itself, and the editors gratefully acknowledge their invaluable contribution. The opinions, findings and conclusions expressed in this book are those of the authors and should not be attributed either to the NRF or to the Focus Area.

Hein Viljoen
Chris N. van der Merwe

June 2003

Introduction

Learning about Space—and about Ourselves

Hein Viljoen, Minnie Lewis and Chris N. van der Merwe

and in the tree hides
a white ear
no a house crouches there
(and so one learns about space)
(Breytenbach, *Blues* 255)[1]

These charged and enigmatic words by the Afrikaans poet Breyten Breytenbach capture something of humanity's rich and paradoxical experience of space. A tree outside in the winter garden, threatened by darkness, can contain a whole house, and this house, as the poem moves through a series of spatial shifts and invaginations, comes to contain the moon. The moon in the darkest corner of the house is drifting in its own light at night, and this eventually becomes an emblem of the lover's heart drifting through the expanse (*ruim*, "space") of the beloved's love. *Die nag se ruim* can also be glossed as "the night's hold"—the night becoming a ship carrying the moon, just like the beloved carries the lover in her heart according to his wish. The container and the contained are continually switching places.

What do we learn about space here? Firstly, that human spatial perception is changeable and continually shifting. Secondly, that it is intimately tied to the emotional value humans attach to certain spaces and places. And thirdly, that as inner space folds into outer space (and vice versa) people need a sense of belonging, of being at home somewhere. The house is a potent emblem of belonging, just as the moon drifting eerily through the night is a potent emblem of longing, of feeling "*unheimlich*".

What can a disembodied organ of hearing register in such a situation? Somehow, irrationally, the ear, like the telescope, is an organ for apprehending space. The ear certainly implies a human presence of some kind, so that, for our purpose, we can rephrase the question as: how can people come to understand the spaces of South Africa? Is it possible for them to belong here? Or are they forever doomed to keep longing for an impossible home, to keep feeling *unheimlich*? Could they, as long-time settlers, ever feel truly at home in South Africa under a new political dispensation? In more general terms: Who are the people who call themselves South Africans?

To this anxiety about identity and belonging one could add an anxiety about the validity and power of stories, since the current calling into question of the relevance of stories—fictions—puts our jobs as critics on the line.

These are the existential questions hidden behind the careful academic language in which we framed the joint research project that resulted in this book. The aim of the project, under the general title of *Problematics of Space and Identity*, was to study how identity is constructed in a number of literary texts, and to describe how such constructions are represented, reflected, recorded, or even modeled. We aimed to pay special attention to the role of various forms of spatiality, such as land and landscape in these processes. We wanted, through a dialogue between local and global texts and contexts, to contribute to the global understanding of processes of identity construction in literature and of the role that spatiality plays in these processes. Crucial to answering these questions is the way in which we perceive, conceive of and live space and identity. This includes how the authors we write about have reacted to the questions of space and identity and how we in turn reacted to them.

Existential Questions

The existential questions perhaps emerge clearest in Annette Combrink's chapter on Fugard's construction of (Afrikaner) identity in dialectic between external events and internal reality. She writes that Fugard's one reaction to the external events ending apartheid was to start turning his personal stories into public accounts (partly in order to keep his creative energies flowing) in a strongly autobiographical, confessional kind of writing. The end of apartheid meant that he (like many other writers) had to look for a new productive topic and had to find a new kind of hero. His second reaction was to embark on consciously constructing a personal identity as creator of imaginative texts and as an Afrikaner. As Combrink points out, Fugard has always been fascinated by identity, and many of his characters can be read as self-portraits at different phases in his life. His construction of himself as an Afrikaner is as contentious as his turn to inner realities. The picture of that mythical beast "the Afrikaner" that emerges through Fugard's characters is very complex, however, and full of contradictions.

Combrink argues that Fugard's characters are often set in real, but hostile landscapes, but show an intense connection with the land. In returning to Karoo spaces Fugard is returning home, completing the cycle of his life. In recent plays, however, this physical space is turned into sites of interrogation and into liminal space. Turning the inner story into public account boils down to a reinstatement of a "private, interior, even visionary domain" (Walder). This turn might be too personal and too private and the harsh reception of this trend by the critics might point to a dead-end rather than a new beginning.

In the theatre physical space is, by semiotic and linguistic means, turned into dramatic space representative of the dramatic world. Mentioning sheep and lack of water might situate a character in the Karoo. Novels likewise construct fictional spaces—abstracted from "real life". One of the primary means of organizing space is by using the oriented human body (the first of Suvin's axioms about space). We describe things as behind or in front of us, below or above. We give directions by referring to left or right. We deictically organize the space around us from our own point of view, dividing it into in front of or behind us, into here and there, left or right.

As Fugard's spaces indicate, space in a literary text is much more than just a setting for the action. In dramas as well as in novels space is often also deictically organized around a specific point of view or a specific oriented body. Referring to here or there, you or I is one of the principal means of creating places and a dramatic world in the theatre. Deictic organization often lies at the basis of the topology or Bakhtinian chronotope of a specific text, that is, a structure of meaning complementary or in opposition to the verbal meaning of the text (Lotman, *Structure* 231). High places can, for example, be associated with elevation, the gods, or higher ideals. Moral meanings may be associated with spatial dimensions like the horizontal or the vertical, inside or outside, above or below—as is clear, for example, from the fact that we situate heaven above and hell below or describe political parties as left or right. Bachelard's dialectic between cellar and attic that will be discussed below also illustrates this point. The meanings that spatial dimensions acquire are important reasons why the finite text can be a convincing model of an infinite universe (Lotman, *Structure* 210).

These meanings are social meanings, and space in literature as in life is never just an empty, neutral extension but much rather a place that has been named, demarcated, allocated. It is a place that gets its meaning from human experience and memories and from relations between people. It is often a stage where human desires and interests clash.

Cultural Identity

One obvious way of giving meaning to space is through the idea of a national identity. This means that who we are depends on living in a specific country. "We are South African", like we said above. Despite centuries of living together under the African sun, and sharing the disruptive effects of colonization, urbanization, and now globalization, the South African identity remains largely contrived. Since 1994, there has been a deliberate project of unifying a divided nation by means of shared symbols like the new flag, heroic incidents such as winning the Rugby World Cup supported by Nelson Mandela in a No 6 Rugby jersey and the painful process of learning a new democratic ethos.

All South Africans could say: "We are African", claiming a very close connection to the continent of Africa, its climate, its soil, its people. This claim is valid for many cultural groups. For instance, *Afrikaner* literally means "person from Africa", just like *American* means "person from America" (at least in a wider sense than the more usual one of "citizen of the USA") and indicates a close identification with Africa in opposition to an allegiance to the European colonial powers of Britain and the Netherlands in the past. Most Afrikaners can trace their family in Africa back for 200 to 350 years. Calling Afrikaners African raises the vexed question of the place of white people in Africa. Many people question the validity of this claim, using an African simile to ask: "How long does a log have to lie in the water before it turns into a crocodile?" The answer, obviously, is "Forever; this will never happen", but the analogy is misleading, since crocodiles and logs are different, and crocodiles do learn to adapt to different rivers.

To speak of "Afrikaners" is to assume an imagined community that nowadays indicates a diversity rather than a unity, and most Afrikaners today probably would be more than a little ambivalent about the markers of Afrikaner identity that Annette Combrink describes: the Afrikaans language, love of the land (especially the farm), courage and a strong will to survive, earthy humor and warmth, a strong sense of family and a concomitant conservatism (shading over into racism and racial intolerance). To this one might add an ambivalent allegiance to Calvinist Christianity. As is well known, the demise of apartheid and the stories of its atrocities told to the Truth and Reconciliation Commission have discredited the ideals of Afrikaner nationalism to the extent that the hegemonic Afrikaans identity has been discredited and has to be replaced.

How difficult it is to define cultural identities is abundantly clear in the case of the so-called colored identity. The term "colored" has a distinctly South African meaning. It refers to people of mixed origin, whose forebears include the San and the Khoi (indigenous inhabitants of South Africa) as well as Cape Malay Slaves and European setttlers. "Colored" is an apartheid construction for somebody who is neither white nor black, but this pejorative meaning is (in some quarters at least) now being turned into a marker of a distinctive South African cultural (rather than racial) identity. Colored identity is, in other words, a complexly constructed hybrid. The chapters by Minnie Lewis and Louise Viljoen further explore the meaning of "colored".

Complexly Constructed Hybrids

Minnie Lewis' chapter on the construction of colored space and identity in E. K. M. Dido's novel *'n Stringetjie blou krale* (A string of blue beads) is very revealing in this regard. The protagonist, Nomsa/Nancy is a constructed hybrid herself, since she was forced to adopt a colored identity and simultaneously repress her black identity. The book starts with one of the nightmares in which the repressed part of her identity returns to haunt her. She moves through different spaces—Transkei laager, town and big city. In the different spaces she has to adopt different identities, leaving her caught between different worlds, marginalized and displaced, in a liminal state. Her sense of dislocation and alienation can only be overcome by a return to her "black space". Only by returning to this symbolic space of the past and recovering her cultural memory can she overcome marginality and reach wholeness and independence.

Her journey through different spaces, overcoming her double marginalization as a colored woman and adopting different identities, deconstructs the commonly accepted identity markers like naming, clothing, language, hair and skin color, since her changing cultural identity escapes definition in these terms. She breaks through the boundaries of race and gender marginalization. As Lewis points out, Nancy has "to recover a discarded past, accept a fragmented present and embrace future with some kind of newfound happiness" while realizing that her new identity and its markers will also change in time. Her life has come full circle, and this is symbolized by the recurrent motif of the string of blue beads. It symbolizes completeness but also recurrent movement, "a never-ending state of flux".

Dido's novel highlights human adaptability. Although the hidden influence of Nancy's black cultural identity seems to suggest some kind of essence, knowing one's roots is but one factor in the complex set of relations that constitute cultural identity. It is a dynamic, relational concept. As has been said many times, the challenge for South Africans today is to confront the past and to construct new identities related to our living experience in South Africa in an age of growing global economic integration. This is a continuous process.

Cultural Identity between Localization and Globalization

Segers' chapter on cultural identity in an age of globalization goes a long way towards explaining why one's roots are so important. In his view culture is a deep systemic construct, linking up with Hofstede's definition of culture as "the collective programming of the mind which distinguishes the members of one group or category from another". This means that culture denotes the shared learning of a given group (and is not innate) and shows a structural stability in which different levels of culture are interrelated. A person belongs to different levels—a national level, an ethnic or linguistic level, a gender level, a generational level, etc. The implication is that one cannot speak of "the" identity of a person, since it may change according to circumstances.

Hofstede thinks that culture at all these levels shows an onion-like layering of symbols, heroes, rituals and, as the deepest layer, values. This idea is very useful in describing the construction of identities, as Heilna du Plooy's and Hein Viljoen's chapters show. Our analyses of narrative identity show that one further element should be added, and that is stories. Symbols, heroes, rituals and values are emplotted together into meaningful stories. This partly explains the power of stories and the need for significant stories, or myths: through them individuals seek to achieve coherence and psychological wholeness.

Segers underwrites Bloom's view that identification is "an inherent and unconscious behavioral imperative". Even in a so-called post-national age, the "imagined community" (Anderson) of the nation remains one of the most visible and most self-conscious of our identifications, as indicated by national flags, sports colors and international sports events. Segers argues that cultural identity is a broader concept than national identity since it goes further than essentialist national stereotypes. It is a relational construct that has to take into account three factors: the facts or statistics about a certain group of people, the mental programming of that group, and the outside image (*Fremdbild*) of that group (that is, how people outside the group interpret the in-group's specificity).

Most of the chapters in this book have a local focus: South African texts and South African issues form the main points of analysis although they are situated in wider international contexts like that of postcolonialism. In the latter part of his chapter Segers takes up the issue of identity in a global world characterized by a shared global or "McWorld" culture of McDonalds, Macintosh and MTV that creates "a common world taste around common logos, advertising slogans, stars, songs, brand names, jingles and trade marks" (Barber 25). He points out that the globalizing tendency is opposed by an equally strong localizing tendency: a search for roots and cultural authenticity. The South African phrase "Local is lekker" (that is, local is good and enjoyable) captures this succinctly. An inner sense of cultural identity often clashes with a global outer culture. In W.B. Yeats' terms—race clashes with soul. Segers argues that the dialectic between localization and globalization and the serious conflicts that often arise between smaller communities and bigger constructed ensembles can best be understood through cultural identity.

In support of his argument Segers cites Huntington's view that the post-Cold War world is a cultural world divided into nine different major civilizations and that conflict between cultures and civilizations will become more prominent in future. The present conflict between the USA and Iraq can also be understood in terms of one (global) culture's (imperial) insensitivity towards the inner tenets of another culture. This cultural turn, that is, the recognition of the socio-political relevance of culture makes research into cultural identity imperative, according to Segers.

This book displays the tension between the local and the global. It is part of reaching out to the global world by telling about fascinating South African stories and texts. Many of the writers discussed here have become part of global literature through translation. We discuss these works in translated form in the global language, that is, English, but much of our effort is aimed at discovering the inner sense of our own specific cultures. However, in their specificity, they reveal a Diaspora found all over the world. All the chapters engage with the dialectic between localizing and globalizing.

Memories of Place

Breyten Breytenbach is one of those nomadic South African authors who seem to be at home everywhere, were it not for the strong sense of exile in his work. In *Dog Heart* he returns to the local, to the region of his heart, perhaps in search of a new identity.

We live in space, grow emotionally attached to particular spaces and places, associate them with particular events of our personal history and connect joyful or sad emotions to specific localities. But such a return to one's region of origin is mostly a return to memories. In memory space is obviously "figurative" and not "literal" or physical. As "normal" humans we cannot live, experience or remember outside the realm of space or time, but memory "recreates" rather than represents lived geographical space. It transforms space into nostalgic places of memory. Reminiscing about times and places gone by always seems to be painted in rosy colors. This 'lost' space and time are then experienced as glorious, something to be sorely missed, but the actual experience at the time (not nostalgically (re)lived) was often harsh and anything but wonderful. Memory of past hardships is highly selective in its reconstruction.

Returning to the Region of Your Heart

A complex mixture of love and hate characterizes Breytenbach's relations with the country of his birth, and his return to the region of his origin in *Dog Heart* enacts many of the paradoxes of identity. The title, as Du Plooy glosses it in her chapter, means "the innermost pain of pain", and thus captures something of the pain of trying to belong yet at the same time being in exile, nowhere at home. She calls the book an "extended poetic exploration of the relations between the individual, his identity and space". The narrator emphasizes that memory is a dark or distorting mirror, empty of sensory experience, and that the process of writing the identity of the I is a mixture of suspect flashes of memory, meanings imposed from outside and the unforeseen events and reactions of the present. For the narrator language is the fundamental medium of human life. That is why the book is written in a studiedly transparent kind of English that lets the underlying Afrikaans structure and idiom shine through.

The book calls into question both the identity of the narrator and the process of representation, since both place and I can be but a series of fleeting images, collections of stories. "Writing is an after-death experience" (Breytenbach *Dog Heart*). The task of the narrator is to keep in touch with history while allowing new experience to shine through. He does this by taking up multiple positions but also by a scrupulous respect for the other. Du Plooy concludes that the book shows how the strangeness of our inner life (the semiotic or preverbal—Kristeva) is continually transposed into signs (the symbolic, or the structures and language of society), keeping the psyche alive. The narrator is a subject-in-process-of-writing—the same, but different; in exile and not quite belonging; nowhere at home. As this chapter shows, identity is a production of the misleading process of memory, the paradoxes of belonging and not belonging, and of collective stories. Place, just like the self, is a series of stories (not a state but a process of interaction between the semiotic and the symbolic).

Personal Memories Subverting History

In her chapter Marita Wenzel compares the role of the personal memories in Isabel Allende's *Eva Luna* and André Brink's *Imaginings of Sand* and shows up the subversive and constructive influence of the alternative women's histories presented in these novels. Wenzel points out that South African and Latin American fiction shares, despite many differences, the need to deal with the colonial past in a postmodern situation where definitive boundaries and fixed interpretations of events are being questioned. Writers face a common need for new identities in dealing with an oppressive colonial past and adjusting to a multicultural situation.

An important common strand is a preoccupation with the past. In a number of novels the national past is re-examined and re-created in a way that highlights the underestimated role of women. The past is recreated by many voices and from multiple perspectives—as typically happens in these two novels. The personal memories and points of view of different generations of women are intertwined with national history. The female family sagas in these novels thus contest the validity of documented history as the only version of the past. History becomes a troubling pluralist construct of many intertwined stories and many different versions of reality that have to be acknowledged.

The different versions of reality that the characters present and the contrast between narrated account and lived experience have the force of meta-history, reflecting on the dialectic between fact and fiction. This underscores the role of narrative in identity construction. Memory combined with the power of the imagination has the ability to create a new reality, like in the case of Ouma Krissie's tales of heroic women in *Imaginings of Sand*. Gender norms are subverted, while fiction provides space for creating a personal identity—for the characters as well as for the reader. These novels thus show that identity is a dynamic process of telling stories.

Inhabiting Space (Bachelard)

...the real beginnings of images, if we study them phenomenologically, will give concrete evidence of the values of inhabited space, of the non-I that protects the I. (Bachelard 5)

In searching for identity and a place to belong, rather than returning to the region of your heart, another reaction might be to take shelter in your own little corner of the world, your own little shell. A house is in this regard the essence of inhabited space—the place we call home shelters us and forms a kind of shell for our solitude and our daydreams. Finding shelter in the world into which we are cast is for Bachelard the essence of "the primary function of inhabiting" (4). That is why the shell is the root metaphor of his phenomenology of inhabiting. The shell gives shelter to individual solitude, just like the human equivalent, the hermit's hut, does. Its essence (which is "the essence of the verb 'to inhabit'") is that it is "centralized solitude" (32). The places we call home are shell-like in the way that they protect our solitude and our "spaces of intimacy" (8). The house itself is a primary space of intimacy, mainly because it shelters our intimacy and solitude and gives us space to daydream, for it is in daydreams that for Bachelard thoughts, memories and dreams are integrated (6). The quintessential house, therefore, is an oneiric house—a space of wishes and daydreams.

Bachelard further claims "a house constitutes a body of images that give mankind proofs or illusions of stability" (17), mainly for two reasons: that it appeals to our consciousness of verticality and of centrality. The vertical dimension has to do with the way in which the daydreamer constructs the upper stories and the attic—and the attic is specifically shell-like in that it is a space of cosmic dreams. At the same time the dreamer is also digging the cellar, so that the meaning of a house lies in the dialectic between cellar and attic—psychoanalytically spoken, between the unconscious and the conscious, between the rational and the dark mysterious depths below. Even in an electrically lit house the cellar retains this unconscious mystery. "The unconscious cannot be civilized. It takes a candle when it goes to the cellar", Bachelard writes (19). Houses with strong subterranean elements are houses with cosmic roots for Bachelard. They are like stone plants "growing out of the rock up to the blue sky of a tower" (22).

The dimension of centrality returns us to "a house's situation in the world" (27), to the essence of inhabiting—to the hermit's hut, in other words. The hermit is alone before God and the hut is an image of the "center of concentrated solitude" around which radiates as it were "a universe of meditation and prayer, a universe outside the universe" (32).

Bachelard writes from a European situation of multi-storied city houses. It is not self-evident that the same values would apply to houses in South Africa. André Brink attempted to create such a house in *Donkermaan* (translated as *Rights of Desire*) where the dark secret of the cellar is the skeleton of the mal-treated slave Antje of Bengal, but Brink's attempt is too contrived to be con-vincing.

The individual shell (or cell) that enables solitude—the "room of one's own" so essential for reading and writing, the place needed to mold, to become a self, to create an identity, especially that of a writer—does not seem to be a central principle of inhabiting in most Afrikaans novels. "To inhabit" rather seems to mean to be sheltered from the heat and from the vast, open veld—a garden or a farm, in other words. Horizontality seems to be more important than verticality, so that the cellar and the attic are translated into their horizontal equivalents: the mysterious, *unheimliche* veld and the safely enclosed garden where the ear can be lulled by the sound of water.

The Farm as Local Habitation

Far more than a city house or a shell the farm can therefore be regarded as the essential South African form of habitation—a collection of simple, fragile struc-tures, surrounded by some kind of garden, set in a wide empty space. In Bache-lard's terms it is closer to a hermit's hut, in other words. The farm is an icon of Afrikaner identity symbolizing a heroic struggle against the wilderness. How-ever, it is marked with ambivalence: on the one hand it is a safe place, home; on the other there is a constant fear of loss, an anxiety about the land, a feeling of insecurity. Safety from the forces of nature and the threat of wild animals and "uncivilized" men is only temporary.

No wonder then that the farm novel has developed into a prominent sub-genre in South African fiction both in English and in Afrikaans. In recent years the farm novel has become an important vehicle for the criticism of the patriar-chy and its racist ideology. The farm is now a prime site of injustice and iniquity and a stage for the age-old struggle with the father (an important farm novel topos from the beginning).

In his chapter Hein Viljoen analyzes the construction of space and the links between space and identity in two traditional farm novels, *Die meulenaar* and *Somer,* and one recent novel that rewrites parodies and mocks this tradition, viz., Etienne van Heerden's *Leap year.* In the first two novels Afrikaner identity is strongly associated with land and land ownership. Lack of land means lack of identity. Both show the typical patriarchal and idyllic space of the farm and in both the idyll is under threat. In both novels landless characters play an important role, however. Space is gendered and racialized: the farm is primarily a male space, and women play subsidiary roles. There is a social as well as an actual distance between owners and colored workers who in both novels are represented stereotypically as jolly, flamboyant figures with disgraceful drinking habits, though there is some attention to their personal struggles and feelings. An important point of difference is that the loss of the land is presented in *Die meulenaar* as a religious inversion and a renunciation of earthly things, whereas in *Somer* nature and humankind are closely identified and the transience of all natural things is the central theme.

Leap year parodies the farm novel by driving one important farm novel theme, that of heredity, to absurd lengths in the central artifice of the fall-goat—the goat that faints when predators approach and is thus killed instead of the valuable livestock. The novel evokes different identities—British settler identity, Afrikaner identity and Xhosa identity. All these identities are in some sense rooted in the harsh land but are also constructed in the novel by means of different stories of the past, rituals (like the fox hunt or playing with toy trains), symbols (the fall-goat, the river) and values (like mutual respect). The main characters' identities are also linked to memorial sites. The contest for the land where oil has been discovered threatens to plunge the whole Kei region into chaos and bloodshed, but this is averted by the sacrifice of a new scapegoat— Seer Wehmeyer, prototype of a cynical life-weary Afrikaner. The novel ends in a mythical reconciliation between a black and a white woman in the river.

Seer's identity is contained in the ramshackle house of his parents where he still lives, surrounded by his rose garden. It is remarkable that gardens seem to constitute the spatial heart of all three novels. They are all lost paradises, but in the first two novels they still bear fruit. In *Leap year* the garden, which forms a sharp contrast with the harsh environment of the region, is a decadent site of nostalgia.

Bachelard's phenomenology of space thus seems to break down in the South African landscape since the modalities of habitation are different. The 'I' in Bachelard's system seems to be born fully-fledged in its house, in its shell where solitude is possible. It is a bourgeois 'I'. The cogito that contemplates the essence of inhabiting has already been formed. Some elements of Bachelard's view point in another direction, however. He emphasizes memories and "the complexity of mixed reverie and memory" that we find in daydreams (26). "To inhabit" is after all also an active verb, and the history of the 'I' is (among other things) the memory of the series of places of its intimacy. Knowing ourselves means knowing "a sequence of fixations in the being's stability" (8). "In its countless alveoli space contains compressed time. That is what space is for," Bachelard writes (8). The mixture of reverie and memory points in the direction of stories. The series of intimacies the 'I' remembers might well be a series of stories. The cogito in its solitude in other words presupposes a narrative process of formation—it is a narrative identity, since for Ricoeur, it is narrative that connects the discontinuity of the 'I' to its continuity.

Narrative Identity

In contrast to the tradition of the cogito and to the pretention of the subject to know itself by immediate intuition, it must be said that we understand ourselves only by the long detour of the signs of humanity deposited in cultural works. (Ricoeur, *Time and Narrative* 3 143)

In Bachelard's work space and identity are closely linked. The spaces of intimacy occupied at various moments help in molding and determining the "self". Both the concept of space and that of identity have to do with our experience as human beings. The very spaces we occupy form our identities, and these identities determine our perceptions and representations of those spaces and varying spatial experiences. We can thus view the relationship between space and identity as a symbiotic relationship, a mutual dependency creating meaningfulness.

Ricoeur points out that identity ("Narrative identity") means both "sameness" (Lat. *idem*) and "self" (Lat. *ipse*). To him selfhood means continuity over time, since he connects it to human *Dasein*—the state of being cast in the world. It indicates the ontological state of being able to interrogate one's self and to enter into a relationship with being qua being. Selfhood is an authentic state of living and experiencing in time. By connecting sameness (continuity) and selfhood (discontinuity over time) narratives therefore reconfigure different states of selfhood, of sameness and of the world, and this can lead to a reconfigured view of the self and of the world. Therein lies the power of narratives.

The Power of Stories

This power is demonstrated in Willie Burger's chapter on Karel Schoeman. Burger emphasizes that identity, as Schoeman's autobiography proves, is always an interpretation—a reconfiguration of events (and of people and places) based on memory and on our pre-understanding of events, symbols, structures of meaning and temporality. Burger writes that "the 'I' as a character in the plot(s) is interpreted by the 'I' as subject, but this interpreting 'I' "is constituted through the process of narration and interpretation". It is, in other words, a narrative that opens a possible world for the reader. The reader has to merge his own world (the horizon of pre-understanding) with the world of the text (the horizon of the imagination), in the process changing his own world and his own 'I'.

In Schoeman's *Voices* trilogy we have different voices telling their stories, and in the telling constituting themselves and their worlds. At the same time, they open the lost world of the past to the reader, if only fleetingly. Ultimately they confront the reader with his own history as part of the history of South Africa and question his identity as African of European descent as well as the morality of his actions. "The function of fiction is to discover by invention", Burger writes. *Verliesfontein*, the first book of the *Voices* trilogy, confronts the reader with the immorality of the killing of the colored man Adam Balie by Boer occupying forces during the South African War, but also questions the morality of the three speaking voices' reactions to that event and thus the morality of the reader's own reactions to events like these in her life.

Just as Ricoeur argues that human *Dasein* is necessarily temporal in nature, one could argue that human existence is equally spatial in nature. We do live in space and utilize different spaces in different ways, but living space is also crucially conditioned by our conceptions and interpretations of space and by our own stories as we remember them in spaces of intimacy. In Schoeman's work the voices telling their stories are constituted in space and at the same time constitute the space of the novels. By naming and describing spaces containing people and events, spaces become meaningful places. For instance, the "lost" fictional space of Verliesfontein becomes a place where humans live and die. The different voices give different names and meanings to the same spaces, so that they record the different values and appropriations of a specific locality like Verliesfontein through history. Its official name of Fouriesfontein records the strong influence of the Fourie family, but its alternative name of Verliesfontein (spring of Loss) refers to an event in the past when the original San inhabitants lost a lot of their cattle to the white farmers. Verliesfontein thus is a palimpsest from which different namings and occupations of the land can be read.

The Power of Myth: Striving for Personal Truth

Kallie, the young clerk who is one of the speaking voices in *Verliesfontein*, spends his life copying in longhand the words of important writers, but never gets around to formulating his own response to their words. The narrator, in the end, leaves him to his writing and withdraws like some kind of ghostwriter. Though he calls writing "liberating", the narrator can offer no liberating truth beyond that of writing itself and leaves it to the reader to find a liberating reconfiguration, a personal truth for her. The end remains open.

Leaving the reader to fend for himself probably spurs him on to find the personal truth he needs, for no one can live in a meaningless void. Finding such a truth might well entail finding a suitable myth and a suitable hero as guide. As Marianne Dircksen argues in her chapter, myths are ways to comprehend life, enabling us to establish secure relations with other people and to discover a meaningful place in the cosmos. She also argues that comparative mythology is a useful tool for discovering this function of myths. A comparative study of myths from different cultures reveals how similar heroes' journeys towards self-discovery are and confronts us with our personal and collective identities.

Following the socio-functionalist view of myths, she argues that myths and rituals provide the social cement that binds societies together—something that the pluralistic South African society sorely needs. The crux of the matter is that myths are essential ingredients of our cultural identity, since they enact a psychodrama that is essential for constructing both personal and collective identity. Losing touch with the myths of one's culture leads to sterility and loss of identity. As Dircksen demonstrates, the Zulu myth of Usikulumi contains all the essential elements of hero myths as they are found the world over—also in Classical Greek and Roman myths. She argues that many young black South Africans have lost contact with their cultural myths and are identifying with global culture, since an essential concomitant of colonization has been denigration of indigenous cultures. They are ignorant of their cultural tradition and deny its integrity. In other words, their local inner culture and their global outer culture are out of kilter. In these circumstances comparative study of African, Greek and Roman myths can lead to a revaluation and recentering of traditional African myths.

In accordance with Jung's and Eliade's views, Dircksen argues that it is the loss of the center, the zone of the sacred to which the hero's arduous journey leads, that is ultimately at stake. Modern societies have become desacralized, and people have lost knowledge of their cultural heritage and its meaning-giving stories, thereby losing a sense of belonging. Restoring myth and ritual to its proper place can counteract this loss of meaning. In the final analysis Dircksen regards this as a spiritual journey that modern people have to undertake to satisfy their need for centering, meaning, coherence in life.

At this point we are very near the centered feeling of the hermit in his house—the essence of centrality as Bachelard sees it. Given the importance of the center, the situation of postcolonial subjects would be dire indeed: Their situation could be described as one of feeling perpetually that the center is elsewhere, of feeling permanently displaced.

The (Dis)place of Postcoloniality

A major feature of postcolonial literature is the concern with place and displacement. (Ashcroft et al., *Empire* 8–9)

Space in the most abstract, theoretical sense, is pure extension—an open area without boundaries, a limitless expanse, and the contemplation of such a limitless space might seem extremely difficult. But as soon as we inhabit certain spaces, experience them, start telling stories about them, they are transformed into places with boundaries and associated with emotions and meaningful events. As Schoeman's voices reveal, space is coded, overwritten by naming, demarcation, allocation, charting. In these processes power and knowledge, especially the power to make representations, play a significant role. This is one of the reasons why a study of space and identity in literary texts yields important results: it reveals the demarcations, values and discourses of space and place and how these constructs are linked to identity. It reveals important aspects of the social imaginary, in other words.

One is often tempted to limit space to a specific location, a given (physical) place. But space is much more encompassing than 'literal' space. Like identity, space is a (social) construct (Lefebvre 26). Ashcroft et al. (*Empire* 8–9) argue that a concern with space is a highly significant aspect of postcolonial discourse and also that space has an important role to play in the construction of identity and the finding of one's place in society. It is a complex issue, involving more than mere physical surroundings or "landscape" as Ashcroft et al. (*Reader* 391) term it. They underline the fact that space is infinitely more than physical locality when they write "By 'Place' we do not simply mean 'landscape'. ...Rather 'place' in postcolonial societies is a complex interaction of language, history and environment. ...The theory of place does not simply propose a binary separation between the 'place' named and described in language, and some 'real' place inaccessible to it, but rather indicates that in some sense place *is* language, something in constant flux, a discourse in process" (Ashcroft et al., *Reader* 391).

Geographical space is tied to emotions as well as ideology. Geographical space refers to a physical space, but it can never be divested from that which ascribes meaning to that physical space, among others the ideology and emotions tied up with memories of that space. As humans our reality and lived experiences are understood in spatial and temporal terms, but they are ever changing and interacting, constructing new and different spaces that are linked in some way. In this regard Ashcroft et al. write: "Place is also a palimpsest, a kind of parchment on which successive generations have inscribed and reinscribed the process of history." (Ashcroft et al., *Reader* 392).

Ashcroft's view of space as a palimpsest calls to mind a view of space as a constantly changing process—space as produced by society (Lefebvre 26). "Scrapping" the old and reinscribing space with something different illustrate the interaction between various spaces and different processes. These processes of construction by which the varying spaces are brought into existence are much more complex than meets the eye. They are intricately linked to a given identity at a specific moment and woven into an already existing space. Space, much like identity, is not static, but rather changeable and dynamic. It is by naming, mapping, imagining, remembering, writing, and representing it that space is transformed into lived space, or place. Space is coded in different ways, not the least by racializing, gendering or politicizing it.

Ashcroft et al. indicate that when space is accepted as more than physical location, its key role in constructing identity becomes clear.

> In the case of diasporic peoples, place might not refer to a location at all, since the formative link between identity and an actual location might have been irredeemably severed. But all constructions and disruptions of place hinge on the question: 'Where do I belong?' The place of a diasporic persons' 'belonging' may have little to do with spatial location, but be situated in family, community, in those symbolic features which constitute a shared culture, a shared ethnicity or system of belief, including nostalgia for a distant homeland. It is when place is least spatial, perhaps, that it becomes *most identifying*. (Ashcroft, *Transformation* 125, our emphasis) .

Ashcroft et al. (*Empire* 8–9) argue that the concern with place and displacement within the postcolonial discourse is where "the special post-colonial crisis of identity comes into being; the concern with the development or recovery of an effective *identifying relationship* between *self and place*" (our emphasis).

Displacement signifies the absence of an identifying relationship. It implies an initial space being occupied as well as a new and/or different space to which displacement leads. Displacement can be experienced as a most traumatic event. It dislocates and alienates and interferes with identities, creating that state of crisis (concerning identity) which Ashcroft et al. (8–9) link to the postcolonial concern with place and displacement. This aspect of displacement is one that is known the world over, and many "non-white" South Africans are all too familiar with this concept. Displacement has to do with giving up, usually not voluntarily, the familiar and dealing with an unknown space.

Symbolic Space of Power—Center vs. Periphery

> Asymmetry is apparent in the relationship between the centre of the semiosphere and its periphery. (Lotman, *Universe* 127)

A sense of displacement, like exile, presupposes a yearning for an absent place or center where a meaningful relation to space is deemed to exist. Postcolonial writing as writing back to the center enacts a kind of dialectic between imperial center and colonial margin—a yearning for that elusive significance, miming it while trying to wipe it out, and at the same time feeling displaced at your own location. A struggle for power between the center and periphery has been one of the key features of the recent postcolonial discourse on space. This struggle for power is necessitated by the opposing nature of these symbolic spaces, of having and lacking power.

Between center and periphery obvious differences are found. They include opposing positionality, centrality as opposed to marginality, and acceptance versus rejection. These differences initiate dialogue between the two opposing spaces, which further enhances the asymmetric nature of the relationship that exists between them. It is exactly because of the oppositional 'relationship' between the center and periphery that asymmetry becomes evident.

The dialogue between center and periphery takes place across boundaries. An interesting aspect of boundaries is their ambivalence. As Lotman describes it, a boundary "both separates and unites" (Lotman, *Universe* 136), and it is exactly this undecidability of the boundary that necessitates and encourages dialogue between the center and periphery, since the periphery is the zone where control from the center becomes weaker, resulting in the increase of semiotic activity. Center and periphery enter into an incessant dialogue that gives rise to the ever-changing nature of both center and periphery.

In the sphere of symbolic space liminal space is born. It is in this in-between space, neither in center nor periphery, that much creative energy is released. This energy flows between center and margin and not merely from the center to the margin. This space is one that has been most significant in Afrikaans literary contributions in recent years, especially with the "inflow" of Colored writers, their "new" voices and "untold" stories. So too it has been in many previously colonized places, where the postcolonial voices of those on the margin have flowed "inwards", making the margin-experiences known, challenging the position and representation afforded them for many (colonizing) years. This energized space is one of the focal points in the postcolonial discourse at present.

The Transformative Power of the In-between

The transformative power of the in-between can be seen at work in Chris van der Merwe's analysis of two stories in which such marginal states play a central role. He compares two very different works by two authors practically at opposite ends of the racial and classes' divides, yet with a shared discontent with the present and nostalgia for a more harmonious and morally sound past. He shows how both Boerneef's *Teen die helling* and A.H.M. Scholtz's *Vatmaar* break down stereotypes and dissolve the boundaries between self and other, white and colored. Both texts point the way for modern people towards a more meaningful life.

Both narratives deal with outsiders—in-between characters in in-between spaces. The slope ("helling") is in-between city and farm, and Vatmaar is literally a piece of land that was left over, a piece that nobody wanted, beyond accepted categories. Van der Merwe emphasizes the "multiple belongings" of South Africans and their complex array of identities. *Vatmaar* itself is woven from many voices and different perspectives. These different stories reveal the humanity of the people and how silken threads of responsibility and love tie them together. Taken together these two writers relativize the racial and class boundaries that are regarded as central to the South African situation, pointing to a world where boundaries are freely crossed and people inhabit in-between spaces in meaningful interaction where new identities, relations to the other and to space and place can be formed.

Liminal Space; Ritual Space

...[liminal space] a marginal, *ambiguous space* in which *constructions* of home and away are temporarily disrupted, before being reinscribed or reordered, in any case *reconstituted.* (Phillips 13, our emphasis)

As these narratives illustrate, the hero in a story often has to move into such an in-between or liminal zone where his identity might be analyzed into factors that can be recombined in new ways (Turner 28). In this sacred space, beyond normal time and space, he can be changed before being re-integrated into society. This is typical of initiation rites and of rites of passage in general. A liminal zone is in other words a zone of playful transformation. Like any boundary, it is a zone of heightened semiotic activity (Lotman, *Universe* 136). Liminality is the result of processes of separation, transformation and re-incorporation. Periods of ambiguity, transition and marginality can be termed liminal in this sense. Creativity as such and creative reading processes are related to liminality, since the text itself is a liminal space where meaning can be created and where creative new identities and relationships between space and identity can be dreamed and produced.

The liminal space, thus termed by Phillips, can be seen as a very creative space, a space caught between various, and often opposing, spaces, being neither one nor the other, but rather borrowing useful characteristics from both, in order to "reconstitute" this "new" marginal and "ambiguous space". The ambiguity of this space lies in the fact that it does not belong to either one or the other, but is formed by the dialectic between the two. Although ambiguous, this space is most illuminating in the discourse of identity. Not only does it concern an "undominated" space, but also a relatively "unidentified" space. The liminal space ties in strongly with the concept of boundaries, because the liminal space comes into existence at the border of that which is found at the center and that which belongs to the periphery. In the light of this notion of liminal space, it is quite understandable that this is the space often, if not always, occupied by the hybrid, the hybrid also belonging to neither of the opposing worlds, but rather existing in the space that comes into being by the dialogue between them.

Wilderness and Civilization: Deconstructing Spatial Binaries

The transformative power of the dialogue between center and periphery emerges tellingly from Louise Viljoen's comparison of André Brink's *'n Oomblik in die wind* (1975) and Kirby van der Merwe's *Klapperhaar slaap nooit stil nie* (1999).

She regards the second novel as a post-apartheid answer to Brink, since it reverses the colonial spatial binaries that are still evident in Brink's work. Both novels deconstruct the spatial binary between wilderness and civilization in order to envision a transformation of the South Africa of their time. She argues that *'n Oomblik in die wind* can be read as implying a natural bond "between the identity constituting categories of race (the colored), class (the slave), space (the wilderness) and a certain kind of sexuality (instinctive and uninhibited)" and its opposite (146). The paradisiacal ideal space (clearly liminal) that the novel visualizes for South Africa partly breaks down these associations, representing identity as a *tabula rasa* free from the restrictions of race, class or gender. However, the ending of the novel presents "a concentrated image of the opposite" of this ideal state: the Cape society to which the characters return is racist, classist and patriarchal. In the end the narrative imagination breaks down in confrontation with reality. The imagined transformations in liminal space clash with the ingrained habits of the center. At the same time it could be contended that Brink's reconfiguration of spatial binaries in one of his most popular novels affected the reader and led her to a reconfiguration of her conceptions.

Viljoen argues that *Klapperhaar* is in many respects the reverse of Brink's novel. The colored woman protagonist crosses the boundary fence between white and colored, yet also has to make peace with her colored family and her memories of colored life.

Both these novels are concerned with the way in which spaces, both physical and metaphorical, impact on the construction of South African identity. Van der Merwe's novel almost reads like a re-working of or answer to Brink's novel. *'n Oomblik in die wind* uses the relationship between a colored slave and a white woman in the eighteenth century to comment on the way in which colored and white identities should interact in an idealized post-apartheid South Africa, finally conceding that it is not a workable idea by devising a tragic ending for the narrative. *Klapperhaar slaap nooit stil nie* uses the relationship between a colored woman and several white men to comment on the complexity of the interactions between colored and white identities in the realities of post-apartheid South Africa. The way in which the novel conceives of its heroine Kinta Januarie's identity indicates that colored identities should not be seen in terms of mixed racial identities but rather as cultural identities comprising "detailed bodies of knowledge, specific cultural practices, memories, rituals and modes of being" (21). In the final analysis one can say that Van der Merwe's novel is more inclined than Brink's to emphasize the specificities of South African identities and less prone to fall into the trap of honoring colonial discourse's interpretation of the binary opposition between the spaces of wilderness and civilization, reserving the former for colored and/or women and the latter for whites and males.

In their reenacting of crossing boundaries and the transformative power of the in-between, both novels imaginatively reconfigure the relations between space and identity.

Some Important Conclusions

There is another important conclusion that emerges from these essays. Our analyses bear out Ricoeur's views about the power of stories to reconfigure our life-world imaginatively and, in so doing, to re-create new places, heroes, histories and identities. Stories are subversive, constructive and do suggest ways toward new racial, gender and cultural identities. Re-telling stories that address the plight of women or of the oppressed in general presents alternative histories in which colonial binaries are reversed or deconstructed so that the voice of the other can be heard and perceptions about him can change. What emerges strongly is the important role of memory as a re-creation or re-imagining and not just a reflection of the past. Narrative emplotment does pave the way for new ways of emplotting individual, place and society in order to overcome the uncertainty and insecurity of our globalized postcolonial condition. The wounded heroes who have passed here in defile—a formidable list, from Faans and Leonora, through Adam and Elizabeth, BB Lazarus, up to Eva Luna, Ta-Vuurmaak, Kallie, Kinta and Nomsa/ Nancy—all hint at the production of new identities, the writing of new histories, the living of new lives.

Many of the chapters are fine-grained studies of how specific sites—farm, garden, mythical paradise, house, an unwanted piece of land—acquire emotional, ideological and literary meaning. Many of them emphasize that identity is not a stable essence, but a dynamic process. The unchanging cogito is a mirage. Instead, identity seems to be a narrative process that ties together memories, fleeting images and reveries in language—the centrally important medium of representation. At the same time there are in our corpus strong indications of a deep sense of selfhood linked to one's history, one's identification with specific places and their moral values that cannot be ignored.

For Bachelard the history of the 'I' is the memory of the series of places of its intimacy. These are sheltered spaces that you inhabit where you feel safe, which means that identity is a result of a history (story!) of sheltered spaces of reverie. A sense of self seems to require a sense of belonging at least somewhere, even if temporarily. Breytenbach's *Dog Heart* demonstrates that identification with a place is a complex dialectic between feeling secure and being alienated. The processes of constructing different spaces are much more complex than meets the eye. They are intricately linked to a (narratively) constructed identity at a specific moment and woven into a (discursively) constructed space. This again emphasizes that both place and 'I' are dynamic processes mediated by codes, conventions, discourse in which the empty mirror of memory plays an essential part.

Virtually all the chapters underline the role of these codes and conventions, which Lefebvre calls representational space. Rituals, stories/myths, symbols, values, heroes can be seen at work in the construction of identities. There is a need for memorial sites—sites of regret or guilt—and a common identification with a region. Land is of central importance, both as marker of identity, as heritage, as political issue and as commodity. Boundaries, values and demarcations of land—and the identities associated or based on land in various forms—are important clues to the social constructions we make.

On the other hand it is clear that subversion and transformation especially take place in the in-between spaces, in liminal spaces. Liminal space is crucial for the adaptation and transformation of identities. In places beyond the limits, beyond the usual categories (like the wilderness or *Vatmaar*), the polarities can be reversed and subverted, borders crossed, new connections of love and responsibility created. The literary text itself is liminal in this sense—it opens an in-between space where imaginative reconstruction and transformation can take place that can lead to re-inventing the ingrained habits of the center.

At the same time this collection of essays, in one way or the other, points to the human need for coherence and significance. Significant places acquire mythic proportions—in Bachelard's terms a centrality—that satisfy the deepest human yearnings even if only temporarily. This is crucial in a world where localizing and globalizing tendencies vie with each other. In dealing with the oppressive colonial past and adjusting to a multicultural situation a sense of centrality—of meaningful relatedness, of being meaningfully cast in the world—is essential. We need both the hermit's hut open to the cosmos and the enclosed safe space of the garden.

Note

1. My translation. The original reads: "en in die boom skuil/ 'n wit oor/ nee daar hurk 'n huis/ (en so leer mens van ruimte)". It is from poem 6.2 in the collection *Lotus* (1970).

Works Cited

Anderson, Benedict. *Imagined Communities*. Rev. ed. London and New York: Verso, 1996.

Ashcroft, Bill. *Post-Colonial Transformation*. London: Routledge, 2001.

——, Gareth Griffin, and Helen Tiffin, eds. *The Post-Colonial Studies Reader*. London: Routledge, 1995.

Bachelard, Gaston. *The Poetics of Space*. Trans. Maria Jolas. Boston: Beacon Press, 1969.

Barber, Benjamin. "Jihad vs. McWorld." *The Globalization Reader*. Eds. Frank J. Lechner and John Boli. Malden, Mass. and Oxford, UK: Blackwell, 2000. 21–26.

Breytenbach, Breyten. *Dog Heart. (A Travel Memoir)*. Cape Town Pretoria Johannesburg: Human & Rousseau, 1998.

———. *Ysterkoei-blues: Versamelde gedigte 1964–1975* [Ysterkoei-blues. Collected Poems 1964–1975.] Kaapstad Pretoria Johannesburg: Human & Rousseau, 2001.

De Klerk, W. A. *The Puritans in Africa; A story of Afrikanerdom*. Harmondsworth: Penguin, 1977.

Hall, S. "Cultural identity and diaspora." *Contemporary Postcolonial Theory. A Reader*. Ed. P. Mongia. New York: Arnold, 1996. 110–121.

Lefebvre, Henri. *The Production of Space*. Trans. Donald Nicholson-Smith. Oxford, UK & Cambridge, USA: Blackwell, 1991.

Lotman, Jurij. *The Structure of the Artistic Text*. Trans. Gail Lenhoff and Ronald Vroom. Michigan Slavic Contributions 7. Ann Arbor: U of Michigan P, 1977.

———. *Universe of the Mind: A Semiotic Theory of Culture*. Trans. Ann Shukman. Bloomington and Indianapolis: Indiana UP, 1990.

Phillips, R. *Mapping Men and Empire*. London: Routledge, 1997.

Ricoeur, Paul. "Narrative identity" *Philosophy Today* 35 (1991): 73–81.

———. *Time and Narrative*. Trans. Kathleen McLauglin & David Pellauer. 3 vols. Chicago: U of Chicago P, 1984–1988.

Suvin, Darko. "Approach to topoanalysis and to the paradigmatics of dramaturgic space." *Poetics Today* 8.2 (1987): 311–334.

Turner, Victor W. *From Ritual to Theatre. The Human Seriousness of Play*. New York: Performing Arts Journal Publications, 1982.

Venter, L. S. "Ruimte (epiek)." *Literêre terme en teorieë* ["Space (narrative)." Literary terms and theories.] Ed. T.T. Cloete. Pretoria: HAUM-literêr, 1992. 453–455.

Walder, D, ed. *Literature in the Modern World*. Oxford: Oxford UP, 1990.

Part I

Stories and Identities

Chapter 1

Listening to the Voices: Narrative and Identity in the Work of Karel Schoeman

Willie Burger

Construction of Identity

Manuel Castells defines identity as "people's source of meaning and experience" (6). This source of meaning and experience is a cultural attribute, or set of cultural attributes, that determine the way that people understand themselves and their world. For Castells (7) "it is easy to agree on the fact...that identities are constructed. The real issue is how, from what, by whom, and for what." Castells goes on to explore the "building materials" used to construct identities, ranging from history, geography, biology, and productive and reproductive institutions to collective memory, personal fantasies and religious revelations. His aim is to understand identity construction in a globalized world ("the network society"). Although I share the view that identity is constructed, the aim of this chapter is only to explore the role of narrative literature in the construction of identity. The role of narratives in the construction of identity is explored by an analysis of the autobiography of the prominent Afrikaans novelist and historian Karel Schoeman. Then, by turning to Schoeman's novels, the role of fiction in identity construction is considered.

The view of narratives that serves as a point of departure for this chapter is that language, specifically the narrative use of language, is not merely a medium that we use to express and understand ourselves (not merely another kind of "building material" in Castells's words), but that the self (and identity) is constituted in and through language, especially through narrating (see also Kerby, Gergen). The self, identity, is not simply described by a pre-existing self in a narrative, but this description, in the end, constitutes the self, as Ricoeur puts it:

> Our life, when then embraced in a single glance, appears to us as the field of a constructive activity, borrowed from narrative understanding, by which we attempt to discover and not simply to impose from the outside the narrative identity which constitutes us. ("Quest" 32)

Since the early 1970s there has been a growing interest in narratives in the human sciences. Before the seventies narratives had often been regarded as the exclusive domain of literary studies. By the end of the 1980s, however, narrative had become so important in the human sciences that it has even been described as an "obsession of the era" (Nash xi). Research methods that originated in literary studies and linguistics received more and more attention in other fields of inquiry—even in the "hard sciences" and in economics (Nash). The growing awareness that all our observations and the ways in which we understand the world are irrevocably part of our sign systems (especially language) underlies this focus on narratives that has been described by Kreiswirth as the "narrativist turn" in the human science.

Narrative Identity—Paul Ricoeur

Ricoeur links life and narrative at the end of volume 3 of *Time and Narrative* (*TN*) when he concludes that narratives, by providing an historic awareness, provide us with identity:

> The state of identity of an individual or a community is to answer the question, "Who did this?" "Who is the agent, the author?" We first answer this question by naming someone—that is by designating them with a proper name. But what is the basis for the permanence of this proper name? What justifies our taking the subject of an action, so designated by his, her, or its proper name, as the same throughout a life that stretches from birth to death? The answer has to be narrative. To answer the question, "who" as Hannah Arendt has so forcefully put it, is to tell the story of a life. The story told tells about the action of the "who." And the identity of this "who" therefore itself must be a narrative identity. Without recourse to narration, the problem of personal identity would in fact be condemned to an antinomy with no solution. (Ricoeur, *TN 3* 246)

For Ricoeur, personal identity is inherently narrative. To understand who we are is to be able to follow a story. Narratives provide the link between continuity and discontinuity of the self. The self is historical and therefore constantly changing, but it seems to stay the self. On the one hand I can say that I am not the same person as the teenager in the 1970s. On the other hand, if I commit a murder and I am brought to book only twenty years later, I could hardly expect to be released on account of the fact that I am not the same person anymore. This accountability is the result of an acceptance of identity as something that does not change, in contrast to the idea that I could change over time; that I do not have any of the cells in my body that I was born with. For Ricoeur, narratives provide the best way to mediate and express this continuity and discontinuity. Through narratives, the episode is provided with coherence. The episode, the single event, is configured in time through the story. That is why narratives can express the self as something present (this episode) but also as something with a history (a self that used to be different). But the narrative can also express the future potential of the self (Ricoeur, *TN 3* 244–249). The concept of a narrative identity means that it is not necessary to "posit a subject identical with itself through the diversity of its different states" and that it is also possible to reject the idea that the identical subject is only a "substantialist illusion." Narrative identity avoids the problems that arise from a notion of identity as "being the same" (*idem*) and rather makes possible a notion of identity as "oneself as self-same" (*ipse*). In other words, identity as "self-sameness" has a temporal structure that "conforms to the model of dynamic identity arising from the poetic composition of a narrative text" (Ricoeur, *TN 3* 246). A narrative identity can include changes within the cohesion of a single life and the story of a life continues to be refigured by all the stories (fictive or truthful) that a subject tells. In this regard it is instructive to analyze an autobiography to demonstrate especially the influence of the culture of narration that the subject finds himself or herself heir to.

When a life is refigured in narrative, it leads to an "examined life" in the sense that Socrates meant. This narrative refiguration differs from the egotistic and narcissistic ego:

> An examined life is, in large part, one purged, one clarified by the cathartic effects of the narratives, be they historical or fictional, conveyed by our culture. So self-constancy refers to a self instructed by the works of a culture that it has applied to itself. (Ricoeur, *TN 3* 247)

To this idea of a self, instructed by the works of a culture, I will return at the end of this chapter.

Karel Schoeman and Self-narrative

Karel Schoeman is probably one of the most important Afrikaans (and South African) novelists. Since his debut in 1965 he has published 17 novels, 10 biographies and 12 historical works. He has received several prestigious prizes and awards. As Schoeman is both historian and novelist, it is interesting to note how he combines the rigor of the historical research with his narrative ability as novelist to construct his autobiography. Close to the end of his autobiography, *Die laaste Afrikaanse boek. Outobiografiese aantekeninge* (2002) (The Last Afrikaans Book: Autobiographical notes[1]), he remarks: "Reality, fiction and imagination have caught up with each other and they overlap, and the different aspects of my life have merged to a single unity" (676—my translation). He wrote his autobiography after retiring from his position as researcher in the archives of the South African library. He reflects on his life and his work as if it has been completed. He describes his life in Jungian terms as a process of individuation—a long "labyrinthic journey to self-realization" (Schoeman 405). The autobiography itself becomes his *mandala*, a symbolic pattern representing the whole self, carefully constructed like a mosaic. This mosaic consists of (often seemingly insignificant) incidents from his life and a myriad of references to other texts. His meticulous descriptions of specific, seemingly insignificant incidents often seem irrelevant or unimportant. These incidents are related in a process reminiscent of free association, often seemingly undermining the central plot.

of free association, often seemingly undermining the central plot. Schoeman feels compelled to relate these events or images that he remembers, frequently reminding the reader that nothing is coincidental—that there must be some reason for the fact that he remembers these fleeting images, that these "irrelevant" memories of seemingly unimportant events or images "are presented to him" (Schoeman 272—my translation). These memories are often accompanied by quotations from literary texts or references to other texts. Together, these references and memories form a pattern. The pattern emerges through the narrative process.

Schoeman's methodology in the autobiography serves to explain narrative identity. A biography is after all an explicit representation of a life. In an autobiography the subject is self-consciously constructing itself. The self that emerges from this self-narrative is not, however, a pre-existing subject that is simply represented in the narrative. Such a view would imply a pre-linguistic *cogito*—a metaphysical presupposition. The self, identity, is not readily available for scrutiny by the self. From a hermeneutical point of view, the self is always an interpretation. Paul Ricoeur's distinction in *Time and Narrative* between three instances of mimesis (which he names $mimesis_1$, $mimesis_2$ and $mimesis_3$ respectively) can be used to describe the process of identity construction through narration.

Mimesis₁. Schoeman's self-narrative consists, in the first instance, of memories of specific incidents that are related. The narrating 'I' of the autobiography (the retired writer and historian) is the 'speaking subject' (Kerby 140). This 'speaking subject', Schoeman, stands in a tradition ($mimesis_1$). He knows, for example, the conventions of the genre of autobiography. He draws on a vast knowledge of literature and literary conventions—for example the quotation that marks the end of his autobiography is from Virgil's *Bucolica* X. In these last lines of the last poem in his pastoral cycle, Virgil takes leave of the pastoral genre. The quotation therefore suggests that Schoeman is also taking his leave—not only from the autobiography, but also from writing altogether. He also has a wide range of memories of events or mere images to draw from—not only his own memories but also knowledge of the history of the country, its architecture, its political and socio-economic situation at various times, and so on. The reader shares this knowledge (or at least some of it), and this makes it possible for the reader to understand him. This "prior knowledge" corresponds with Ricoeur's concept of $mimesis_1$.

To represent action, according to Ricoeur, is to have a previous knowledge of human actions and the symbolic codes through which these are represented. The plot is founded on a previous understanding of the world of events, symbols, structures of meaning and temporality. We have a kind of pre-under-

standing implied by mimetic activity, a structural, symbolic and temporal understanding that makes emplotment (mimesis$_2$) possible: "If, in fact, human action
can be narrated, it is because it is always already articulated by signs, rules, and
norms. It is always already symbolically mediated" (Ricoeur, *TN 1* 57).

Ricoeur makes use of the work of anthropologists like Clifford Geertz to
support this argument. A symbolic system provides a descriptive context for
actions. Symbols do not have immanent meaning but are reliant on a community's symbolic norms. The author and readers share these norms. The community knows these norms even before the story is narrated. In this sense mimesis
is the representation of pre-existing norms.

Mimesis$_2$. Drawing on these conventions and knowledge, the "speaking subject", Schoeman, creates a plot (Ricoeur's *mimesis$_2$*) in which he is a character
signified by the personal pronoun 'I' ("oneself as another"—as Ricoeur puts it
in the title of one of his books). Through the process of emplotment (mimesis$_2$)
the story of the "self" emerges. Mimesis$_2$ has a mediating function between mi-
mesis$_1$ and mimesis$_3$—emphasizing that mimesis (and the three instances of
mimesis) is a dynamic process rather than a passive representation. Ricoeur employs Aristotle's concept of *mythos*, emplotment, to describe mimesis$_2$. Emplotment is "a synthesis of heterogeneous elements" (*TN 1* 21). Divergent events
are turned into a meaningful story by emplotment. The single event only becomes meaningful in the plot.[2] A plot is more than just an enumeration of
events in succession—it creates meaning: "In short, emplotment is the opera-
tion that draws a configuration out of a simple succession" (*TN 1* 65).

Configuration is the "grasping together" of divergent events, made possible
by the reader's ability to follow a story. Following a story is to understand how
all the events lead to a conclusion that could not be foreseen but is plausible in
the light of all the preceding events. Schoeman emplots his life by selecting certain moments, specific memories, and organizing these events in a certain
way—with a beginning, middle and a meaningful end.

Mimesis$_3$. But Schoeman also reflects explicitly on the memories narrated. In
other words, the subject (narrating 'I') reflects on the actions and feelings of this
signified 'I'. The narrating subject thus also turns into a reader of his own narrative. In this process an interpreted 'I' (the "spoken subject" in Kerby's terms)
emerges. But, as Ricoeur describes when he explains the third aspect of mimesis, the interpreter, the reader is not unaffected by the process of reading. Ricoeur states that understanding (in the hermeneutical sense) is more than simply
the (structural) analysis and description of the plot:

> The hermeneutical problem begins, then, where linguistics leaves off. It attempts to
> discover new features of referentiality which are not descriptive, features of communi-

cability which are not utilitarian, and features of reflexivity which are not narcissistic, as
these are engendered by the literary work. ("Quest" 27)

To understand is therefore more than merely describing or analyzing the plot
(mimesis$_2$). The configuration described as mimesis$_2$ has to be re-figured (mime-
sis$_3$) through the reading process. This refiguration is the third instance of mimesis that involves "application." Narrative is restored to the time of action and
suffering in mimesis$_3$. Mimesis$_3$ is the intersection between the "world of the
text"[3] and "the world of the reader." The world configured by emplotment is
refigured by the reader (which does not mean that it is discovered in or behind
the text, but it is an active process of re-figuration, not re-storing something
inherent in the text). The narrative process (configuration/composition/em-
plotment) is not completed in the text, but by the reader and it has an effect on
the reader; it changes the reader: "My thesis is here that the process of composition, of configuration, is not completed in the text but in the reader and, under
this condition, makes possible the reconfiguration of life by narrative" (Ricoeur,
"Quest" 26).

Through the reading process a possible world is opened up in front of the
text, and the reader enters this possible world by means of the imagination. The
reader thus experiences the horizon of experience (the world of the reader) and
the horizon of imagination (the world of the text) simultaneously, and these
horizons merge, leaving the (world of the) reader changed. When it is said that
one is *moved* by a work of art, in this sense it would mean that one has moved
out of one's world into another and that this experience changes one as one's
worldview and perception of oneself are changed in the process.

In application (mimesis$_3$), when horizons merge, a "new I" emerges—
constituted through the reading process. Ricoeur uses Gadamer's term *Aneig-
nung* (appropriation) to explain how the interpreter, the reader, is changed by the
experience of the world that "unfolds" in front of the text:

Ultimately, what I appropriate is a proposed world. The latter is not behind the text, as
a hidden intention would be, but in front of it, as that which the work unfolds, discovers, reveals. Henceforth, to understand is to understand oneself in front of the text. It is
not a question of imposing upon the text our finite capacity for understanding, but of
exposing ourselves to the text and receiving from it an enlarged self, which would be
the proposed existence corresponding in the most suitable way to the world proposed.
(Ricoeur, *Hermeneutics* 143)

The 'I' as a character in the plot(s) is interpreted by the 'I' as a subject, but this
interpreting 'I' is not a fixed, pre-existing subject in a metaphysical sense. The
interpreting 'I' is constituted through the process of narration and interpretation
and is constantly changing. The implication of mimesis$_3$ is that the reader has to
appropriate the meaning of the text, but in order to achieve this, the reader has
to distance herself from her own position. "If fiction is a fundamental dimen-

sion of the reference of the text, it is no less a fundamental dimension of the subjectivity of the reader. As a reader I find myself only by losing myself" (Ricoeur, *Hermeneutics* 144). This process can obviously never be completed. Reinterpretation, re-telling of events remains possible. A Proustian *"madeleine"* experience could bring lost memories back that could change the self-narrative once again, while the significance of events could change in the light of later experience. This process of constant change in self-understanding is what Ricoeur calls "narrative identity":

> [A]llow me to say that what we call the subject is never given at the start. Or, if it is, it is in danger of being reduced to the narcissistic, egoistic and stingy ego, from which literature, precisely, can free us. …In place of an ego enamoured of itself arises a self—instructed by cultural symbols, the first among which are the narratives handed down in our literary tradition. And these narratives give us a unity which is not substantial but narrative. ("Quest" 33)

The emphasis that Ricoeur places on "the narratives handed down in our literary tradition" is what I would now like to turn to. In his autobiography, Schoeman constantly refers to other texts in order to express himself and to clarify certain ideas. He explicitly shows how his self-narrative is informed by "our literary tradition."

Turning away from Schoeman's autobiography, I will try to show how the literary tradition (which could be understood as mimesis₁) could influence the construction of narrative identity. I will explore this by referring to the possible effect of Schoeman's novels on an individual's (or the Afrikaner community's) construction of identity.

Voices

It is interesting to note that Schoeman's autobiography (as well as biographies like *Merksteen* [Marking-stone] and historical works like *Armosyn van die Kaap* [Armosyn from the Cape]) and his novels are narrated in a similar fashion. He often uses the same metaphors in his autobiography that he employs in his fictional and historical works—for example, that memory or any attempt to know the past is like seeing something revealed by the momentary flicker of a candle before it is blown out. This metaphor of the candle is often repeated in *Hierdie lewe* (This Life⁴), and the novel even has a picture of a candle on the cover. The past is often described as darkness or as a different, foreign country. To remember, to reconstruct the past, is like pushing against a heavy door, trying to enter a dark room (especially in *Verliesfontein* and *Verkenning* [Reconnaissance]), like swimming against a heavy current to a foreign destination. The image of a jigsaw puzzle is also employed, especially in *Verliesfontein*, where a past is reconstructed by making use of the imagination to fill the space between the few available pieces of the puzzle.

In the three novels known as the "Voices trilogy," *Hierdie lewe* (This Life), *Die uur van die engel* (The Hour of the Angel), and *Verliesfontein* (Spring of Loss), Schoeman focuses on unimportant individuals' recollections of the past. In *Hierdie lewe* an old lady looks back on her life. She has always been on the periphery of her family and the community. Nobody ever really took note of her. On her deathbed she takes stock of her life, of all her experiences. In *Die uur van die engel* the life of a humble nineteenth-century shepherd who wrote a few forgotten poems on visitations by angels is reconstructed by a researcher visiting the small rural town where the shepherd had once lived. Although *Verliesfontein* was published last of the three novels, it is called "Voices 1" and as such should be read as an introduction to the trilogy. In this novel three "voices," which narrate their different experiences in the same town during the South African War (1899–1902), are framed by the narrative of a researcher who visits the town almost a century after the war and tries to capture a specific event in the town—the death of one of the rebels during a battle outside the town.

In all three novels there are "voices" speaking from the past—sometimes almost inaudible, often difficult to understand and they almost never provide the information searched for by the listener. The motto in *Verliesfontein* (and as *Verliesfontein* is called "Voices 1," this could be seen as a motto for the trilogy) is a quote from the German author Christa Wolff's *Kindheidsmuster*. It reads:

> Solche Stimmen nun, haufenweise. Als hätte jemand eine Schleuse hochgezogen, hinter der die Stimmen eingesperrt waren.

> These voices now, piled up. As if someone opened a sluice gate behind which the voices had been blocked. (*Verliesfontein* 5)

The motto seems to suggest that in these novels, the insignificant voices from a forgotten past and the voices of those unimportant figures, forgotten by history, have been blocked off from our memories and from our history for long enough for these novels to open the sluice gates so that we can start listening to them.

The "voices" are prominent in all three novels, but my focus will be on *Verliesfontein*, a metafictional novel where comments are made explicitly on the process of writing history and fiction. In *Verliesfontein* the narrator (a historian), accompanied by his photographer, travels through the Karoo on a mission to collect information and to take pictures for a book on the South African War. The planned book deals with the part of the war when Boer forces from the Orange Free State invaded the Cape Colony. The Boers occupied several Karoo towns in this British colony for short periods of time. This invasion put the Afrikaner population in the Cape Colony in a difficult position. Even if many were sympathetic towards the Boer cause, they were British subjects and support for the Boers was regarded as treason; rebels who joined the Boer forces were tried and some were executed.

The historian/narrator in *Verliesfontein* has done extensive research on the history of the war in the town of Fouriesfontein/Verliesfontein before undertaking the journey. Although the town is officially known as Fouriesfontein, named after the influential Fouries who "founded" it, older people (according to the narrator's research) often referred to the town as Verliesfontein. (A compound which would literally mean "spring of loss"—*verlies* means "loss" and *fontein* means "spring.") This name was given to the place after the substantial loss of stock as a result of skirmishes between early white settlers and the San who populated the area. This unpopular name for the town is the title of the novel, introducing and strengthening the idea of loss—the loss not merely of material means, but also of traces of the past and the inability to recover the (lost) past. The writer and his photographer fail to find the town; it is lost to them. Although loss (*Verliesfontein*) is an important theme in the novel (i.e., loss of evidence of the past, etc.), the title also suggests the opposite, a spring. This second part of the compound (*Verliesfontein*) could refer to the life-giving force of remembering, of recalling "lost" events, especially by making use of the imagination (in the form of the novel) that leads to the achievement of a new moral identity. Literature is like a spring that provides the reader with possible ways of understanding, of creating his or her own identity.

A well-preserved photograph of a good-looking young rebel from Fouriesfontein, Gideon Fourie, triggers the narrator-character's initial curiosity about the town. His research has shown that Gideon Fourie was the only casualty during the Battle of Vaalbergpas outside the town. In search of interesting pictures for his book, he wants the photographer to take a picture of the memorial that was erected for Fourie in front of the church. They are unable to find the town, however, and the frustrated historian walks into the veld at the place where the town is supposed to be. Walking into the open space, in the hot afternoon, he suddenly finds himself in the summer of 1901, in the town of Fouriesfontein. In the words of the opening line of the novel, he becomes a traveler in "another country." He gets to know the town (although everybody is unaware of his presence) and hears three of the inhabitants' accounts of the short siege of the town by Free State forces. These three narrators' accounts make up the bulk of the novel. At the end he reminisces about the meaning of these voices and on his own (and the reader's) experience of the past.

The historical "facts" presented in the novel and the three voices that narrate three different versions of the events during the war are fictional. Verliesfontein does not exist (is "lost" as the name of the town and title of the novel suggest). The Battle of Vaalbergpas never took place; no rebel by the name of Gideon Fourie was killed in action, and the Free State forces did not execute a

colored community leader by the name of Adam Balie.[5] That is why the writer
and his photographer cannot find the town. Only the writer experiences the
town by means of his imagination. The photographer, who is simply interested
in the latest cricket score and not in the past, is unable to share in this experience. However, the narrator's experience is not "merely fictional." It offers a
possible history of a town, similar to so many other towns on which the narrator has done research:

> A handful of obscure notes, newspaper clippings, photos and facts I can remember,
> and then I have to improvise, with the certainty that the events during the war did not
> differ significantly from one small town to the next, Roggeveld, Hantam, Namakwaland
> or Boesmanland, Vanrijnsdorp or Victoria West, Fouriesfontein, Fraserburg or Suther-
> land. . . . and finally it's probably also not important, a few yellowed newspaper clippings
> and two or three old photographs of an empty street, trees, a village square; Victoria
> West, Williston or Fouriesfontein. What does it matter in the end, and who, a century
> later, still remembers or even cares? It has all become interchangeable. (*Verliesfontein* 69–
> 70[6])

The "voices" are simply "heard" by the writer. All three of them are unimportant people in the small town: Alice is a juvenile girl protected from the impact
of the war by her aunt, and she never directly experiences anything of the brief
occupation. Kallie is a crippled son of an Afrikaner farmer who is excluded
from the Afrikaner farming community because he prefers reading to farming,
but he is also not accepted in the English-speaking community. Miss Godby is
an old spinster. No comments are given on their versions of their experiences.
The three "voices" exist only in their own narratives. They are constituted by
these self-narratives.

The voice of Kallie is particularly interesting as the writer (and in the end
even the author) identifies closely with Kallie. Kallie (like the Schoeman described in the autobiography) is an outsider. He does not belong to either the
English- or Afrikaans-speaking part of the community. He spends most of his
time reading and copying out parts of the books that he reads in a book that he
calls his *Epitome*. His intention is to write a second book, *Reflections*, in which he
will write down his own ideas. He never reaches this point and remains copying,
by candlelight, striking parts and ideas from borrowed books. This seems to
suggest that copying narratives of others could be a way of avoiding a confrontation with the self. Kallie often repeats that he is recounting his experiences of
the war under duress. He refuses to talk about the central event (that the colored man, Adam Balie, his childhood friend, was killed by the Boer forces after
he had tried to muster resistance against the Boers in the colored community)
and relates many other insignificant events. He feels guilty that he didn't do anything to help Balie and insists repeatedly that he had only done his duty, that
nothing more could have been expected of him.

In the last chapter of the novel—a metafictional chapter in which the narrator discards "anonymity" and is revealed as the author—the author walks into Kallie's room—without Kallie noticing—and he bends over Kallie where he is sitting at his desk, writing by candlelight deep in the night. He even puts his hand on Kallie's writing hand, and their hands keep on writing together: "his hand holding the pen under mine as if it is me who moves it" (264). Just before daybreak, the narrator (who at this stage is the author) stands up and walks out into the early morning. He leaves the door open behind him, walks through the garden and does not close the garden gate behind him and walks off, stating in the final words of the novel: "the job is completed, the instructions carried out" (264). The open gate and door seem like an invitation to the reader. The past has been opened up. The voices have been made audible. The reader can now listen. Kallie has never reached the stage of writing his *Reflections*, and this is now left for the reader. The reader has contact with the "voices from the past" and then has to apply these, appropriate these in the way that Ricoeur suggests with his concept of mimesis$_3$.

What would such an application entail? It becomes clear in his biography that Schoeman uses references and quotations from literary texts in at least two ways: on the one hand these quotations often seem to provide a conceptual framework that he uses to express his own thoughts or feelings. On the other hand literature provides insight. We usually do not have access to people's thoughts and motivations. In literature these thoughts and motivations are explained and therefore can assist us to understand ourselves. Ricoeur explains how literature assists us in self-understanding:

> In contrast to the tradition of the cogito and to the pretension of the subject to know itself by immediate intuition, it must be said that we understand ourselves only by the long detour of the signs of humanity deposited in cultural works. What would we know of love and hate, of moral feelings and, in general, of all that we call the self if these had not been brought to language and articulated by literature? Thus what seems most contrary to subjectivity, and what structural analysis discloses as the texture of the text, is the very medium within which we can understand ourselves. ("Quest" 143)

Part of mimesis$_3$ is that the reader becomes involved in the world of the text—and in the process discovers the self that had been "brought to language and articulated by literature." This opportunity to discover the self is opened up by the voices in Schoeman's trilogy. The question is what the influence of these voices is. What kind of self is to be discovered by the reader of these novels?

An answer to this question will ultimately have to be answered by each individual reader, but certain suggestions can be made. In Schoeman's novels, the voices confront the reader with the history of South Africa—specifically of what it means to be an African of European descent. In *Verliesfontein*, readers are confronted with a rendition of the South African War that differs from the nationalistic narratives on this war. It also confronts the reader with the negative effect of divisions in a community, whether these divisions are the result of racism or cultural differences. By understanding the motivations of the three different voices—Kallie, who explains that he has done his duty, Alice, who claims that she didn't know anything and Miss Godby, who feels that she should have done more—readers can gain insight into their own feelings and motivations. These voices also provide a way of articulating the self.

The function of fiction is to discover by invention. By inventing a "story" a discovery is made. Each fictional narrative invites the reader to look at the world from the perspective of the story. The reader's focus on his or her experiential reality is changed, and in this way fiction "remakes" reality. According to Ricoeur fiction has two functions: to reveal and to transform: "Revealing, in the sense that it brings features to light that were concealed and yet already sketched out at the heart of our experience, our praxis. Transforming. In the sense that a life examined in this way is a changed life, another life" (Ricoeur, *TN 1* 158).

This is what happens in the Schoeman text. On the one hand the novel reveals—it reveals the traces that were overlooked, the whispering voices, not the story of the rebel hero, but the forgotten story of Adam Balie. The novel is also transforming, in the sense that the reader is changed.

Fiction refigures the world in order to make it possible for us to see the world and ourselves in new ways. The difference between fiction and history is also found at this point. History moves from life (traces, experience of the past) to literature—past events are remembered by being written down; the writing takes the place of the past. Fiction moves from literature (imagination) to life—by means of narratives that influence the reader's life. The patient reader experiences the past with the time-traveling narrator (who leaves the doors and gates to the past open for the reader).

This does not mean that the gates are open for any interpretation. Narratives are also a means of searching for a new morality. Ricoeur points out that the appropriation of a fictional world goes together with a process of distanciation, of taking leave of your own world. In this process of distanciation and appropriation a critical moment is included. A fictional history like *Verliesfontein* challenges traditional ways of remembering the war. The South African War, as recounted to Afrikaners, is often the story of resilience, defiance and an ultimately brave attempt to maintain freedom. Although this valued end point of freedom was not achieved by the war, the narrative served to inspire Afrikaners to attain freedom at a later stage (and to justify the Afrikaner's seizure of power). It has provided a collective identity to the Afrikaner community and to individuals. The loss of life and the often inhuman suffering did not lead to a moral identity similar to the history of the Holocaust, which led to a cry for humane conduct. The incoherent accounts in *Verliesfontein* undermine the traditional "taken-for-granted past" by introducing the unvoiced history of Adam Balie. A clear-cut end point is absent from this narrative that does not ascribe to the "well-formed narrative" but does propose a new valued end point to the history of the South African War—that is, humane conduct. The reading of a novel could thus lead to the constitution of a changed identity. Ricoeur (TN 3 247) states that "[s]ubjects recognize themselves in the stories they tell about themselves"—whether these stories are about individuals or communities. But they tell the stories about themselves, according to the conventions, following examples of the stories that they already know the tradition. In that sense Schoeman's novels and fiction in general, always influence narrative identity. In the case of *Verliesfontein*, in particular, it can also lead to a revision of previous narratives about the Afrikaner community's identity. Ricoeur points out that "the story of a life comes to be constituted through a series of rectifications applied to previous narratives."

Schoeman's fictional works continue to influence possible ways of narration (and thus forming identity) while suggesting alternatives to previous narratives.

Notes

1. My (Willie Burger's) translation of the title.
2. See also how David Carr, MacIntyre and others support this idea.
3. By "world of the text" Ricoeur means (following the reader response theory of Jauss) that the meaning of the text is not hidden inside or behind the text—waiting to be discovered by the reader—but through the process of reading, a world comes into existence in front of the text, as a result of the text and the reader's response to the text.
4. The English translations of the literal meaning of the Afrikaans titles are my own—English translations of the "Voices" trilogy and *Verkenning* are not yet available.
5. These incidents coincide with historical events in several other towns, and the character of Adam Balie and the events described in the novel are probably based on Abraham Esau, a blacksmith from Calvinia who openly resisted the Boer campaign (Weideman).
6. In subsequent paragraphs page numbers in parenthesis, without author or date, refer to Schoeman, *Verliesfontein*. (My own [Willie Burger's] translation from the original Afrikaans.)

Works Cited

Carr, David. "Narrative and the Real World: An Argument for Continuity." *Memory, Identity, Community: The Idea of Narrative in the Human Sciences*. Eds. Lewis P. Hinchman and Sandra K. Hinchman. New York: SUNY Press, 1997. 7–25.

Castells, Manuel. *The Information Age: Economy, Society and Culture II: The Power of Identity*. Malden, Mass. Oxford: Blackwell, 1997.

Geertz, Clifford. *The Interpretation of Cultures: Selected Essays*. New York: Basic Books, 1973.

Gergen, Kennith J. *Narrative, Moral Identity and Historical Consciousness: A Social Constructionist Account*. 6 March 1999 <http://www.swarthmore.edu/ SocSci/kgergen1/text3.html>.

Kerby, Anthony Paul. "The Language of the Self." *Memory, Identity, Community: The Idea of Narrative in the Human Sciences*. Eds. Lewis P. Hinchman and Sandra. K. Hinchman. New York: SUNY Press, 1997. 105–14.

Kreiswirth, Martin. "Trusting the Tale: The Narrativist Turn in the Human Sciences." *New Literary History* 23.3 (1992): 629–657. Summer.

MacIntyre, Alisdair. "The Virtues, the Unity of a Human Life, and the Concept of a Tradition." *Memory, Identity, Community: The Idea of Narrative in the Human Sciences*. Ed. Lewis P. Hinchman & Sandra K. Hinchman. New York: SUNY Press, 1997. 26–50.

Nash, Christopher, ed. "Slaughtering the Subject: Literature's Assault on Narrative." *Narrative in Culture: The Uses of Storytelling in the Sciences, Philosophy, and Literature*. London: Routledge, 1990.

Ricoeur, Paul. *Hermeneutics and the Human Sciences*. Trans. Kathleen McLaughlin & David Pellauer. Cambridge, U.K.: Cambridge UP, 1981.

———. *Time and Narrative*. Trans. Kathleen McLaughlin & David Pellauer. 3 vols. Chicago: U of Chicago P, 1984–1988.

———. "Life in Quest of Narrative." *On Paul Ricoeur. Narrative and Interpretation*. Ed. David Wood. London: Routledge, 1991. 20–33.

———. "Narrative Identity." *Philosophy Today* 35.1 (1991): 73–81.

Schoeman, Karel. *Hierdie lewe*. [This Life.] Kaapstad, South Africa: Human & Rousseau, 1993.

———. *Die uur van die engel*. [The Hour of the Angel.] Kaapstad, South Africa: Human & Rousseau, 1995.

———. *Verkenning*. [Reconnaissance.] Kaapstad, South Africa: Human & Rousseau, 1996.

———. *Merksteen*. [Marking-stone.] Kaapstad, South Africa: Human & Rousseau, 1998.

———. *Verliesfontein*. [Fountain of Loss.] Kaapstad, South Africa: Human & Rousseau, 1998.

———. *Armosyn van die Kaap*. [Armosyn from the Cape.] Kaapstad, South Africa: Human & Rousseau, 2001.

———. *Die laaste Afrikaanse boek*. [The Last Afrikaans Book.] Kaapstad, South Africa: Human & Rousseau, 2002.

Weideman, George. "Schoeman dwing om te besin oor versoening." [Schoeman forces one to rethink reconciliation.] *Die Burger*, 4 November 1998. 14.

Chapter 2

To Belong or Not to Belong

Heilna du Plooy

When the Afrikaans poet Breyten Breytenbach was asked by Hanser Verlag to write about "his Africa" as part of a series of books by well-known authors on favorite or special places,[1] he wrote about the Little Karoo, the region in South Africa where he was born and spent his childhood. He called the book, which was published in 1998, *Dog Heart*, adding a subtitle in parenthesis, namely (*A Travel Memoir*).

The text is no ordinary account of someone's travels; in fact, it defies being categorized. On a superficial level it is a collage of descriptions and stories of places and people, using anecdotes from the present and the past to represent the region and its history. Despite the variety of materials used (anecdotes and stories of personal and political and communal nature, folklore, philosophical remarks, poetical interjections and even poems), the text maintains its coherence through the constant juxtaposition of memory and present experience and through the use of metaphor. Breytenbach creates a network of metaphoric links, a web of metaphors that connect and interconnect narration, description and comment. In this way metaphoric and metonymic connotations and associations are activated in an increasingly complex tapestry of meanings, so that the text becomes an extended poetic exploration of the relations between the individual, his or her identity and space.

Breytenbach's concern with issues of identity and the self in *Dog Heart* can be examined by analyzing the use of narrative as constitutive of identity as well as the complex relationship between humankind and the spaces of the individual's past and present as recreated in memory.

This chapter focuses on the issue of narrative identity but the interrelatedness of all the aspects of the text forms the backdrop of the interpretation and arguments put forward. The metaphoric web not only keeps the collage of discourses together but also distinguishes the text as a poetic enactment of the holistic nature of human existence. The Self and its relations to the Other are not merely explored in the text but are constituted by the textual and poetic activity.

The first part of the chapter presents a brief sketch of Breytenbach's life. Because *Dog Heart* is to a large extent autobiographical, contextual knowledge is necessary to understand the nature and intensity of the conflict of the narrator. This will be followed by a discussion of the painting on the cover of the book and the epigraph. The discussion of the way in which narrative is used in constituting aspects of identity in the text *Dog Heart* forms the central part of the chapter. In conclusion I will make a few remarks about the poetic nature of the text.

Biographical Background

Breyten Breytenbach's relation with his country of origin has been complicated by the dramatic facts of his life. His work, that includes painting, poetry, narrative, essays and philosophical writings, is mainly autobiographical (Sienaert, "Africa and Identity" 80). It has been described as being preoccupied with exile and imprisonment and the resulting issues of problematized identity (Reckwitz 90).[2]

Breytenbach left South Africa at the age of twenty in 1959 to travel and work in Europe. Settling in Paris, mainly for artistic reasons, he married a Vietnamese girl, Yolande, in 1962 (Galloway 1). Yolande was repeatedly refused a visa to enter South Africa by the apartheid government because she was not considered white (Galloway 43–62). Consequently Breytenbach became involved with the international wing of the liberation movement and on a mission in South Africa to recruit members for the organization *Okhela*, he was arrested for traveling with a false passport. He was put on trial for taking part in terrorist activities, and though there was sympathy for him to the extent that even the prosecutor believed that a fairly light sentence would be given, he was sentenced to nine years of imprisonment in November 1975 (Galloway 169–172). He served seven years of the term before he was released.

Breytenbach has lived mainly in Paris since then, and though he has repeatedly resolved to cut all ties with his past, with South Africa as a country and with the Afrikaans language, he is still writing poetry (and drama) in Afrikaans and is at present generally regarded as one of the greatest, if not the greatest, poet in Afrikaans. Since the political changes in South Africa, he has visited the country regularly and has become a prominent figure on the cultural (and even to a limited extent, on the political) scene in South Africa, giving voice to a very particular form of reconciliation and reconstitution (see also Lazarus 158–161; Sienaert, "Africa and Identity" 81–82).

The complexities inherent in the relationship between Breytenbach and the country of his birth should not be underestimated. Golz (15) speaks of "the fundamental and schizophrenic split within the feeling of identity" that was brought about by apartheid and that affected both oppressors and oppressed. Ethnically, Breytenbach belongs to the racial minority group of the oppressor but he sympathized with the oppressed. After his release from prison he wrote in *The True Confessions of an Albino Terrorist*:

I believe, more than ever, that the system existing in South Africa is against the grain of everything that is beautiful and hopeful and dignified in human history; that it is a denial of humanity, not only of the majority being oppressed but of the minority associated with that oppression. (59)

Although he has never been able to sever his ties completely with either the African continent, South Africa as a country or the Afrikaans language, his writing reflects a fragmented psyche, since he never speaks from one position or in a single voice (Sienaert, "Africa and Identity" 80–85).

Dog Heart and Textual Multiplicity

The multifaceted face of reality and the multiplicity of positions from which the past and the present can be viewed are prominent themes that feature strongly throughout *Dog Heart*.

The Painting on the Cover of the Book. The painting by Breytenbach himself on the cover of *Dog Heart* immediately confronts the reader with multiplicity in various ways. This painting, like all the other paintings on the covers of his books, is an important signifying element of the text, because in Breytenbach's oeuvre there is always interplay between text and image. Marilet Sienaert ("Interrelatedness" 11) explains this relationship between writing and painting in Breytenbach's oeuvre as follows: "The one does not strive to elucidate the other; for him writing is simply a continuation of painting, just as painting is a prolongation of writing. As a means to consciousness or awareness they are in fact one and the same 'umbilical cord of survival.'"

In the painting on the cover of *Dog Heart*, there is a yellow moon with dramatic mountain peaks just like the peaks above the town of Montagu, which is the town described in the book. A human figure with the face of a donkey stands in the center of the painting. The face is averted and the eye closed, perhaps sleeping or dreaming, but it seems to me that the posture of the head indicates tentativeness, sensitivity and vulnerability. It is as if the figure is in the landscape, but not fully part of it, turning away or holding back. Behind the figure two feathered arms are held up, while the figure's "normal arms" are crossed in front of the body. One feathered arm holds up a hand with two fingers stuck out in the gesture for peace, and the other hand is a closed fist, which indicates violence and resistance, but somehow, looking at this hand, it seems to me that the closed fingers at the end of the outstretched feathered arm may also be holding or hiding something secret. The most prominent feature of the painting is the bright red heart on the white shirt, a heart clearly divided (torn or broken) in two.

The painting contains a number of elements that have come to be associated with Breytenbach's oeuvre, for instance the colors white and red and blue, the feathers and the idea of flight, the animal face. The defamiliarizing feathered arms foreground the feathers and the hands as powerful metaphors for writing. The feathers are also metonymically associated with the wings of birds and angels and with flight. In Breytenbach's oeuvre the freedom of flight is achieved by writing, and writing is done with the hands. Writing brings about freedom but the freedom is associated with peace (or longing for peace) as well as aggression (the inevitability of violence). Writing is also associated with love that includes the pleasure of the text, the ecstasy of writing. The ecstasy of flight is therefore linked to the ecstasy of writing, but both are determined by the inevitable tension between peace and violence. The other two arms and the face seem to be turned inward, the hands, looking more like animal paws than human hands, passively at rest.

The figure in this painting can therefore be associated with a series of attributes and attitudes: activity (including aggression), peace, creativity, love, pleasure and freedom, as well as restraint, passivity and distancing. There is a striking contrast between the warm colors—red and orange and yellow—and the cool blues and greens. There are even green shadows on the white shirt. The divided red heart is the clearest indication of the complexity of the emotions experienced by the figure in the painting: all relationships are fraught with heartbreak, pain, division, with blood and cruelty as well as with glowing (or bleeding) love.

It is abundantly clear that the painting activates contrasting codes and that these codes will influence the reader on an intellectual as well as a subconscious psychological level when the text is read. As will be illustrated further on in this chapter, this multiplicity is developed and complicated to an even greater extent in the text itself.

The Epigraph to Dog Heart. The relativity and complexity of feelings of belonging and identity are underlined by the epigraph that consists of three quotations (Breytenbach, *Dog Heart* 7). From *Un Captif Amoureux* by Jean Genet there is a quotation suggesting that writing, which revives the delicious moments of memory, hides the truth that memory is empty of sensory content and meaning. The second quotation is from Erich Auerbach and refers to the ideal state of that person who is nowhere at home, who sees the whole world as a foreign country, thus suggesting humankind's estrangement in the world. The author then quotes the simple words of an ordinary woman from Bonnievale about the colored people of the region: "Those who are here are just like us."

The first quote has to do with writing and the emptiness of memory, the second suggests that it is good to be without a country (probably also that humanity is destined to be without a place in the world) and the third refers to the similarities between people. Then the author of *Dog Heart* proceeds to write a book about memory, about feeling bonded to places and about the inability to relate to people whom one also regards as one's own people.

When considered together, the painting on the cover and the epigraph clearly indicate the undeniable multiplicity that is ingrained in all relationships and all experiences. The text becomes the site where discrepancy and multiplicity of meaning are accommodated and represented in such a way that an even greater complexity is generated.

Identity

In much of his narrative work, Breytenbach is almost obsessed with identity and self-representation (Reckwitz 90–93), and in *Dog Heart* the contemplation of the possibility of reclaiming an almost lost identity becomes a fascinating process, incorporating a number of techniques of which narrative is an important component.

According to Hofstede (4) the sources of the mental programming that underlies cultural and individual identity are to be found within the social environment and include the family, the neighborhood, the school, youth groups (friends), the workplace and the living community. Though all people have human nature in common and therefore share the basic human faculties in experiencing fear, pain, anger, love, the need for other people, and so forth, their actions and reactions to these experiences differ on account of the mental programming they receive in different cultures (Hofstede 6–7). Though individual identity is determined to a certain extent by an inherited genetic uniqueness, it is partly learned in the collective processes of cultural activity and partly influenced by personal experience.

In *Dog Heart* the narrator searches for connections with his own past by re-imagining his childhood and adolescence and by recalling incidents and images, namely of his parents, brothers and sisters, grandparents, uncles, aunts, cousins and friends. He takes note of many things in the day-to-day life of the community in the region he is writing about, but he also examines the past of this community by re-capturing old stories and reviving almost forgotten heroes.

The descriptions of places and the stories he tells are in no way idealized versions of places and people. This text is not a nostalgic journey either in the present or into the past. It is a complex juxtaposition of flashes of memory and dream with the present experiences of a man. He is confronted with scenes that are partially known to him but which have become filled with a different content, mainly because he himself has changed too much. A sense of belonging and a sense of estrangement are both inherently part of the present experience, and the text confronts the reader constantly with the inability to pin down emotion or meaning.

In the first brief chapter of the text of *Dog Heart*, the narrator says: "To cut a long story short: I am dead" (9). Added to the fact that the titles of all chapters are given in parentheses to suggest the provisional nature of all statements, the narrator declares himself dead. He does say that he is writing—that is the one thing that he allows himself to say—and adds that he does not want anything from his readers. It is as if he wants to eliminate the person behind the words, as if he wants to declare this person harmless or absolve himself by presenting only the words. And yet the narrator is looking for that person, for the boy that he used to be and the man that he has become:

> But no, when I look into the mirror I know that the child born here is dead. It has been devoured by the dog. The dog looks back at me and smiles. His teeth are wet with blood. This has always been a violent country. Writing is an after-death activity, a sigh of remorse…I return to this land now that time has gone away. (9)

The identity of the narrator as well as the process of representation is problematized. The past is irretrievable and the act of writing only takes place once the immediate meanings have receded into the domain of memory. There are only reflections available, reflections in a dark mirror that distorts and presents an inaccurate and unfathomable image:

> Is what we call identity not that situation made up of the bits and pieces which one remembers from previous encounters, events and situations? Is memory not hanging from the branches?…Now I am dead, and distance and space will be dust. Memory will be emptied like a glass held to lifeless lips. (17)

Violence is an important theme in the text and is also introduced on the first page. It is suggested that violence is the reason for the death of the child the narrator used to be. And violence is associated with the dog. Later on the narrator refers to Nietzsche, who decided to call his pain "Dog" (58). Associations of pain and violence can be linked to the dog and the heart of the dog, the dog heart. It is as if the narrator sees himself as the heart of the pain, as the innermost and most vulnerable aspect of pain, thereby suggesting the exquisite sensitivity with which intolerable pain is experienced.

Because of the pain caused by violence, the boy has disappeared: it is as if he has died. He cannot even be recaptured in memory, as if his existence has been wiped out by the pain and violence that befell the man and reigns in the country at large. The pain and the violence are undeniable aspects of the past as well as the present of this country. Innocence can never be recaptured, not even in writing, which is at best an approximation. But words are all one has and are therefore not only necessary but also indispensable: "Language is the live topography of a history of specificity. When words are forgotten an awareness disappears" (24).

Yet recapturing the images of youth from bits of memory is impossible, because time and experience have made the man almost unrecognizable to himself. Identity is thus constantly in flux, to the extent that the self can be regarded as a mere series of fleeting images.

The narrator also revisits the places of his adolescence. When he is invited by the staff of the high school he attended to be honored retrospectively, he accepts the invitation, but instead of finding traces of his youth, he experiences a deep sense of estrangement: "These are my people and I do not know them …We remember past one another" (22).

He remembers too well how these people, who are now trying to compensate for past injustices, previously ostracized his parents on account of what happened to their son. He says about his parents: "You were the ones to be injured by what was bound to happen to me" (23). Though he is fully aware of the shortsightedness and constricted conservatism that determined this society in the past, he also sees the anguish and fear that they experience in the present. In an ironic way it is as if he allows them to reown him, to connect themselves to him. This happens in a limited way, but he still makes himself available to them. It is as if he feels he has to do this in order to be able to understand them as the Other (24, 30). They are also part of this process of recapturing memory and investigating the possibility of re-inserting himself into this place of the past (25, 31). Later on he even says of the people of Montagu: "I recognize how much I resemble my people" (67), a formulation that refers both to identification (in the sense of sameness) and distance, because he is not like them, he only resembles them. He remains the outsider.

What becomes clear here is that on his present journey, the narrator delves not only into his own memory but also into the collective memory of the people of the region. Therefore he explores his present experience of a place he used to know well, accompanied by the anecdotes of people from the past and by his own memories.

Collective and individual memories sometimes become fused with dreams. He often dreams about his parents, sometimes he imagines them in visionary recreations of the past. He traces his family history and the genealogical heritage on both sides of his family (96–104), and is delighted to find that his great-grandmother was a well-known midwife who attended to people of all racial backgrounds with equal devotion. He is proud to claim such a person as his ancestor. But in the same way that he tries to recapture his own youth and some essential facts about his parents by means of retelling or searching for their stories, this woman comes into existence for him mainly through stories and anecdotes about her life that are remembered by people and that have been written down (44–47; 91–95).

Anecdotes about picaresque figures of the region, people like Koos Sas and Gert April, who have become part of the folkloristic tradition of the region, are also recounted. Koos Sas could run so fast that it was almost impossible to catch him. He escaped from custody repeatedly by dodging the hands of the police. Gert April was a "cocksure braggart," but a scoundrel with such flair that people were sorry when he was killed.

The narrator of this text is intensely conscious of the position of others, of the Other. It is almost as if he exchanges positions with a number of Others. Therefore he does not shy away from even the most horrible events, either in the past or in the present. Noteworthy events and even ordinary news (the more shocking because it is so common) are told in a conspicuously objective style, like journalistic reportage (cf. the chapter Transition, 127–132). Though an ironic tone can be noted and is used to indicate indignation, he undermines any fixed position, any unchanging point of view deliberately by juxtaposing the multifarious stories. He even describes himself in the present and the past such as he would be or is seen by others. The impression is that the narrator attempts to present what is experienced by ordinary people as lived experience, without filtering the experience through the ideological lenses of either the past or the present, thereby trying to avoid appropriating the experience of others for some form of gain.

The assault on the daughter of Alex Boraine, who is one of the commissioners of the Truth and Reconciliation Commission, is for instance presented as a factual report (in the chapter The Absent Face, 27). That she is beaten and left for dead, left without a face (by a murderer who has been released before the expiration of his sentence), is not mediated by political rhetoric. All people are human and all people deserve to be respected for their humanity, even the rich and the privileged. Therefore he writes in turn about famous people, like the philosopher Marthinus Versfeld and the painter Francois Krige; and unknown people, little people like Rachel Susanna Keet, Gert April and Koos Sas. Value or humanity is not determined by political systems and ideological frameworks, but by a value system that respects human dignity, which is shared by people from all walks of life and all ranks of society. But though the narrator broaches uncomfortable information about the present situation in South Africa, he also acknowledges the complexities behind the facts:

> (At this point one reflects that there must be a puzzling link between effect and cause, between the calamity of pathological alienation and white wealth, but one would have to let them all lay themselves open on a couch to caress the somber secrets from them.) (29)

The tracing of identity in this text correlates to a remarkable extent with Hofstede's description of the elements of identity (Hofstede 6–8), though in the artistic text the division between categories of identity disappears. According to

Hofstede identity is determined by the symbols, the rituals, the heroes and ultimately by the value system of a community. In the narratives in *Dog Heart* the holistic nature of existence is foregrounded by the network of stories that continuously reflects the variety and the numerous faces of life, but also indicates how the same experience repeats itself irrespective of historical time or of social and political categories. The stories told here indicate clearly that behind the superficial appearance of reality, people indeed "resemble" one another as the quotation in the epigraph suggests, therefore the symbols, the heroes and the rituals can change while the core values of humanity are respected and provide a bond that can withstand the distances of time and place.

The narrative, for instance, provides the community with heroes who were not previously regarded as heroes (Rachel Susanna Keet, Gert April and Koos Sas) and indicates resemblances between people of all racial backgrounds and people from the present and the past irrespective of social or political status.

Hofstede (9) provides a diagrammatic representation of the elements of identity (symbols, rituals, heroes and values) with the elements resembling layers like the rings in an onion. This diagram also refers to the manifestation of culture at different levels. In Hofstede's diagram language is placed under the category of symbols in the outer layer of the onion, but Breytenbach sees language differently, almost as the basic medium of life. The importance of language, of narration and metaphor, of words as such, is stressed throughout the text. Writing (the visualization of language) is an integral aspect of the most basic experience and of awareness as such. The narrator speaks of the "tongue of memory" and says that "[i]t pronounces us" (*Dog Heart* 38). Therefore we are not constituted by memory alone, but by the act of language, by the enunciation of memory in and through language. He also says that he wanted to return to this "paradise…[t]o write myself one last time" (172). In a recent letter Breytenbach explains something of his writing process:

> I increasingly find that a book is the representation/the residue of the period of physical origin: all the senses (existential sensors) are turned in towards and woven into the process as it is delimited by the beginning and the end of the writing period, no matter what the writing is about. ("Letter")

Breytenbach furthermore uses a very specific form of English in this text. When asked about it at the publication of the book, he explained that though he used English, the linguistic style of the text had to reflect the fact that the region and the people he was writing about were inherently Afrikaans. Because of the language spoken in the Little Karoo, the region, its history and its people can only be represented faithfully in a type of writing that reflects the language in which the region exists and comes into existence in the mouths of the speakers of the place. Therefore he uses a "transparent" English in which the underlying Afrikaans grammar and idiom are clearly perceptible. He even uses the present tense for narrating as is customary in Afrikaans, rather than the past tense, which is generally used for narration in English.

The inseparability of language and life is repeatedly referred to in *Dog Heart*, and has to do with individual identity (the author is "writing himself") and space: "Language is made from the need to digest a new environment. I know this land, and yet I am a stranger here. I have been away too long. I have to find a way of getting under its skin. One moves forward and backward over the soil, over the page" (41).

Language can also not be conceived of without taking into consideration the collective experience of space by a community:

> Why could one not be easy in a borrowed tongue…? But language is not just a tool, it is perhaps the closest we can come to a communal "soul"—because the sounds and the rhythms (all that is not conveyed by epistemological "meaning") flow, on the one hand, from a shared environment, and on the other from shared attitudes and knowledge conditioned by this environment. And because a language should not just be about communicating effectively, however sensitive a form of expression it may be, but also the contact with the inchoate, the pre-rational, the dark shadows flickering around the words. (184)

It is as if the narrator regards the specific sounds, rhythms, words, sentences and expressions of a specific language as the medium through which life is experienced and remembered.

Narrative Identity

The narrative density of *Dog Heart* is an important signifying aspect of the text. Narrative does not only carry content and meaning; it is not only the vehicle of meaning, but the narrative mode as such should be interpreted to understand the text better.

Narrative as Rewriting. The narrator in *Dog Heart* is acutely aware of the impact and the effect of stories:

> I have been putting it off. I close my eyes to the outside world in order not to see the rhythms and the shapes. Will it help not to tell these stories? Will I understand this land any better? But it is unfair. It is not *right* to bring people to look and to look, and then expect them to continue living as if they haven't seen. People turn their glazed eyes to me. Who made the bed in which we must now all lie down? This has always been a violent country. (127)

The stories construct a reality that does not necessarily coincide with the view of reality reflected in newspapers and official historical documents either in the past or in the present. The text presents an alternative history of the region. It tells about things that have remained undocumented, about people whose voices have been forgotten. The people of the region and their history are represented from a series of different points of view, through the eyes of an insider who has become an outsider and now tries to look from both inside and outside at the same time. Moreover, everything is regarded through the eyes of one who has come to accept and appreciate his own chameleon-like identity. And therefore he also tells the stories of contemporary horrors, because all the stories together make up the fabric of identity of the country.

The telling of stories, in and through the activity of writing, becomes a complex process of identification and acknowledgment as well as questioning and distancing. Eventually the text enacts Julia Kristeva's notion that art is constitutive of the subject rather than constituted by the subject (see also Lechte 24).

Whereas official history is determined by the ideological power structures of the day, as was the case in the past and unfortunately in the present South Africa as well, the narrator of *Dog Heart* writes against the discourse of the day. This is what Breytenbach has been doing since the beginning of his writing career, trying to keep his eyes clear and his senses alive to the textures of experience and by probing the memory as honestly as possible.

What Breytenbach says in the following quotation with regard to the ability of art to expose, problematize and undermine the syntactic and semantic procedures in processing material reality, relates to his view of writing and is exactly what he has been doing in the old as well as in the new South Africa: "I tried writing subversively. What I could and did try to do was on the one hand to undermine the petrified positions, the cultural stratagems and institutions, the retarded conceptions of the dominant Afrikaans culture, and on the other hand to sharpen the knowledge of the implications of the South African regime" ("Statement" 193).

Consequently history is rewritten in a regenerative way, not giving way to external structures and matrices that would distort and dictate meaning from outside. This approach determines the structural organization of the text. The text is arbitrarily organized as far as chronology and causality are concerned. The only principles for selection and presentation of material are the highly suspect flashes of memory and the unpredictable irruptions of present experience. The world is brought into being through new words, and the text becomes a place where old perceptions and hardened attitudes and prejudices are cleared away so that the present can be experienced and explored as directly and honestly as possible.

Narrative and the Self and the Other. The narrator in *Dog Heart* says: "When the stories die, we no longer exist" (42). Paul Ricoeur (73) formulates a notion of narrative identity that is the "sort of identity to which a human being has access thanks to the mediation of the narrative function." According to Ricoeur human lives can be better understood and interpreted and be more readable

"when they are interpreted in function of the stories people tell about themselves" (73). Narration can play a significant role in the resolution of difficulties
related to personal identity, and here Ricoeur refers to *identity as self* rather than
to *identity as sameness*. In *Dog Heart* there are passages that can be seen as referring
to sameness ("I recognize how much I resemble my people," 67), but sameness
as well as individual identity is undermined constantly. Breytenbach indeed constitutes the self in and through narration, but at the same time a perspective on
reality is developed in which the self and the community can be regenerated.
The narrator says:

> I walk and sit like these people, and speak the same sounds. …When we came around
> Vrotkop and look down upon the pattern of vineyards, the shade of the prickly pears
> merging with the soil, the movements of squat bushes, then I know I'm looking
> through my grandfather's eyes. And when I put a blade of grass in the mouth to chew I
> taste my father's spittle. (68)

The relation between Self and Other is not simple, since the self is constantly
shifting its position in narrative terms. The narrator finds satisfaction in claiming Granny Keet as an ancestor because her life becomes part of his story when
he asks: "Am I not allowed to mark out my history?" (203). But in the present
she exists only in stories. In the same way that the boy he used to be, has disappeared, memories of this woman have also become empty. He cannot find her
grave. The narrator and his wife, Lotus, have to appropriate a place and imagine
it to be her grave (202–203). He needs to belong; yet he knows that in belonging or in experiencing kinship, even to a limited degree, "there's an ambiguity…a painful uncomfortableness". He explains: "Partaking of the known can
be a very effective way of camouflaging the unknown, or rather the unspeakable. It is like hiding in the light. Too much "understanding" leads to compla-
cency and then corruption" (185).

Therefore the narrator keeps his distance. The stories in *Dog Heart* are based
on memory: "To write is to make memory visible…" (16). The narrator adds
directly after that: "and this memory uncovers a new landscape" (16). In the
book memory is repeatedly associated with mirrors, especially a dark mirror:
"the ways of the mirror are dark to the eye" (173). Memories are stories dark-
ened by distance and the lapse of time. They are written down from imagination. They create new landscapes from which no fixed meaning or content can
be derived and the narrator repeatedly says that he cannot even find himself in
his memories. There is a constant awareness of the relativity of all things and all
experiences. Trying to remember and to write down memory and imagination
can also be deceptive and undermining to the self: "Intense remembering has
scorched one's memory. I insert too much meaning in the gaps and the cracks.
Without knowing it I have become my own other. The heart has seasons which
the trees will not colour"(22).

But sometimes memory presents more than what is expected as well: "Is this not what life is about: to leaf through the book of yourself and come upon known stories you've never read before?" (67).

The narrator understands the identity crisis suffered collectively by Afrikaners in particular in South Africa: "We are painted in the colors of disappearance here. At best we are destined to become other (while even now not knowing who we were): it is 'good' in a practical and possibly moral sense, but it is painful" (151).

With these words he warns his daughter not to let this South African landscape enter her memory, not to become attached to it, but he goes on to describe that which she has to forget in glowing and poetic terms, thereby disclosing his own attachment and the passion in his own vision of the place:

> Above all, don't let this décor, these expanses of light and darkness, enter your memory. Look at the surroundings as pleasant postcards; let not this shimmering snake of a river soak your imagination, close your eyes so that these mountains cannot rise and imprint themselves upon the back of your eyes as fortresses of transcendence, be careful not to allow the ocean to lay down patterns of an interior rhyme, don't look at the fire in the clouds and rather pretend that you can neither see nor hear nor smell the wind. Do not let any of these odours become as familiar as forgetting. We only visit here. It must die away. (151)

Ultimately nothing is unilateral, nothing is uncomplicated and life cannot be written about in a simple and direct way. The narrator does not merely deconstruct reality in a superficial way. He tells many stories and recounts many anecdotes, adding up to a mosaic of information that reflects the complexity of reality and the multiple meanings that can be ascribed to or deduced from what happens every day and from what has been happening for decades and centuries before.

Ultimately he also knows that even these stories are unreliable, just as unreliable as memory and imagination: "the momentary and fragmentary fixing in words of letting-go time" (69).

Conclusion

From this analysis of narrative patterns in *Dog Heart* it seems to me that Breyten Breytenbach writes a narrative text in what can be described as a poetic mode. He exploits sensory and emotional experience in the present and attempts to experience human existence as directly and uncompromisingly as possible. The poetic quality of impressions captured in language transcends fixed semantic categories. He does this without abandoning a sense of context and history.

This correlates with what Julia Kristeva (*Desire* 133; *Revolution* 68–72, 127–139, 214–225) describes in her theoretical work, namely the relation between the semiotic, which is associated with the pre-verbal aspects of human existence and the symbolic, which is associated with structure and language and society. The semiotic challenges the restrictions of the symbolic and the syntactic stability of constructions of identity proper to the symbolic (including social and political structures). According to Kristeva, retaining contact with the semiotic is essential for the functioning of the psyche.

In this sense the shifting identity of the narrator in *Dog Heart* is "a subject-in-process of writing...a subjectivity in revolt against constraint and against the signifier which announces fixed identity" (Smith 24). In Kristeva's own words, "If we did not ceaselessly expose the strangeness of our internal life—and transpose it ceaselessly into other signs, would there be a life of the psyche, would we be living beings?" (quoted in Smith 97).

Breytenbach's artistic practice, in this case especially the poetic use of narrative in *Dog Heart*, is clearly related to Kristeva's views on the revolutionary nature of poetic language. The text also underscores Kristeva's notion that though the uniqueness of the self is constituted in language, the individual has to retain contact with the social structures so as to transcend loneliness. This notion can be described as follows: "Our only hope is to hang onto a sense of history, both personal and social, and to insist upon the creation of a time and place in language, in culture, for the experience and processing of the sensible, the intimate, the imaginary" (Smith 96).

Breyten Breytenbach creates the present and the past in language and though he acknowledges the relativity and multiplicity of the things he writes about as well as of writing itself, writing remains an essential activity to him. It is life itself.

Notes

1. The series includes books newly written as well as new editions of older works such as *The Voices of Marrakesh* by Elias Canetti, a memoir by Marguerite Yourcenar, Werner Hertzog's account of a journey to Paris on foot and Joseph Brodsky's essay on Venice (letter from Breytenbach to the author—June 9, 2001).
2. In the novel *Memory of Snow and of Dust* (62) the character Barnum says: "The magic of the writer is that he can slip into the skin of his making," and Breytenbach repeatedly refers to the constitution of the self through literature and memory:

    > ...The biography
    > I am repeatedly in the process of
    > writing is always the same one,
    > and it may be described
    > as a variously sliced-up or torn-apart
    > book of myself as the essential
    > apocryphal memory.
    > (*Memory of Snow and of Dust* 3)

3. In the following interpretation I do not intend to analyze all aspects of the cover painting or refer to the relation of this painting to other cover paintings in Breytenbach's oeuvre. The discussion is limited to those issues that are developed in the rest of the chapter.

Works Cited

Breytenbach, Breyten. *Memory of Snow and of Dust*. London: Faber & Faber, 1989.

———. *The True Confessions of an Albino Terrorist*. Emmarentia, South Africa: Taurus, 1984.

———. "Statement." *Crossing Borders: Writers Meet the ANC*. Eds. Ampie Coetzee and James Polley. Johannesburg: Taurus, 1990. 190–196.

———. *Dog Heart (A Travel Memoir)*. Cape Town: Human & Rousseau, 1998.

———. Letter to author via e-mail. June 9, 2001.

Coetzee, Ampie, and James Polley, eds. *Crossing Borders. Writers Meet the ANC*. Johannesburg: Taurus, 1990.

Galloway, Francis. *Breyten Breytenbach as openbare figuur.* [Breyten Beytenbach as public figure.] Pretoria: HAUM-Literêr, 1990.

Golz, Hans-Georg. *"Staring at Variations": The Concept of 'Self' in Breyten Breytenbach's* Mourior. Mirromotes of a Novel. Aachen British and American Studies 5. Frankfurt: Peter Lang, 1995.

Hofstede, G. *Cultures and Organizations: Software of the Mind.* London: HarperCollins, 1991.

Kristeva, Julia. *Desire in Language: A Semiotic Approach to Literature and Art.* New York: Columbia UP, 1980.

———. *Revolution in Poetic Language*. New York: Columbia UP, 1984.

Lazarus, N. "Longing, Radicalism, Sentimentality: Reflections on Breyten Breytenbach's 'A Season in Paradise.'" *Journal of Southern African Studies* 12.2 (1986): 158–182.

Lechte, John. "Art, Love and Melancholy in the Work of Julia Kristeva." *Abjection, Melancholia and Love. The Work of Julia Kristeva*. Eds. J. Fetcher and A. Benjamin. London: Routledge, 1990. 24–41.

Reckwitz, Erhard. "Breyten Breytenbach's 'Memory of Snow and of Dust'—A Postmodern Story of Identiti(es)." *AlterNation* 6.2 (1999): 90–102.

Ricoeur, Paul. "Narrative Identity." *Philosophy Today* (1991): 73–81. Spring.

Segers, Rien T. "Inventing a Future for Literary Studies: Research and Teaching on Cultural Identity." *Journal of Literary Studies* 13.3-4 (1997): 263–283.

Sienaert, Marilet. "The Interrelatedness of Breyten Breytenbach's Poetry and Pictorial Art." *De Arte* 51 (1995): 11–20.

———. "Africa and Identity in the Art and Writing of Breyten Breytenbach." *AlterNation* 6.2 (1999): 80–89.

Smith, Anne-Marie. *Julia Kristeva. Speaking the Unspeakable*. London: Pluto Press, 1998.

Chapter 3

External Events and Internal Reality: Fugard's Construction of (Afrikaner) Identity in the Plays of the Nineties

Annette L. Combrink

One typical mode of autobiographical writing practiced in South Africa at the moment is to write life stories that proclaim one's liberation from the bonds of the past. Another, perhaps produced more often by white writers, is the adoption of the mode of the confessional. (Nuttall & Coetzee 6)

This is a particularly apt introduction to the work of Athol Fugard in the nineties. Indeed, he has interwoven to such an extent the personal and the public in his latest work that the dividing line has become very tenuous. This has had the effect that his work has been met by a marked degree of reservation by some critics while still being rapturously accepted by his faithful following. This chapter will seek to investigate the extent to which he has further explored two established concerns in his work, namely, Afrikaner identity and the space within which characters are located, in his latest work in different genres, most notably autobiography and drama.

In Fugard's most recent writings there is a strong suggestion of the confessional, which also has the concomitant effect that his work has become increasingly interiorized, with an almost insistent concern for turning the "personal story into the public account" (Ray vi). Fugard justifies this by saying, in *Cousins* (the first of an intended four-part autobiography) that "secrets have an ambiguous nature, however, and as important as it is to lock them away safely, so also is there the compulsion to share them. A very necessary skill for a writer is to judge when that moment has come. I know it is time now to share this one…" (*Cousins* Foreword 2).[1] In Fugard's case this project has been a matter of embracing the "motherland" and adopting the identity suggested by his roots, a conscious re-inscription of himself into the history of the country that has provided him with abundant raw material for his dramatic career. Interestingly enough, though, in the work and public utterances of another icon of South African (especially Afrikaans) literature, Breyten Breytenbach, the same issue has become a love-hate relationship centering on an insistence on flight and repudiation. What will follow in this chapter is how, at the beginning of a new millennium, Fugard has in a wide range of writings spelled out his stance on the adoption of identity as located within the ambit of language and culture and firmly anchored in physical and liminal space.

About forty years after his debut as a significant playwright, and in view of the recent developments within his oeuvre hinted at above, it is apposite to stand back and look at the work of Athol Fugard, directing a fresh gaze at what is by most standards a prolific author output, spanning the genres of drama, fiction, autobiography and random prose writings such as notes. Fugard has for a long time figured prominently both nationally and perhaps especially internationally, addressing an audience that has been assiduously and consciously cultivated. He has been the object of fulsome praise on the one hand, and sometimes virulent criticism, on the other, and a whole range in between. Dennis Walder, in a 1999 article, has called for "a re-siting of the boundaries of critical and theoretical discourse" (50) in the reading and critical assessment of South African drama. In view of the developments in this formerly highly productive area of South African drama, this is both necessary and inevitable.

This chapter is an attempt, within a specific context, to offer perspectives on Fugard's work that have been hinted at often and tentatively explored in a number of studies.[2] It is constructed within a frame created by a number of statements made by Fugard himself and by critics that center on his fascination with identity, his role as a playwright, his standing as a creator of imaginative texts, dark personal and other forebodings about his continued success as a playwright and a number of increasingly personal or interiorized issues drawn from his personal life and incorporated with a greater or lesser degree of success into his creative works. It is also built on the premise that Fugard has embarked on a more overt project of identity construction using particular cultural markers (especially language and personal history) located within particular localized spaces. In the consideration of his claims fairly extensive use is made of material drawn from his non-dramatic writing, as it impinges so directly on the dramatic work. It is a hallmark of Fugard's work that in the construction of the identity of his characters he tends to locate himself in a character to the extent that an overt correlation can often be established between personal events at a given time and the character that emerges from the play of the same period.

A few examples that spring to mind immediately include Don (*People Are Living There*—the early Fugard where a concern with existentialism is made very overt); Hester (*Hello and Goodbye*, where the indomitable but devastatingly lonely individual sets out with courage to continue existing in a hostile world); Hally (*Master Harold...and the Boys*, where deeply felt and long-hidden personal trauma emerges in almost excessively candid autobiographical fashion); Miss Helen[3] (*Road to Mecca*) and more recently as The Author (*Valley Song*) and The Author/Tiger (*The Captain's Tiger*). Critics who have been less than impressed with Fugard have over the years commented on this adversely. The often seemingly unmediated turning of the personal story into the public account has seen the "raw" transfer of his personal concerns into the plays in a number of instances.

In an address to the University of the Witwatersrand (Johannesburg) convocation in March 1990, upon receiving an honorary doctorate, Fugard himself said that "thinking [about the political events of early 1990] has involved something in the nature of a stocktaking of the ideas, values, prejudices, ideals that I have as a political animal. And a few questions. What do I need to keep? What should I get rid of? And the possibly most important of all, what do I need that I haven't got?" (*Playland* 67).

The unhappy clue to this riddle could perhaps be considered to lie in the last line: at the time when this speech was made, the entire political, social and economic scene in South Africa was in an unprecedented flux that could conceivably have provided very fertile ground for playwrights in which to locate dramatic responses of the kind envisaged in *Hamlet* when he enjoins Polonius to treat the players well, as "they are the abstract and brief chronicles of our times" (II.ii, lines 519–20). André Brink complements this sentiment when he maintains that "an artist is a problem-finder not a problem-solver" ("Stories of History" 163) and problems of the most fascinating kind abounded at the time, but as a crowning irony South African playwrights did not rise to this occasion in a way that their earlier involvement might have suggested. Following the events of February 2, 1990, a veritable curtain came down on the production of what had up to then been a vastly productive field of dramatic creation.

The announcement by F.W. de Klerk of political liberation, perhaps in part because of its unexpectedness among the ordinary population of the country, seemed to preempt the need for politically aware drama (which had found its whole reason for existence in the context of the struggle against apartheid). South African drama entered the doldrums and playwrights seemed to lose momentum and become silenced—the enemy, the apartheid state that had provided the target for protest theater, for committed theater that had been the staple for many years, had at least temporarily been defeated.[4] In a documentation project on South African drama that was being concluded at the time,[5] both publication and performance of protest theater pieces were observed to have suffered a dramatic decline after February 2, 1990. Irene Oppenheim brought this problem close to home for Fugard in an article titled "Fugard in Need of New Kind of Hero to Fuel the Flickering Creative Fires"—the title derived from a quote by Andrzej Wajda, the Polish filmmaker, to the effect that, after the drama generated by the Polish political upheaval "now that we have freedom, perhaps we are going to need a new kind of hero" (Oppenheim 11). It has been in the process of moving towards the creation of a new kind of hero that Fugard would experience more acutely the searing doubt that he expressed in no uncertain terms in non-dramatic writing—an awareness also fuelled by certain events in his personal life.

In an address to students at Rhodes University in 1991, Fugard, while stressing that he was more committed than ever to his craft as a playwright, expressed his fear quite openly: "One of the great fears of my life has been the possible drying up of my creative energy. What would I do if I ever found that I could not write again and there was still a lot of time left to live?" (*Playland* 76). This sentiment is echoed in a 1997 interview with the Afrikaans theatre critic, Paul Boekkooi, and Oppenheim picked up this angle again, for she ends her article by saying that: "*In Road to Mecca* and *Valley Song*, Fugard appears to be bidding a farewell to the stage. But he may discover that his muse is only temporarily dormant and that, like the seeds in *Valley Song*, it will emerge again and thrive" (Oppenheim 12).

Thus the idea that the creative fires might be burning out has emerged quite insistently in writings both by and about Fugard. In view of the fact that, by his own admission, his work has always been strongly influenced by autobiographical detail, by the personal story needing to become the public account, I would like to look at two particular areas in this context, concentrating on the 1990s plays and other writings but drawing on apposite material from some of the earlier plays as well.

The analysis of issues of space and especially identity is intriguing as they have insistently and, as suggested earlier, overtly surfaced again and again— especially in Fugard's work of the last decade of the twentieth century. Throughout this discussion I will attempt to analyze the way in which he has incorporated in his plays ideas agonized over in other texts by and about himself. The focus is therefore to some extent on the way in which he has created in the plays sites of interrogation for ideas developed in the socio-political, social and especially the personal spheres.

The personal concern with identity emerges revealingly in a statement contained in his autobiographical work *Cousins* as to how he had changed his name from Hally to Athol (3):

> This photograph has been hanging on walls in my life for all the time there is between me, as I sit writing these words at the age of sixty-one, and that little boy squatting on the bottom step on the extreme right. I think he is seven years old. Harold Athol Lanigan Fugard according to the birth certificate—but as far as the family was concerned, I was just plain "Hally."[6] I changed all of that six or seven years later when I bullied, blackmailed and bribed everyone into calling me Athol, a small but possibly significant act of rebellion. My dad's name was also Harold, and I wanted to be different.[7]

What already emerges here is the issue of both name and family and the vexed relationships that would haunt him throughout his life.

Walder (51) says that "Fugard's interest in questions of identity, bound up as much with the inheritance of Calvin as with Camus, is well enough known, although it has yet to be adequately analyzed", and he goes on to point out that "Fugard has increasingly come to identify himself as an Afrikaner, an identity explored in what I am calling his plays of the interior"(55).[8] This view of his identity has been emerging more and more insistently, although he has had to shake off another persistent personal concern in the address to the Rhodes students:

> I must also tell you that I find myself very frustrated by the label "political playwright" which I have ended up with...there is a very obvious political spin-off to the plays I write. But then my work is not unique in that regard. I don't think it is possible to tell a South African story accurately and truthfully and for it not to have a political spin-off. (*Playland* 72)

He goes on to lament that "even though I can understand how I have ended up with that label I still find it very frustrating because I think it creates an expectation that gets in the way of people receiving the play that I have written. Even more seriously, I think, is the way that it tries to take away certain freedoms from me as a writer" (*Playland* 73).

In an interview with Charles Fourie he is even more insistent. To Fourie's question, "South African theatre is dangerously moving into a sphere of guilt and over-compensation, trying to come to terms with a national identity rather than a personalized one. Phrases like 'socio-political responsibilities are thrown around," he exploded: "Oh Jesus. Oh Jesus. Please Charles. What is that? The death of theatre is when academics, philosophers, critics and politicians try to create agendas for art" (Fourie 4).

How could one, then, construct a picture of Fugard as he sees himself? Clearly, he (now) perceives himself as an unwilling political animal, even though a large part of the Fugard mystique rests on precisely that view of him.[9] His unequivocal criticism of the previous political dispensation would be the single strongest picture that the public would have of him, and his most powerful and haunting characters are those who emerged over years as victims of the system.[10]

Increasingly, over time, two aspects of his publicly perceived and consciously constructed personal identity have been developing: as a creator of imaginative texts, and as an Afrikaner. In his handling of the notion of creativity in two specific plays, interestingly enough, he has dwelled on the extinguishing of the creative fires. In talking about *The Road to Mecca*, he says:

> [I]t was only after I had written the play that I realized what I had been trying to do. I used the symbolic vocabulary of the play to understand my own dreaded moment of darkness—the extinction of my creativity. What happens when all the candles go out? What Miss Helen realizes of course is that to be a true master you have got to know not

only how to light them, but also how to blow them out. This recognition has, I think, been the inspiration behind some of the most moving works of art. When you listen to Strauss's four last songs or Mahler's *Das Lied von der Erde* you are in fact in the presence of artists who have recognized the need for renunciation. The affirmation of my play is Miss Helen's recognition and acceptance of that necessity.[11] (*Playland* 77)

In *The Captain's Tiger*, after speaking of "creative authority...the freedom and authority of the creative artist to go in any direction his imagination chooses" (9), he comments on the fact that "my job as a writer is to make reality dramatic" (36)—but it is up to Betty to tell him, *very* significantly, that "a real writer wouldn't have worried about happy endings you know—he would let the cripple go on the dance floor" (74). In the final scene but one, Betty says "you're old you know. Aren't you tired? Don't you want to make my story your last one? Your first failure, your last great success?" (78). The author responds that "If I knew there was only one story left to tell, I'd be too frightened to tell it. I'd feel like a condemned man who had reached his last day" (74).

A far more difficult and contentious issue is the one attached to his view of himself as an Afrikaner. Within the context of the cultural and social realities of South Africa this is a fraught and hotly debated issue, one that is likely to incense many. "The Afrikaner" is a mythical beast, glimpsed only imperfectly through the dense undergrowth of stereotype, convention, ignorance and hostility. Brink (36) says soberingly that

> [T]he apartheid memory, reshaping history around the *largely imagined national consciousness of the Afrikaner*, was constrained to forget large tracts of the South African past (the shaping of the Afrikaans language in the mouths of slaves; slave revolts; the enslavement of indigenous people; the role of Colored and black laborers in the service of Boers in the Great Trek; collaboration between black nations and Afrikaners on the Eastern Frontier during the nineteenth century; the part played by women in conserving certain standards of education and morality in the deep interior, or in the Great Trek)...and to suppress the key roles played by "outsiders" to what came to be construed as the master narrative (Krotoa, Andries Stockenstrom, Coenraad Buys, Estienne Barbier, Susanna Smit, Nongqawuse, Christiaan de Wet's "traitor" brother Piet). By the same token it would be possible for the newly emerging post-apartheid memory conveniently to forget or underplay other events and characters in the overall narrative, ranging from collaboration with the oppressor to atrocities in training camps in Angola and elsewhere. ("Stories of History" 36, my emphasis)

The way in which Fugard moves from personal story to public account (Ray vi) is perhaps the most rewarding route to investigate the present issue, and in trying to distil from Fugard's work (dramatic and otherwise) the image or myth of the essential Afrikaner, it might become possible to determine what would be the picture of the Afrikaner that underlies the insistence that it is now (more) possible for him to call himself an Afrikaner.

In trying to construct a working definition or image of the Afrikaner, one could consider the following:

First, to be an Afrikaner the bottom line that one could expect would be for the individual or group concerned to speak Afrikaans as a native language—the language and the people have been indivisibly linked. Language is therefore the foremost marker used to construct identity within this cultural context.

Second, a persistent stereotype construing the Afrikaner that one could not get away from is that of the white descendants of the Huguenots and the Dutch from who would be descended the Voortrekkers (colonizers all), who have generally been perceived as dour, puritanical and conservative people with a passionate attachment to the land and a sometimes obsessive racial intolerance. Add to this, following the South African War, a strong Anglophobia linked by extension to the poor white problem as experienced in the first third of the twentieth century. This stereotype is an enduring one that is still persistently extant in certain areas in South Africa.

Add to the above considerations other qualities popularly associated with the Afrikaner over time, such as stolid courage in the face of adversity, moral rectitude, an indomitable will to overcome, an often earthy if not scatological sense of humor, and you have "the salt of the earth." Notions of family are crucial and are tied in seamlessly with the land and with naming.[12]

One could then bring in another ingredient of Afrikaans-speaking people— in postcolonial jargon, the Other—the colored people, that heterogeneous grouping made up of the descendants of the Cape Malay slaves (with a strong Muslim presence but Afrikaans-speaking) as well as other constituent groups making up the group of people of mixed race described by Venter (13) as emanating from a disparate background: "From where do the Coloured people of South Africa come—Who were their progenitors?...For many years a formidable and polyglot array of 'experts'...have sought to clarify the issue. ...What is true is that few communities in the world can claim origins as disparate, widespread and complex as the South African Cape Coloured." The issue becomes even more vexed when one realizes that all the members of this group, until recently, shared the misfortune of being dispossessed in terms of land—in some instances particularly poignantly, as in the case of District Six in Cape Town. Carli Coetzee has argued persuasively (118–119) that "Krotoa offers Afrikaans-speaking South Africans a way into a South African identity, rearticulated in an African context...the admission of, or the claim to, hybrid identity and Khoikhoi blood can have a conservative impulse: it risks forgetting the conflict and destruction involved in the mix."

Within this context religion has always played a crucial role. The traditional white Afrikaner has mostly belonged to one of the "sister churches"[13]—and the very distinct Calvinist-Protestant slant of these churches added its own flavor to the identity construction of the Afrikaner. Popular (mis?)perceptions about Calvinism and Protestantism of this particular brand have perhaps contributed most strongly to reigning stereotypes about the (white) Afrikaner. A strong sense of being the "elect" among the more conservative Afrikaners (the pioneer stereotype) would be inextricably woven into the issue of apartheid vis-à-vis church. Colored Afrikaners had also traditionally been relegated to the indignity of belonging to the "mission" branch of especially the Dutch Reformed Church—a further divisive wedge between different groupings of Afrikaners.[14]

In trying to find some common denominators of what the Afrikaner is popularly considered to be constituted of, one would then resort to denominators such as:

- the Afrikaans language;
- the Afrikaans church(es);
- love of the land (however popularly and stereotypically construed);
- courage, an indomitable will to survive;
- earthy humor and warmth;
- a strong sense of family in which the issue of "naming" is central (naming people, naming the land);
- a concomitant conservatism expressed often as racism and racial intolerance.

These are the qualities that Fugard has invested his characters with over the years—at times with one-sidedness, as in the case of the brutal policemen in a number of plays, most notably perhaps Prinsloo, the sadistic warder in *The Island*, called by the inmates Hodoshe, a word used to denote an obnoxious insect, at other times with considerably more nuance and sympathy, as in the case of the sincere but misdirected minister in *Road to Mecca*, the suffering Piet Bezuidenhout in *Lesson from Aloes*, and Betty in *The Captain's Tiger*. Moving from the early period to the present, to the decade under consideration in this chapter, he has made some shifts, and these are what will be considered further on. The quality of the confessional, leading to his more overt embracing of the notion of the Afrikaner, will emerge more and more strongly in the plays to be considered.

Who Are the (Putative) Afrikaners[15] in the Plays?

In *Boesman and Lena* the titular characters are colored, dispossessed, in their own terms the "rubbish of the earth." Hester and Johnny, and their absent dead parents in *Hello and Goodbye* belong quite unmistakably to the poor white Afrikaans-speaking segment of the population. Philander, the colored protagonist of the searing indictment of the Immorality Act in *Statements*, is Afrikaans-speaking. Prinsloo, the sadistic prison warder in *The Island*, is the archetypical conservative Afrikaans-speaking racist. Piet Bezuidenhout in *Lesson from Aloes*, married to a fragile Englishwoman, is one of his more sympathetic, salt-of-the-earth Afrikaner characters. Hally's mother, in *Master Harold...and the Boys,* is the most overt of his personal creations, a direct, unmediated portrait of the mother whom he adored and to whose memory his latest reconstruction of Afrikaner identity is owed. Marius Beyleveld is the sincere, but conservative and misguided Afrikaans minister in *Road to Mecca*—unable to plumb the depths of suffering of either Miss Helen or Elsa, and doomed to remain unredeemed in dramatic terms—a fairly stereotyped Fugard solution when it comes to such characters. Gideon, in the more recent *Playland,* is also a stolid stereotype, a soldier returning from the senseless and wasteful war in Angola. In this play Fugard forces a dramatic solution between white and black that borders on the ludicrous and in so doing loses an opportunity to forge a convincing resolution within the context of the new South Africa.

Oupa/Buks and Veronica in *Valley Song* are stereotyped colored characters embodying the dispossessed of the earth, located more promisingly in an environment where ultimately their dispossession will be alleviated (unlike the total lack of prospects experienced by Boesman and Lena in the play of the same name). Betty le Roux, alias Potgieter, in *The Captain's Tiger,* is the embodiment of Fugard's mother, and early portraits of his mother are used as concomitants to the text to locate it in terms of place and time.

The whole range of Afrikanerdom is to some extent represented here— from the insensitive bully (Prinsloo), dispossessed colored people (Boesman, Lena, Buks, Veronica), inarticulate males (Piet Bezuidenhout, locked into the land), the stereotyped, well-meaning minister Marius Beyleveld, the soldier returning from a bewildering, ultimately senseless and wasteful war (Gideon) to the women: Hester, Hally's mother and Betty le Roux. It would not be preposterous, I think, to hazard a guess that when Fugard aligns himself with the Afrikaner, his picture is of a strong, indomitable morally upright Afrikaans-speaking woman with an earthy sense of humor, strong family values, and an attachment to the land (the Karoo).

Njabulo Ndebele (24–25) has captured much of what Fugard aspires to by referring to the "Afrikaner" in the context of the Truth and Reconciliation Commission in the following terms: "The ordinary Afrikaner family, lost in the illusion of the historic heroism of the group, has to find its moral identity within a national community in which it is freed from the burden of being special. Afrikaner culture and its language will triumph from the resultant honesty of self-revelation, the resonances of which will appeal to many others whose humanity has been newly revealed by a liberated present. ...Somewhere the story of the agony of the contemporary Afrikaner family will converge with the stories of millions of those recently emerged from oppression." What has been happening in Fugard's most recent plays would seem to resonate quite closely with this.

Having said all this—the range of people who are "Afrikaans-speaking South Africans" is wide, complex and always shifting. The easy distinction often made between white Afrikaners who are reactionary and white English people who are liberal is a facile and unsophisticated one as is acerbically highlighted by Ndebele when he speaks of "the archetypal image of the bleeding-heart, English-speaking liberal South African, who has no understanding of why he is hated so much when he sacrificed so much for the oppressed" (26).

In terms of space, it is possible to identify physical spaces used as settings and other "ritual" spaces. Fugard, in common with a number of other South African authors, uses space as a concrete context for his characters. His use of space is at times utterly redolent of places that one knows, and he refrains from idealizing any of the physical spaces that he evokes—in fact, he has quite successfully evoked, in naturalistic detail, landscapes and interiors that are depressing, hostile and totally inimical to being idealized, and yet the landscapes especially have been shown to have a hold on characters and keep them in thrall.[16] The estranging quality imparted by the hostile landscapes creates a powerful tension when seen in concomitance with the characters' intense connection with the land.

Fugard has long used the Eastern Cape as a space in which to locate his plays. From the earliest works such as *Boesman and Lena* and *Blood Knot,* there is a recognizable feel to the landscape inhabited by the characters who blend effortlessly into the landscape. The names are redolent of the area around Port Elizabeth and lend a local habitation to the plays. Fugard has now turned full circle and has returned to the world of his youth, significantly saying to an audience at Rhodes University that "Nieu [sic] Bethesda is important to me because it is the Karoo. Why the Karoo[17]? I have a sense of going home. I was actually born in the Karoo…I have to start with a sense of returning and it's interesting that the older I get, the more important becomes that idea of returning, of the wheel turning its full cycle, of going back to where you came from, that sense of completion" (79). He goes so far as to say that "the only truly safe place I have ever known in this world, in this life that I have lived, was at the center of a story as its teller" (76), but links this geographically with the Karoo and New Bethesda, where he has bought a house.

This physical setting has served for most of the recent plays—except that *My Life* takes place in a neutral setting, and *Tiger* is situated on a ship, although the Port Elizabeth flavor is tangible. It becomes more interesting, however, to investigate space in other terms. Temporal space is increasingly important in the period from 1990 onwards, especially when seen in conjunction with Marcia Blumberg's view that "the notion of the liminal proffers a space for the negotiation between fixed and often antithetical positionings of threshold states with potential for various and shifting perspectives." (457)

This is a most useful and illuminating notion to use with regard to the plays of the 1990s, poised as they are in an uncertain no man's land. Myles Holloway captured this well with reference to *Playland*, seeing it as "the product of an era of change where the rigidities of the past are slowly giving way to the possibility of a more equitable, democratic future" (36).

When looking at what has transpired in terms of Fugard's dramatic achievement post-1990, some representative views will be considered that center essentially on *Playland* and *The Captain's Tiger* as representing specific areas of contention.

Playland, located as it is in a temporal space (Holloway), is considered in many ways to be highly problematic. The critic Barry Ronge commends it highly, calling it a landmark work, but Myles Holloway, in a carefully reasoned analysis of the liberalism evident in the play, perhaps best sums up the uneasiness engendered by the play; for after voicing concerns about the appositeness of the parable and the symbolic and metaphoric value of the characters, he states that "not only is the play typically liberal in its impulse, but liberalism has earned for itself a reputation in the popular imagination for effeteness, shallowness, incompleteness and inefficacy, especially when confronted with the strident demands of political extremism"(38). He finds that the play ultimately does disservice to the liberal cause espoused by Fugard and his supporters, and, more damningly, concludes that the political message is "disturbingly inadequate given the exigencies of our society," and that in the play we are dealing with "a failure in writing, rather than ideology" (41). This is precisely the kind of damning indictment that Fugard has so evidently feared and to which he increasingly falls prey, I suspect, because of the unmediated transfer from the private to the public that increasingly is a problematic feature of his playwriting.

My Life has similarly had very mixed receptions. One interesting point is that in an essay on the genesis of the play (introducing the written version) Athol Fugard informed the theater critic Pat Schwarz that there had been a fairly rapturous reception by young people and that "some critics suggested that in a very quiet way the programme was a little truth and reconciliation commission on its own. It certainly was an attempt at discovering and telling the truth which, as we all know, is a process that is going to be important in our immediate future" (*My Life* xii). The triteness that speaks from this remark was perhaps what relegated this play, in my opinion, fittingly, to a place at schools festivals. He is more successful in locating *Valley Song* into a recognizable space (a physical space in the Karoo, with strong emphasis on land ownership and working the land). In this place he does succeed in creating a microcosm of land ownership and the concomitant problems, and he does, even though still in a self-consciously direct way, effect the closure that he seeks when he says "Tell me the truth now Buks. Think back to your young days and tell me. ...Did a woman ever smell as good as the Karoo earth after a good rain? Or feel as good?" (*Valley Song* 86).

Responses to and views about *The Captain's Tiger*, to my mind, sum up the present state of affairs when it comes to Fugard and the vexed matter of his transmuting of the personal concerns, especially with identity, into the public. Certain developments in his public and personal agonies about creativity have come back to haunt him and cause critical opinion to become either harsh or elegiac—and it is difficult to decide which is worse.

In an anonymous article on Fugard in the *Mail and Guardian*, Vandenbroucke is quoted as saying that "many writers begin their careers autobiographically and become more 'objective' through time. For Fugard, the process has been the reverse" ("Voyage" 64). This was said in connection with *Master Harold...and the Boys*, and it is considered a laudatory statement, because he goes on to maintain that it is good because "the actions have a more cohesive form and clearer meaning than the actual events of Fugard's life, because they have been ordered to a work of art rather than a precise historical recapitulation" (64). The author of the review in the *Mail and Guardian* of *The Captain's Tiger* is quite adamant that "one gets the impression that the reverse is true, and that the actual events were more cohesive and carried more meaning than the theatrical version...[it is] essentially untheatrical theatre" (64). He ends the review by saying that it militates against "the text's desire to confide in the audience in very personal messages. Although Fugard's return to his beginning is interesting, in this form it is perhaps too private and personal to enlighten or entertain beyond itself-as-event" (65).

This statement carries within itself some kind of dire prognostication in reverse when one thinks of what Fugard said in the Foreword to *Cousins*: "there is only a hint of what are unquestionably the biggest and best of the stories of my childhood: those about my mother and my father. I am not yet up to telling them" (2). It would seem, from the responses cited, that the telling of them has been less than successful in terms of the dramatic realization than Fugard might have hoped himself. In a review elegiacally called "Fugard, My Fugard" (with a forlorn allusive echo of *My Children, My Africa*, perhaps?), Peter Marks (16) notes that *The Captain's Tiger* "is a bit of a letdown. It founders in the effort to achieve the kind of narrative force and effortless grace of Fugard's earlier plays." He ends the review on a note of sad but firm dismissal: "*The Captain's Tiger* is an excursion that takes longer than is necessary"—and when Fugard himself is quoted in a review of *Tiger* by Paul Boekkooi as saying that "nou kan ek persoonlike, genotsugtige stories vertel" ("now I can tell personal, utterly indulgent stories"), he unwittingly gives voice to the central problem involved in the indulgence that he claims for himself, giving rise to what Raeford Daniel has asked uncompromisingly, and in line with the *Mail and Guardian* critic, "What is not so certain is that *The Captain's Tiger* is really a play. It has many of the essential elements—situation, finely honed dialogue efficiently delivered in nicely tempered performances and, in the end, catharsis and resolution. What is lacking is any tangible evidence of conflict" (25).

While it was said in a somewhat different context, the following comment by Irene Oppenheim is almost achingly apposite: "The problem posed by Fugard's artist-as-warrior persona is that his creative *raison d'être* remains dependent on the existence of a *palpable enemy* [my emphasis]. Fugard is not the only artist to be confronted by this dilemma" (11). When tied in with the concerns raised in this chapter, the troubling implications of the way forward for Fugard are brought into sharper focus. Walder, in a 1999 article in the *South African Theatre Journal* (49–57) proposes a "redefining of the role of theatre in the 'new' South Africa…[involving]…a re-siting of the boundaries of critical and theoretical discourse" (49). His proposal for a move to a reinstatement of the "private, interior, even visionary domain" (49) would seem to be in line with what Fugard himself has fairly ostentatiously declared to be his intention. In the conclusion of this article, Walder expresses the wish that "if we accept the case for new bearings I am proposing for theatre criticism, and foreground the claims of interior space, we may be led towards a more inclusive, but still informed awareness of the theatre of the 1990s" (55). Walder takes up the concerns that have become so permanently highlighted at the TRC[18] and links them to the issues under consideration in this chapter—especially Afrikaner identity. If there is a definitive move towards a more interiorized drama, what are the standards that we judge it by? Political standards? Artistic standards? Is this a play that I see before me?

A shift to the mellower, to indulgent optimism, to a release from anger—but at the price of not identifying a "palpable enemy"? Fugard said, in 1991, that "there is an extraordinary and regrettable paradox about the literature in our society—that so often trouble and pain are the alchemical agents that produce significant literature—it is the old story that out of repressive societies come highly energetic literary events, significant writing. Pain is of course not the only alchemical agent in the crucible, but it's an important one and more often than not it is the elements that do it. God knows, one wishes somehow that art could work in some other way, but maybe then it wouldn't be art any more" (*Playland* 80).

Fugard has, in his own terms, and perhaps as a defensive counter to his own premonitory sense of artistic atrophying, become indulgent and his personal utterances have perhaps become a self-fulfilling prophecy.

Notes

1. In the same address to the Rhodes students, he quotes the Swedish poet Tranströmer to the effect that "when the external event coincides with the internal reality the poem happens. That is how it works for me as a playwright" (*Playland* 76).

2. In a session at a world conference called "Fugard at 70" one cannot escape from the imperative to do a recapitulation, a stock-taking—but also a looking forward. This chapter was a paper first read at the annual conference of the MLA in New Orleans (December 27–30, 2001). The whole panel had been devoted to Fugard.

3. "The Miss Helen of my *The Road to Mecca* is actually a self-portrait. It was only after I had written the play that I realized what I had been trying to do. I used the symbolic vocabulary of the play to understand my own personally dreaded moment of darkness—the extinction of my creativity" (*Playland* 77).

4. One notable exception to this has been Pieter-Dirk Uys, who has maintained his momentum and now uses his considerable skill as a satirist and a public conscience-raiser in the fight against HIV/AIDS. A less fortunate episode in this saga has been the Ngema/Sarafina II debacle, where a project costing millions and intended to be used in AIDS awareness-raising ended in a messy financial scandal.

5. Annette L. Combrink, South African Drama: 1960–1990. Project funded by the Centre for Science Development (now National Research Foundation).

6. In *Master Harold...and the Boys* the main character is called Hally; and this play, as indicated elsewhere, is overtly autobiographical and confessional.

7. This problematic relationship is dealt with throughout his dramatic oeuvre—and emerges very tellingly in plays such as *Hello and Goodbye* (in the characters of both Johnny and Hester) and in *Master Harold...and the Boys*. In his personal life his relationship with his mother was markedly different and is tied into his virtual idealization of the persona of the strong, indomitable Afrikaans woman.

8. *Statements, The Guest, Dimetos, A Lesson from Aloes, Road to Mecca, Valley Song.*

9. His early works were in fact very politically oriented, and plays such as *The Blood Knot, The Island, Statements* and *Sizwe Banzi Is Dead* could in fact only be understood by someone with a fairly good understanding of the South African political landscape of the sixties and seventies. Even later plays, such as *My Children, My Africa*, from the late eighties, cannot be seen as being other than overtly political in inspiration.

10. Characters such as Boesman and Lena, the actors in *The Island*, the brothers in *The Blood Knot*, the teacher in *My Children, My Africa.*

11. The acceptance of that necessity, in the case of Miss Helen, would inevitably lead to suicide—as also in the case of the real Miss Helen on whom the play is based, and whose owl house can still be visited in New Bethesda. The existentialist preoccupation with suicide as a courageous option is still clearly an echo of his earlier fascination with Camus and others.

12. Land, naming and family are important notions in Fugard's work. Apart from issues already pointed out, the issue of the name as attached to the land comes out particularly poignantly in Piet Bezuidenhout in *A Lesson from Aloes.*

13. The three Afrikaans churches are the Dutch Reformed Church (Nederduits-Gereformeerde), the Reformed Church (Gereformeerde or Dopper) and the Nederduitsch Hervormde (also Reformed but a distinctly different configuration, with a politically fraught background as well). The history of division among these groupings makes fascinating reading and sheds a great deal of light on some Afrikaner traits.

14. Marius Beyleveld in *Road to Mecca* is a typical stereotyped minister in the mold described in the previous note.

15. It is, of course, also a critical commonplace that although Fugard writes in English, many of his characters (and this would be true of Boesman and Lena) actually "speak" Afrikaans. It is a particular characteristic of Fugard's work that the English spoken by some characters has a very distinct Afrikaans flavor.
16. Arid farmland in *Lesson from Aloes*, dry and forbidding Karoo land in *Road to Mecca*, dismal and smelly mudflats in *Boesman and Lena*, sordid and forlorn in *Playland*, for example.
17. "I think it is the most spiritual of all South Africa's landscapes" (*Playland* 79).
18. These are the corrosive effects of guilt, forgiveness, reconciliation; a new negotiation of imprisoning guilt's forging of new nationhood (Walder 55).

Works Cited

Bentley, Kim. "Fugard's Song for African Odyssey in US." *Eastern Province Herald* 153.30 (1997): 5.

Blumberg, Marcia. "Negotiating the In-Between: Fugard's *Valley Song*." *Journal of Literary Studies* 12.4 (1996): 456–469.

Boekkooi, P. "Nou kan ek persoonlike, genotsugtige stories vertel." [Now I Can Tell Personal, Indulgent Stories] *Beeld* 5 August 1997: 11.

Brink, A. P. "'No Way Out': *Sizwe Banzi Is Dead* and the Dilemma of Political Drama in South Africa." *Twentieth Century Literature* 39.4 (1993): 438–454.

———. "Challenge and Response: The Changing Face of Theatre in South Africa." *Twentieth Century Literature* 43.2 (1997): 162–176.

———. "Stories of History: Reimagining the Past in Post-Apartheid Narrative." *Negotiating the past.* Eds. Sarah Nuttall and Carli Coetzee. Cape Town: Oxford UP, 1998. 29–42.

Coetzee, Carli. "Krotoa Remembered: A Mother of Unity, a Mother of Sorrow?" *Negotiating the Past.* Eds. Sarah Nuttall and Carli Coetzee. Cape Town: Oxford UP, 1998. 112–119.

Daniel, Raeford. "Fugard in Retrospect." *The Citizen* 8 March 1997: 15.

Durbach, E. "Paradise Lost in the Great Karoo: Athol Fugard's *Road to Mecca*." *Ariel* 18.4 (1987): 3–20.

Foley, A. "Fugard, Liberalism and the Ending of Apartheid." *Current Writing* 9.2 (1997): 7–76.

Fourie, C. 1997. "Interview with the Outsider." *Mail and Guardian* 13.32 (1997): 4.

Fugard, Athol. *Boesman and Lena.* Cape Town: Buren, 1969.

———. *People Are Living There, Hello and Goodbye, The Bloodknot (Three Port Elizabeth Plays).* London and Cape Town: Oxford UP, 1974.

———. *Statements after an Arrest under the Immorality Act.* Oxford, UK: Oxford UP, 1974.

———. *Dimetos.* Oxford, UK: Oxford UP, 1977.

———. *The Guest.* Johannesburg: Donker, 1977.

———. *A Lesson from Aloes.* Oxford, UK: Oxford UP, 1981.

———. *Master Harold...and the Boys.* London: Faber and Faber, 1983.

———. *Road to Mecca.* 2nd edition. New York: Theatre Communications Group, 1989.

———. *Playland...and Other Words.* Johannesburg: Witwatersrand UP, 1992.

———. *The Township Plays. (No-Good Friday; Nongogo; The Coat; Sizwe Banzi Is Dead, The Island).* Oxford, UK: Oxford UP, 1993.

———. *Cousins: A Memoir.* Johannesburg: Witwatersrand UP, 1994.

———. *My Life* and *Valley Song.* Johannesburg: Witwatersrand UP, 1996.

———. *The Captain's Tiger.* Johannesburg: Witwatersrand UP, 1997.

———. *My Children, My Africa.* London: Faber and Faber, 1998.

"Fugard Liberated from Anger." *The Daily News* (Washington) 30 October 1998: 8.

Herbst, T. "Another Gem from the Pen of Fugard." *Eastern Province Herald* 154.84 (1998): 6.

Holloway, M. "*Playland:* Fugard's Liberalism." *UNISA English Studies* 31.1 (1993): 36–42.

Hough, B. "Fugard vlek die derms van kuns oop in dié stuk." [Fugard Dissects the Innards of Art in this Play.] *Rapport* 10 August 1997: 23–24.

Maree, Cathy. "Truth and Reconciliation: Confronting the Past in *Death and the Maiden* (Ariel Dorfman) and *Playland* (Athol Fugard)." *Literator* 16.2 (1995): 25–37.

Marks, P. "Fugard, My Fugard." *The Star* 25 January 1999: 16.

Ndebele, N. "Memory, Metaphor and the Triumph of Narrative." *Negotiating the Past.* Eds. Sarah Nuttall and Carli Coetzee. Cape Town: Oxford UP, 1998. 19–28.

Nuttall, Sarah and Carli Coetzee, eds. *Negotiating the Past.* Cape Town: Oxford UP, 1998.

Oppenheim, Irene. "Fugard in Need of New Kind of Hero to Fuel the Flickering Creative Fires." *The Sunday Independent* 9 April 2000: 11–12.

Ray, W. *Story and History.* Oxford, UK: Blackwell, 1990.

Shakespeare, W. *Hamlet.* Ed. Harold Jenkins. London: Methuen, 1982. Arden Series.

Vandenbroucke, R. *Truths the Hand Can Touch.* New York: Theatre Communications Group, 1985.

Venter, A.J. *Coloured: A Profile of Two Million South Africans.* Cape Town: Human and Rousseau, 1974.

Visser, N. "Drama and Politics in a State of Emergency: Athol Fugard's *My Children, My Africa!*" *Twentieth Century Literature* 39.4 (1993): 486–502.

"Voyage Back to the Start." *Mail and Guardian* 13.32 (1997): 64–65.

Walder, D. "Suffering Visions and Present Bearings: Fugard's Theatre of the Interior." *South African Theatre Journal* 13.1/2 (1999): 49–57.

West, Mary. "Doing it for Athol: Representation and Appropriation in *My Life*." *Literator* 20.2 (1999): 1–15.

Chapter 4

The Latin American Connection: History, Memory and Stories in Novels by Isabel Allende and André Brink

Marita Wenzel

The Postcolonial Condition

As countries previously exposed and subjected to imperialist enterprise, African and Latin American countries have several geographical, social and political issues in common. Apart from physical and topographical features such as extremities in climate, isolation and inaccessibility of terrain, the issues of culture, race and gender and their respective social and political implications remain of paramount importance. Susan Bassnett's introduction to a collection of studies on Latin American women writers gives a succinct summary of the history of Latin American countries that could almost serve as a blueprint of most contemporary postcolonial societies, and in particular South Africa. She maintains that it "is a history of colonialism, of revolution, of emergent nationalism, of tyranny and resistance, of genocide, poverty, economic and ecological crises, but also a history of survival, struggle and triumph and it is a history in which *women have played a crucial though underestimated role*" (1–2, my emphasis).

It is the idea of survival that best describes women's participation in history and highlights their stance of endurance and perseverance in colonized societies. Yet their contributions have remained, for the most part, unacknowledged. Omission from history and official documentation has been one of the main incentives for women in the sixties to start rewriting and subverting history by including the untold stories, individual voices and personal memories that were originally omitted from oral history and formal documentation. By reliving memories and reconstructing their experiences, women are able to deal with problematic issues from their past. Memory is augmented by the imagination that, in turn, leads to the creation of new narratives and the re-assemblage of fragmented identities. In this sense, fiction conforms to the essential functions of revelation and transformation as described by Ricoeur when he states that fiction is "revealing, in the sense that it brings features to light that were concealed and already sketched out at the heart of our experience, our praxis.

Transforming. In the sense that a life examined in this way is a changed life, another life" (*Time & Narrative* 1 65). This form of crusade has since also been taken up by individual men such as André Brink, whose novel *Imaginings of Sand* creates a history of stories to parallel Allende's representation of female identity in *The House of the Spirits* and *Eva Luna*, and his novel *Devil's Valley* shows a similar trend.

Some correspondence in colonial experience is evident in the respective literatures of South Africa and Latin America. During the last two to three decades, the Latin American peoples' reaction to colonial rule has resulted in major socio-political upheavals and shifts in mindset. The fiction, and in particular the novels written in these countries, not only exemplify the postmodern refutation of definitive boundaries and fixed interpretations of events, history and reality, but also embody the identity crisis resulting from an oppressive colonial past and the concomitant reality of adjusting to a multicultural society. De Toro briefly summarizes the situation when he claims that:

> Today, with the blurring of boundaries that once surrounded totalizing discourses…we can only position ourselves with regard to a nomadic subjectivity, in a nonhierarchical space, where discourses are being constantly territorialized, deterritorialized, and reterritorialized, and where the only certainty is that nothing is certain. (39)

The diffusion of demarcated boundaries has created a state of hybridity and liminality not only evident in the fusion of traditional generic categories such as history and fiction, but also manifest in prevalent thematic issues, character formations and identity representations in the novels.

In general, postmodern writers have increasingly reverted to fictional re-examinations of the past in order to "re-imagine" and rewrite a more representative history, to construct an "imaginative creation of a national past" (Balderston 9). The interaction between fiction and history is of specific concern to Balderston, who asserts that "historians need to pay as much attention to historical fiction as novelists have paid to history" (10). In a more creative sense, Marta Morello-Frosch (re)conceptualizes history as a text that enables the rekindling or regeneration of new discourses via fiction (201), while Brink refers to "the story nature of history itself" ("Reinventing" 19). The result has been that traditional perceptions of the authority and validity of historical documentation have been deconstructed to expose the selective quality of historical discourse, equating it with fiction or stories. In the shift from document to context and subjective interpretation, the covert ideological quality[1] of historical discourse and literature has become more pronounced. The relativization of history, the transgression of genres, and application of parody has also been singled out by De Toro as postmodern traits in Latin American fiction (38).

In Latin America, fiction was effectively used as a conduit of political critique to counteract the oppressive political systems during the middle and second half of the twentieth century (in this sense, certain South African novelists followed a similar though less spectacular trajectory in the struggle against apartheid during the sixties and seventies). The fiction created attempted to subvert the status quo through a unique interpretation of the Latin American reality called magic realism.[2] The introduction of magic realism signifies the boom period in Latin American fiction.[3] This element of social critique, also present in South African fiction, is personalized and problematized in contemporary novels by including (multiple) individual voices and perspectives on history. The idea of multiple perspectives is seen as a typical postmodern trait by Gesa Kirsch, who claims that it is an indication of the "collapse" of boundaries between different genres (193). In order to reconstruct the personal and cultural identity of groups such as women who are omitted from official discourse, I will discuss in this chapter how fiction and history play an important role and also constitute a significant aspect of the novels analyzed.

History, Stories and Identity

Revisiting history in Latin American and South African fiction for the purpose of this chapter serves mainly two purposes: to emphasize the role of memory in history (the contributions of individuals and communities excluded from official history), and to explore the influence of histories/stories as subversive and constructive devices. However, before we continue with the comparison between the relevant South American and South African novels, it should be mentioned that there are also many differences between these literatures, and by implication, cultures and histories. Despite similarities in context and themes, Latin American and South African literatures retain their individual characters and should not be seen as parallel in either development or experience. De Toro emphasizes this when he discusses the dilemma of present-day fiction in searching for "authenticity" and directives for the construction of a realistic future. He warns against the dangers of "essentializing" or "universalizing" discourses[4] because such a perception could lead to viewing the past as homogeneous experience (35). Yet, as Allende and Brink focus specifically on individual contributions and narratives within a particular historical context and environment, the tendency to universalize seems minimal.

The focus on personal history intertwined with national history is of vital importance in defining cultural determination, as Nick Couldry clearly indicates when he states that "cultural studies, until recently, has tended [...] to study culture on the scale of wider cultural formations" and cautions that "ignoring the scale of individual cultural experience means missing crucial insights into what culture is" (45). This insight, together with the cultural complexity of South African society, has also been the driving force in André Brink's literary contribution towards a representative historical past in South Africa. Similar to Latin

American fiction in the past, recent South African fiction has also reverted to origins, myths, legends and stories in order to restore coherence to its fragmented society. Afrikaans and English novelists, in particular, have attempted to retrace, merge and integrate indigenous with European and international traditions.

Whereas the literature written during the apartheid era relied on and reacted to historical evidence and ideological concepts on the assumption that such evidence was "an acceptable record of an accessible reality," post-apartheid fiction contests this authority because it perceives history to be a construct, an assembly, of "moments" of experience (Brink, "Reinventing" 18). The result of this paradigm shift has been an ongoing dialectic between the two concepts of "history as fact" and "history as fiction," a process that Brink both explores in his work and experiences as author ("Reinventing" 17). He argues that the dialectic between history and fiction provides for an element of open-endedness that not only gives the reader more creative scope but also confronts "the reader with the need—and above all with the responsibility—to choose" ("Reinventing" 23).

In *The House of the Spirits, Eva Luna* and *Imaginings of Sand,* Allende and Brink inscribe women's omission from history on two levels that, for the sake of clarity, will be referred to as the textual level and the intertextual level. On the textual level, the role of the grandmothers is to convey oral renditions of past events, histories and stories to their granddaughters, Alba and Kristien, respectively, who are entrusted to record them in writing. These contributions in *The House of the Spirits* and *Imaginings of Sand* serve several purposes: they evoke the significance of the oral tradition of storytelling, affirm the position and contribution of women in the historical context, and represent the grandmothers as repositories and custodians of the past who, by recalling "ignored" experience, are able to infuse it with meaning.

The second or intertextual level consists of a particular repertoire of stories which themselves indicate a meta-fictional dimension, incorporating both a didactic and a creative function.[5] Brink explains that this technique "involves an awareness and an implicit or explicit acknowledgement of its own processes of narrativization: every narrative text, I should venture to say, is per definition also a meta-narrative" ("Stories" 38). The stories, which resemble fairy tales, become an implicit means of learning from the past.[6] Yet, in contrast to the standard plot of fairy tales (the predictable exposition of "once upon a time…" and conclusion of "and they lived happily ever after") and their didactic function, these stories are open to change and individual interpretation (similar to life). In conjunction with the fairy tale element, the stories also display strains of magic realism[7] that not only emphasize the role and power of the imagination in the re-construction and interpretation of the past but also intimate the possibilities and choices contained in the present and the future. This juxtaposition of past and present, real and surreal serves to emphasize the relativity of context and intimates the possibility of hope for the future: if stories can be constructed, then so can history.

Another important device that separates these stories from fairy tales is their obvious intertextuality: they evoke and interweave strains from traditional stories, reminiscent of Scheherazade and *The Thousand and One Nights*. The different stories all conform to one big "story," a concatenation of stories similar to Scheherazade that both Brink and Allende consciously emulate and adapt to their own contexts. However, for Brink the allusion to Scheherazade has a dual function: it conjures up stories as a technique of survival (both for the narrator and the reader in the postcolonial context) and inverts the stereotypical role of the woman as victim to become the subject in her own story. While Brink perceives Scheherazade the woman as an important emblem for the role of women in society, the text as a hybrid composition of adaptations and re-writings of stories serves as a bridge between different cultures.[8]

The individual stories in both *Eva Luna* and *Imaginings of Sand* are not only representative of a cultural history but also imply a positive personal element of responsibility in the question of choices that can be made and changes in outcomes that can be affected. Isabel Allende (quoted in Cortínez, "Polifonía" 74) summarizes this aspect in her fiction very well when she asserts that:

> Tal vez lo único que he aprendido en todo este tiempo es que nada es un callejón sin salida, hay una solución, y que con mucho trabajo, o con poco trabajo si uno tiene la inspiración o la suerte, sale…Hoy sé que hay siempre una salida.

> Perhaps the only thing that I have learned in all this time is that there is no dead-end without an exit. There is a solution, and with a lot of work, or with a little work if one has the inspiration or the luck, one will find a solution. …Today I know that there is always an exit. (My translation)

The idea of a solution is also clearly reflected in Ouma Kristina's stories featuring impossible exploits that prove to be a source of constant frustration to her granddaughter, Kristien, because she wants them to be resolved in a satisfactory way. However, Ouma is adamant that the heroine has to find her own solution to her dilemma—however improbable—or else "an elephant came and blew the story away" (*Imaginings* 65).

The House of the Spirits

In *The House of the Spirits* and *Imaginings of Sand,* respectively, both Allende and Brink create the notion of a family saga similar to *A Hundred Years of Solitude* by García Márquez (Agosín 87).[9] However, in this instance the protagonists are all female: grandmothers, daughters and granddaughters. *The House of the Spirits* recounts the history of a family against the backdrop of the history of Chile. Allende traces the individual life stories of mainly three Trueba women (the great-grandmother, Nívea, also evinces some form of social consciousness in her care for the poor) and their fight against oppression: Clara, Blanca and Alba.[10] The novel depicts the transition from old to new forms in women's struggle for equal rights (Rojas 209) as each of the women asserts her independence in a different way to undermine the conventional, stereotypical role ascribed to women by a male-oriented society (Cabrera 41, Campos 23, Handelsman 57–58). Contrary to tradition, they all exercise their own choice in the future planning of their respective lives. This individual aspect emphasizes the interrelationship between personal and political experience. However, the novel is told from two different perspectives, a male and a female one: that of Alba, the granddaughter, and that of Esteban, her grandfather.

The grandmother, Clara, commences her assertion as an individual and a woman when she undermines her parents' and husband's authority through silence. She illustrates and consciously subverts the historical silence of women when she chooses it as a form of opposition to oppression. Her stance effectively counters any form of violence as she does not invoke it and ironically, renders both her parents and her husband Esteban helpless. Silence then also constitutes and implies meaning or repressed meaning, and Clara's silence must be seen as a positive act of self-affirmation; a resort to unconventional means of communication (Meyer 362). Her independence and freedom of choice are then significant indications of her deviation from the traditional role model of the married woman. Yet hers is still a personal world that does not choose to engage with society.

Clara's daughter, Blanca, refuses to view marriage as the ultimate state of fulfillment. Her stance provides an ironic perspective on her own forced marriage as well as the unhappy marriage of her parents. Whereas Clara asserts her personal space, Blanca asserts her sexual liberation (Handelsman 61), thereby illustrating that a woman does not need marriage to define her identity or self-esteem; that personal relationships are not dependent on social sanctions in their success or failure. Blanca is more pragmatic than her mother Clara and consequently views matters differently. She places her emphases differently, creating new versions of Clara's stories. Although Camacho-Gingerich (18) attributes these omissions to Blanca's bad memory, it could also be argued that Blanca simply remembers what appears to be important to her, thereby exposing the role of ideology and personal context in the construction of history and fiction.

The third woman in the matriarchal line, Alba, represents a synthesis of the attributes that are necessary to create an independent lineage of women who take on equal responsibility with men—and with the reader. As Huerta suggests, she displays the political consciousness of her great-grandmother Nívea, the

independent will of her grandmother Clara and the spontaneous and free passion of her mother Blanca (61). However, Clara's rebellion is private, whereas
Alba's act of writing implies public engagement (Meyer 362). Alba is the main
narrator in *The House of the Spirits* and is engaged in reconstructing the family
history by arranging and editing her grandmother Clara's diary.[11] Alba is, however, also influenced by her mother Blanca's account of events as well as her
love for her grandfather Esteban, who recounts his side of the saga. By integrating and adapting Clara's and Blanca's accounts to her own situation, as well as
incorporating Esteban's version of events, Alba's text not only asserts female
identity but also assumes importance by representing another, more inclusive
version of the family history. Alba has the dual task of overcoming and exorcising the past (*House* 491) and constructing a new future as she recognizes at the
conclusion of the novel:

> That's why my Grandmother Clara wrote in her notebooks, in order to see things in
> their true dimension and to defy her own poor memory. And now I seek my hatred and
> cannot seem to find it. I feel its flame going out as I come to understand...(*House* 490)

Thus the various perspectives, woven into the tapestry of personal history, contest the validity of documented history as the only version of events and reflect
Hutcheon's claim that a "pluralist (and perhaps troubling) view of historiography as consisting of different but equally meaningful constructions of past reality—or rather, of the textualized remains (documents, archival evidence,
witnesses" testimony) of that past" is also meaningful (96).

Using a similar strategy, Rosario Ferré employs dual narration in her novel
The House on the Lagoon, emphasizing different perspectives on a shared/ common "history." The female protagonist, Isabel, also composes a family history
only to have her narration interrupted by passages in italics written by her husband Quintín who secretly accesses and appropriates her manuscript and takes
the liberty of correcting her interpretations of his history. Such a dual narration
places responsibility on the reader. As history appears different to different
people, the only solution would be for the reader to interpret the story for herself, like Isabel is doing, because each story will attain a different slant according
to the context in which it is told or read.

Morello-Frosch points out that discourse needs not necessarily be confined
to one person but could be fragmented, be narrated by multiple narrators, or
consist of complementary or conflicting versions which would each provide a
new version of events (203). This perception is also endorsed and illustrated by
Ouma in *Imaginings of Sand*, and by Eva in *Eva Luna* when they tell their respective histories and stories. In fact, Ouma's stories correlate with Schmidt's interpretation of "histories" when he suggests that "the function of telling histories
is not to approach the historical truth as closely as possible, but to integrate our
data and facts into plausible and reasonable stories which do serve as the/a nar

ration of our past" (458). The Personal Narratives Group also defends this point of view. In defiance of stereotypical roles, Allende's heroines assume various modes of independence advocating an androgynous approach to the social dilemma (Camacho-Gingerich 22) and thereby illustrate a fusion of female and male perspectives and voices in the narrated experience (Boschetto 531).

Imaginings of Sand

As an Afrikaans male writer who has always been a champion of the oppressed and openly criticized the injustices of apartheid, Brink has now entered a new phase in his writing by focusing his attention and sympathy more exclusively on the position of women to redress their insignificance in historical documentation. This is especially evident in some of his recent novels: *Imaginings of Sand*, *Devil's Valley*, and *The Rights of Desire*. He is preoccupied with reconstruction by recalling and recording the feats of Kristien's female ancestors in *Imaginings of Sand*, a family saga (similar to Isabel Allende in *The House of the Spirits*), revising the role and position of women in the isolated, bigoted society of Devil's Valley and remembering the slave experience in the story of Antje of Bengal in *The Rights of Desire*.

Similar to Allende, he strives to depict the evolution of a political consciousness in the female members of a specific family in *Imaginings of Sand*.[12] The female protagonist, Kristien, is entrusted by her dying grandmother with the task of recording the history of her female ancestors. Kristien, a liberated young woman living with her lover in London, has been recalled home to South Africa because her beloved grandmother has been in an accident and is on her deathbed. As the old lady is very weak and tires easily, she relates her family history in instalments to Kristien, who is entrusted with the task of scribe.

The stories are characterized by absurdity on the one hand and a sense of pathos on the other. Kristien learns about impossible feats and accomplishments, magical powers and flights of fancy (the stories and their implications will be discussed in more detail later). When questioned as to the veracity of this evidence, Kristien's grandmother informs her that it is not truth per se that is significant but the fact that different versions of reality should be acknowledged. She reprimands her granddaughter by saying: "I'm not asking you to believe me, Kristien. I'm only asking you to listen to me" (109). Yet as her grandmother insists, these stories/memories also signify something because they represent the grandmother's attempt at rewriting her history and she wants to leave her granddaughter this gift. In fact, Ouma wants to sensitize Kristien to her past, or, as her grandmother believes, have her memory restored, so that she (as well as the reader) can understand the present and finally be able to realize that she (like the reader) has a choice to create her own future. To deny her grandmother a voice would not only defeat the purpose of constructing a representative version of history but would also only result in a partial account of the past.

The technique of relating her stories in installments gives Kristien the opportunity to piece together her past as well as to sort out her confusion about her present situation so that the narrated account is juxtaposed with the "lived" experience. Forced to interpret, translate and structure her grandmother's ramblings about the past and unwillingly involved in political events of the present, Kristien becomes aware of her sense of commitment and responsibility. She realizes that the courage and suffering experienced by her female ancestors and the sacrifices they made have made possible her liberated lifestyle in the present. The imminent elections in the country symbolize a new beginning for Kristien and women in general as it contains at least the promise of a small step for women so that they can finally "vote for something, not just against" (*Imaginings* 314). The ignominious position of women is still further brought home to her when she witnesses her sister's disastrous marriage, and she realizes that she has no control over the past but she can attempt to forge her own future, which lies in South Africa. She cannot remain aloof from politics and history because to remain uncommitted is to live in limbo. Thus, the only alternative is to become her own writer of history similar to her female ancestors before her.

Consequently, the original personal account of a family saga assumes the dimension of a meta-history of women in South Africa by including and acknowledging the influence of indigenous women in the shaping of the history of this country. While Brink follows the same structure in relating the lives of several women from one family, he also explores the intricacies involved in the "living" of stories and the "telling" of lives, that is, the ever-present dialectic between history and fiction. In this way Brink not only highlights the importance of voice in history but also underlines the necessity of complementary versions of events.

Allende's preoccupation with memory and the past is closely associated with her identity, because she avers: "when you have to leave everything behind, the past becomes central because you have to put your roots in the past and not in a landscape or in a place" (quoted in Foster 44).[13] She is also particularly firm about the role of memory in keeping the past alive:

> A nivel histórico, a nivel de un país, es grave olvidar el pasado. Hay que recuperar la memoria para sacar experiencia para el futuro. Por eso es importante para mí mantener vivo el recuerdo.

> On a historical level, and for a country, it is serious to forget the past. One has to recover memory in order to extract experience for the future. Therefore, it is important for me to keep memory alive. ("Entrevista" 56)

As Klein observes, memory gives people "a sense of the relevance of history for their own lives" (129). Thus in the persons of Alba, Eva and Kristien, Allende and Brink illustrate how self-expression engenders political accountability that surfaces as an impulse to rewrite history.

Schick also emphasizes the role of narrative in identity construction when he claims that "The informal body of knowledge that determines the limits of the possible and provides individuals with roadmaps to the societal landscape, is acquired, reproduced, and transmitted through narrative. Indeed, not only do such patterns or structures determine individuals' behavior in the world, they also define their identities" (21).

Eva Luna

The idea of stories as maps is clearly illustrated in Allende's and Brink's novels. Not only do the authors themselves rely on memory combined with the power of the imagination to produce their novels, but they also equip their characters with the same powers to navigate their way through life using stories. In *Eva Luna*, Allende creates a protagonist who recounts both her past and present in the form of an intriguing story. Her surname was derived in an arbitrary fashion from the name of the tribe to which her father, an Indian from the jungle, belonged. The trajectory of her life follows a similar pattern, as it is pieced together for the reader from the fragmented account of her life, illustrated by stories. These stories become the protagonist, Eva's, mainstay and lead to her profession as a writer (similar to Isabel Allende's profession as a reporter that stimulated her to write fiction). Eva's life is one long concatenation of improbable characters and stories. Her various employers range from a retired and frustrated couple of siblings—spinster and bachelor—in a neglected household; to a woman with porcelain figures cluttering her house—with a room decorated like a pharaoh's tomb (*Eva* 97); to a cabinet minister, an aristocrat with vulgar habits; to a brothel madam and finally to Riad Halabí who gives her an identity in the form of a birth certificate and educates her. In this surreal existence of bandits, political upheaval and colorful characters, Eva finally meets Rolf Carli whose life story is alternated with her own in the novel *Bolero* that she finally writes—as well as in Allende's own novel. As Rotella remarks, Eva lives in a contradictory world where "the whores and the thieves who populate the red-light district are more honest and better organized than the police force...and in which social outcasts (such as Mimí, a gloriously beautiful and unusually generous transsexual) behave more decently than highly placed government officials" (129).

Eva Luna is written in the tradition of *The Thousand and One Nights*, and the protagonist, Eva, is also aware of the power of the imagination. She subtly warns the spellbound reader that she has a penchant for manipulation when she says, "Porcelana is a dangerous temptation, because once its secrets are known, nothing stands in the way of the artist's copying everything imaginable, con-

structing a world of lies, and getting lost in it" (Eva 98). Ester Gimbernat de
González explains this comment by pointing out that fiction has an enlivening
quality whereas porcelain has a lifeless, fixed quality and shape (118). The reader
therefore has to weigh her story with the necessary care and accept that her stories are inversions and subversions of reality and that "the telling and retelling
of stories affords the opportunity for self-representation through tactics that
reveal and reverse relationships of power" (Barrett 120). The reader is left uncertain about the veracity and validity of her accounts, whether her interpretation of reality is factual or fictional. However, the important thing about her
stories is that they are never the same and can assume different shapes and create different worlds.

This quality is also part of the charm of *The Thousand and One Nights* as the
very composition of the collection indicates. Mia Gerhardt specifically mentions
the varied origins of stories (Indian, Arabic, Persian and Egyptian) in the collection and how they have been periodically adapted and enhanced over the centuries so that the collection has no definitive form as a "closed and well-outlined
whole" (10). The protean quality of the stories can also be attributed to the different creators, repeaters, writers, collectors and translators (Gerhardt 41) involved in its history and the types of stories that appeal to readers and listeners
alike. Like *Eva Luna* and the stories about Kristien's ancestors in *Imaginings of
Sand*, their appeal lies in the association with human aspirations and emotions,
accounts of rogues, distant travels and fairy tales. The interesting fact about this
comparison with *The Thousand and One Nights* is that Gerhardt distinguishes
three basic frame stories: entertaining, time-gaining and ransom frames. The
time-gaining frame is associated with Scheherazade, whom Eva seems to emulate. Similar to Scheherazade, Eva learns that stories help to make life bearable,
to transform reality. Through writing, Eva recreates the past that becomes an
almost tangible presence and she intimates that this exercise also empowers her
to shape her future when she says: "Little by little, the past was transformed
into the present, and the future was also mine" (*Eva* 224).

Eva realizes that one can create one's own story and consequently one's
own ending, but would that be reality? If Eva, in her task as author, wants to be
true to herself, she cannot create a happy ending to her stories because life continues and cannot be predetermined. In the event of devising her own conclusion, Eva's life becomes closely intertwined with her fictional characters who
also shape her life (Gimbernat de González 122). However, life is more complex than a fairy tale and perhaps also more challenging. Eva (271) openly
speculates about the outcome of life and fiction when she concludes the account of her romance with Rolf Carli by saying that:

> Later, for a judicious period of time, we loved each other more modestly until that love
> wore thin and nothing was left but shreds. Or maybe that isn't how it happened. Per-

haps we had the good fortune to stumble into an exceptional love, a love I did not have
to invent, only clothe in all its glory so it could endure in memory—in keeping with the
principle that we can construct reality in the image of our desires.

This extract embodies the thematic and metafictional concerns of the text: the
idea of a love turning sour is countered with an ideal love, "a love I did not have
to invent," which emphasizes that fiction is a construct. Allende manipulates the
dialectic between fact and fiction to illustrate their close relationship, and as
Cervantes's knight, Don Quixote, realized all those years ago, she intimates that
fiction might be preferable to life.

As the protagonist/narrator in *Eva Luna*, Eva successfully asserts a female
perspective by undermining the stereotypical concept of woman and pícara.
First, she creates Mimí, the transvestite who is ironically described by Aravena
the journalist as the "absolute female" who has been "painfully created to satisfy
the dreams of others." Juxtaposed to this "fictional woman" (*Eva* 227), Allende
creates Eva, who is picaresque in spirit but also defies the stereotype of the
pícara who is usually represented as an illiterate prostitute. This implied criticism
of social stereotypes and conventions is further concretized and embodied in
the conscious dialectic between fiction and reality. We are under no illusion that
Eva is engaged in constructing a story like her own, and we are left to draw our
own conclusions about the implications of this creative act.

Boschetto compares Clara in *The House of the Spirits* with Scheherazade and
maintains that they are both "creatures of language, imagination, and invention:
weavers of words, and creators of worlds within words" (54), but this description seems even more appropriate to Eva in *Eva Luna*. In both *The House of the
Spirits* and *Eva Luna* there seems to be a clear incentive for women like Alba and
Eva—as well as other women—to construct their own future, whether by
means of words or some form of artistic expression. Allende's texts then overtly
emphasize the subversion of gender norms and the traditional concept of a "living happily ever after ending" similar to the fairy tale, because that would imply
a static, prescriptive state of existence.

Transforming Reality

The most important feature of stories is that they can create new experiences or
different versions by using the power of the imagination. It is this aspect of
Ouma Kristina's stories that proves irresistible to her granddaughter: "Her stories always resolved everything, without disturbing the miraculous nature of the
world. Which was why I could never have enough of them" (Brink 5). Like *The
Arabian Nights* or *The Thousand and One Nights*, Ouma's memories assume bizarre
proportions, grotesque shapes and surreal explanations, because she is constructing her own reality. As Brink explains, Ouma's "narratives are their own
raison d'être and derive from the individual's need to insert her/himself,

through storytelling, within the larger contexts of space and (historical) continuity" ("Reinventing" 22).

Ouma recounts the history of Kristien's female ancestors to illuminate the
present because, as Sarah Nuttall points out: "Memory is always as much about
the present as it is about the past" (76). The fact that Ouma's stories exceed the
boundaries of normality and verge on the supernatural and that the lives and
demise of Kristien's ancestors tend to assume legendary and fantastic proportions is unimportant, because Ouma wants Kristien to realize that the ending is
a matter of choice. We are taken as far back as the life of Maria-Kamma, who
was of Khoi origin and displayed a miraculous affinity to water and animals as
well as a fascination with mirrors (*Imaginings* 176–193). These character traits
seem to have been inherited by later generations of women such as Lottie, who
was fascinated by mirrors, losing and searching for her shadow till she simply
disappeared one day. We have Samuel with the beautiful hair who decides to die
at the age of fifty-five and Petronella with her religious fervor and affinity with
the sea. Similar to *The House of the Spirits*, the women all manage to express their
individuality in some way and to retain a close bond with animals and nature:
Wilhelmina, who has healing powers; Rachel, who expresses herself in painting;
and Louisa, who prefers singing. Kristien realizes that her personality stems
from this long line of women and that she has the power to express herself as
well. Consequently, Kristien concludes with the following observation:

> The configurations may be interchangeable; the myths persist, she has lived them into
> being. Why demand the truth, whatever that may be, if you can have imagination? I've
> tried the real, and I know it doesn't work. The universe, somebody said, and I know it
> is true, is made up of stories, not particles; they are the wave functions of our existence.
> If they constitute the event horizon of our particular black hole they are also our means
> of escape. (*Imaginings* 325)

In *Imaginings of Sand* and *Devil's Valley* Brink engages with the various means and
dimensions of recording and transmitting human experience: oral accounts
documented and officially recognized history, memory, myth, fiction/stories
and legend. All these "records" perform a role in the story of mankind as Ouma
wishes to illustrate in her reference to Moishe's interpretation of the Talmud:

> It said in the Talmud, he told me, that God had created people to tell Him stories; but
> later, sadly, they forgot about Him, they even forgot that they themselves were stories
> first told by God. And ever since, if old Moishe was to be believed, men and women
> have been telling each other stories. To fill the gap after the Great Storyteller had fallen
> asleep. (*Imaginings* 92)

Allende's technique is special in the sense that she both addresses and redresses
two important postcolonial issues: the exposition of hegemonic systems and
their destructive impact on society and the positive resolution provided by fiction to construct a personal identity. However, this implication is not only valid

for a fictional protagonist such as Eva Luna but is also valid for the reader, who is complicit in the machinations of a critical society. Brink, in turn, implements a new approach to political and social questions in which he aspires to attain a uniquely African element, a synthesis of cultural riches. According to him, "part of the narrative wealth of Africa lies in moving beyond the simple dichotomies of either/or, to arrive at more syncretic and holistic patterns of narrative thinking" (Brink, "Reinventing" 22). In Brink's opinion, the challenge facing South Africans lies in accepting that neither their "history nor its moral boundaries are fixed and final, but remain constantly to be reinvented and, in the process, re-valorized" (23).

Constructing a Future

This preoccupation with the past, and in particular the plight of women and their "underestimated role" in history, also forms the focal point in the Latin American novels mentioned above. Conscious of their respective legacies from a colonial past,[14] Brink and Allende take issue with the officially documented histories of their respective countries as recorded from a predominantly male perspective which precludes and represses multiple facets of experience. (Ironically, Brink is also male, but he uses female narrators to redress that imbalance.) They attempt to trace the roots of dissent and expose structures of power in order to foreground the role of women in South African and Latin American (represented by Chilean experience)[15] history. The implementation of choice, a major theme in these novels, is not only performed on the textual levels but is also enacted on the meta-textual levels. The narrator-protagonists first of all have to reconceptualise and reformulate the past as women and determine their role as women in their respective histories—in both personal and public/national capacities—and finally, each determines her own role in that process by writing her own history and formulating her own stories for the future.

Both Allende and Brink take recourse to alternate voices and narrators, open endings and a combination of conventions such as magic realism, autobiography and fairy tales. Literature, stories, history, and memory create means of understanding life but they are never constant because circumstances change and people are different. Each one has to determine her own history and future. History could then never be static or "original" because, like literature and identity, it has to continuously deconstruct its foundations. Like sand castles that are subject to the vagaries of the tides, history adapts to context. The title of Brink's novel, *Imaginings of Sand*, captures both the substantial and the ephemeral: the reality of sand as substance but also its inherent inability to retain structure, like sand castles (*Sandkastele*, the title of the Afrikaans version of the novel). In conclusion, these novels exemplify De Toro's (39) perception of identity as a dynamic process when he claims that:

Instead we begin to sense that old authority cannot simply be replaced by new authority, but that new alignments made across borders, types, nations, and essences are rap-
idly coming into view, and it is those new alignments that now provoke and challenge
the fundamentally static notion of identity that has been the core of cultural thought
during the era of imperialism.

Notes

1. Ideology is defined by du Plooy (216) as a system of values, ideas, motives and norms that
    strives to understand and interpret reality but also serves to shape and distort it by prioritis-
    ing the specific goals of a community.
2. It was espoused by writers such as Alejo Carpentier, Gabriel García Márquez and, among
    several others, Isabel Allende.
3. This period is discussed in detail by Stephen Henighan, "Two Paths".
4. De Toro (35) cautions against the error of "essentializing" by pointing out that Latin Amer-
    ica still has an undeniable "ancient and still active hybridity" which makes it impossible to
    render the past as a homogeneous construct.
5. Similar to *Imaginings of Sand*, the stories in *Eva Luna* also have a specific function in the text.
6. Mia Gerhardt (275) maintains that the concept of a fairy tale is better expressed by the Ger-
    man term *Märchen* and that Grimm is generally regarded as the creator of fairy tales as we
    know them. Gerhardt (276) refers to various definitions but restricts herself to a story in
    which the supernatural plays a decisive function in the plot, while Cuddon in *A Dictionary of
    Literary Terms* (Harmondsworth, UK, 1986, p. 258) insists that the closure of a happy ending
    should be included in such a definition.
7. Magic realism, used as a mode or genre, "serves as a site for cultural critique and change"
    (Bawarshi 336) because it illustrates the essential duality of existence and the possibility of
    different interpretations of reality; it also creates the opportunity to experience and interpret
    the past (the unimaginable) firsthand to illustrate the inherent complexity and chaotic reality
    of the past and implicitly contest the simplistic, orderly interpretation foisted on the reader
    by historical documentation.
8. This theme of survival through fiction is explored in Brink's article entitled "Die duisend-en-
    tweede dag" (The Thousand and Second Day).
9. Allende has often been accused of emulating *One Hundred Years of Solitude*, but the overt femi-
    nist stance in the novel makes it clear that the text should be read rather as a parody of the
    "master text" and an assertion of feminist innovation. She seems deliberately to evoke the
    similarity between *The House of the Spirits* and *One Hundred Years of Solitude* as a preliminary
    strategy to indicate her novel's literary parentage (Cánovas 121) only to emphasize her sub-
    sequent deviation from it. Whereas Márquez concentrates on male lineage in *One Hundred
    Years of Solitude*, Allende focuses on the female line, which complements the male perspective
    (Cánovas 123). In contrast, she also establishes an implicit dialogue between the sexes in the
    two novels.
10. Coddou (30) observes that their names trace the respective stages of persona and political
    clarity that they attain.
11. The fact that Clara's diary is arranged according to the importance of events and not chrono-
    logically suggests her creative ability and relates to the difference between plot and story,
    which in turn suggests the fictionalization of history (Muñoz 443). Earle ("Literature" 552)
    expresses it as follows: "If observation of what occurs, changing the course of what occurs,
    and understanding what must occur are the three most important attributes of the narrative
    writer, then Clara fully and dynamically symbolizes the narrative writer."

12. A similar strategy is employed by the Afrikaans author Elsa Joubert in her family saga entitled *Die Reise van Isobelle* (translated as *Isobelle's Journey*).
13. Part of her obsession with memory can be attributed to the effects of her self-enforced exile after the political coup of 1973 in Chile.
14. Both are representatives and descendants of former European colonists.
15. Although the countries in Latin America are by no means homogeneous, they all experienced similar political and social problems at different times.

Works Cited

Agosín, Marjorie. *Silencio e imaginación: metáforas de la escritura femenina.* [Silence and Imagination: Metaphors of Feminine Writing.] Mexico, DF: Editorial Katún, 1986.

Allende, Isabel. *La casa de los espíritus.* Barcelona: Plaza & Janes, 1982.

———. "Entrevista." *Historias intimas: converzaciones con diez escritoras Latinoamericanas.* [Intimate Stories: Interviews with Ten Latin American Women Writers.] Ed. Magdalena García Pinto. Hanover: Ediciones de Norte, 1988.

———. *Eva Luna.* Trans. Margaret Sayers Peden. London: Penguin, 1988.

———. *The House of the Spirits.* Trans. Magda Bogin. London: Black Swan, 1990.

———. *The Stories of Eva Luna.* Trans. Margaret Sayers Peden. New York: Atheneum, 1991.

Balderston, Daniel. Introduction. *The Historical Novel in Latin America: A Symposium.* Ed. Daniel Balderston. Gaithersburg, Md.: Ediciones Hispamérica, 1986. 9–12.

Barrett, Estelle. "Dissolving Boundaries: Story-Telling as Self-Representation." *Critical Arts: A Journal for Cutural Studies* 10.2 (1996): 119–137.

Bassnett, Susan. "Looking for the Roots of Wings." *Knives and Angels: Women Writers in Latin America.* Ed. Susan Bassnett. London: Zed Books, 1990. 1–8.

Bawarshi, Anis. "The Genre Function." *College English* 62.3 (2000): 335–60.

Boschetto, Sandra M. "Dialéctica metatextual y sexual en *La casa de los espíritus* de Isabel Allende." [Metatextual and sexual dialectics in *The House of the Spirits* by Isabel Allende.] *Hispania* 72.3 (1989): 526–532.

Brink, André. "Reinventing a Continent (Revisiting History in the Literature of the New South Africa: A Personal Testimony)." *World Literature Today* 70.1 (1996): 17–23.

———. *Imaginings of Sand.* London: Minerva. 1997.

———. *Devil's Valley: A Novel.* London: Secker & Warburg, 1998.

———. "Stories of History: Reimagining the Past in Post-Apartheid Narrative." *Negotiating the Past: The Making of Memory in South Africa.* Eds. Sarah Nuttall and Carli Coetzee. Cape Town: Oxford UP, 1998. 29–42.

———. "Die duisend-en-tweede dag". [The Thousand and Second Day]. T.T. Cloete-erelesing [Lecture in honour of T.T. Cloete], Potchefstroom, South Africa, September 1999." *Stilet* 12.1 (2000): 63–75.

———. *The Rights of Desire: A Novel.* London: Secker and Warburg, 2000.

Cabrera, V. "Modalidades textuales en La casa de los espíritus." [Textual modalities in The House of the Spirits.] *Chasqui: Revista e literatura latinoamericana* 20.2 (1991): 36–45.

Camacho-Gingerich, Alina. "La mujer ante la dictadura en las dos primeras novelas de Isabel Allende." [Women and dictatorship in the first two novels by Isabel Allende.] *Discurso literario: Revista de temas hispánicos* 9.2 (1992): 13–26.

Campos, René. "*La casa de los espíritus:* Mirada, espacio, discurso de la otra historia." [*The House of the Spirits:* Appearance, space, discourse of the other history.] *Los libros tienen sus proprios espíritus: Estudios sobre Isabel Allende.* Ed. M. Coddou. Veracruz, Mexico: Universidad Veracruzana, 1986. 21–28.

Cánovas, R. "Los espíritus literarios y políticos de Isabel Allende." [Isabel Allende's literary and political spirits.] *Revista chilena de literatura* 32 (1988): 119–125.

Coddou, M. "Dimensión del femenismo en Isabel Allende." [The feminine dimension in Isabel Allende.] *Los libros tienen sus proprios espíritus: Estudios sobre Isabel Allende.* Ed. M. Coddou. Veracruz, Mexico: Universidad Veracruzana, 1986. 29–53.

Cortínez, Verónica. "Polifonía: Isabel Allende y Antonio Skármeta." [Polyphony: Isabel Allende and Antonio Skármeta.] *Plaza: Revisita de Literatura* 14-15 (1988): 3-80.

Couldry, Nick. *Inside Culture: Re-Imagining the Method of Cultural Studies.* London: Sage, 2000.

De Toro, Fernando. "From Where to Speak? Latin American Postmodern/Postcolonial Positionalities." *World Literature Today* 69.1 (1995): 35–40. Winter.

Du Plooy, Heilna. "Teks en ideologie." [Text and Ideology.] *Journal of Literary Studies* 6.3 (1990): 215–230.

Earle, P. G. "Literature as Survival: Allende's 'The House of the Spirits'." *Contemporary Literature* 28.4 (1987): 543–554.

Ferré, Rosario. *The House on the Lagoon.* New York: Penguin, 1995.

Foster, D. "Isabel Allende Unveiled." *Mother Jones* 13.10 (1988): 42-46.

Gerhardt, Mia. *The Art of Story-Telling: A Literary Study of the Thousand and One Nights.* Leiden: Brill, 1963.

Gimbernat de González, Ester. "Entre principio y final: la madre/material de la escritura en *Eva Luna.*" [Between Beginning and Ending: The Mother/Subject of Writing in *Eva Luna.*] *Critical Approaches to Isabel Allende's Novels.* Eds. Sonia Riquelme Rojas and Edna Aguirre Rehbein. New York: Peter Lang, 1991. 111–124.

Handelsman, M. H. "*La casa de los espíritus* y la evolución de la mujer moderna." [*The House of the Spirits* and the evolution of modern woman.] *Letras femeninas* 14.1-2 (1988): 57–63.

Henighan, Stephen. "Two Paths to the Boom: Carpentier, Asturias, and the Performative Split." *The Modern Language Review* 94.4 (1999): 1009–1024.

Huerta, Teresa. "La ambivalencia de la violencia y el horror en *La casa de los espíritus* de Isabel Allende." [The ambivalent nature of violence and horror in *The House of the Spirits* by Isabel Allende.] *Chasqui: Revista de literatura latinoamericana* 19.1 (1990): 56–63.

Hutcheon, Linda. *A Poetics of Postmodernism: History, Theory, Fiction.* New York: Routledge, 1992.

Kirsch, Gesa E. "Opinion: Multi-Vocal Texts and Interpretive Responsibility." *College English* 59.2 (1997): 191–201.

Klein, Kerwin Lee. "On the Emergence of Memory in Historical Discourse." *Grounds for Remembering: Special Issue of Representations* 69 (2000): 127–50.

Márquez, Gabriel Garcia. *Cien años de soledad.* London: Pan Books, 1978.

Meyer, Doris. "'Parenting the Text': Female Creativity and Dialogic Relationships in Isabel Allende's *La casa de los espíritus.*" *Hispania* 73.2 (1990): 360–365.

Morello-Frosch, Marta. "La ficción de la historia en la narrativa Argentina reciente." [The fiction of history in recent Argentinian narrative.] *The Historical Novel in Latin America: A Symposium.* Ed. Daniel Balderston. Gaithersburg, Md.: Ediciones Hispamérica, 1986. 201–208.

Muñoz, W. O. "Las (re)escrituras en *La casa de los espíritus*." [The re-writings in The House of the Spirits.] *Discurso literario: Revista de temas hispánicos* 5.2 (1988): 433–454.

Nuttall, Sarah. "Telling 'Free' Stories? Memory and Democracy in South African Autobiography since 1994." *Negotiating the Past: The Making of Memory in South Africa*. Eds. Sarah Nuttall and Carli Coetzee. Cape Town: Oxford UP, 1998. 75–88.

Personal Narratives Group, ed. *Interpreting Women's Lives: Feminist Theory and Personal Narratives*. Bloomington: Indiana UP, 1989.

Ricoeur, Paul. *Time and Narrative*. Trans. Kathleen McLaughlin and David Pellauer. 3 vols. Chicago: U of Chicago P, 1988.

Rojas, M. A. 1985. "*La casa de los espíritus* de Isabel Allende: Una aproximación socio-linguistica." [*The House of the Spirits* by Isabel Allende: A socio-linguistic approximation.] *Revista de crítica literaria latinoamericana* 11.21-22 (1985): 205–213.

Rotella, Pilar V. "Allende's *Eva Luna* and the Picaresque Tradition." *Critical Approaches to Isabel Allende's Novels*. Eds. Sonia Riquelme Rojas and Edna Aguirre Rehbein. New York: Peter Lang, 1991. 125–137.

Schick, Irvin Cemil. *The Erotic Margin: Sexuality and Spatiality in Alteritist Discourse*. London: Verso, 1999.

Schmidt, Siegfried J. "Making Stories about Story-Making, or Why We Need His- and Herstories: An Approach towards a Constructivist Historiography." *Poetics* 28.5/6 (2001): 455–462.

Chapter 5

Myth and Identity

Marianne Dircksen

Types of Myths and Their Usefulness to Modern Society

Studied alive, myth…is not an explanation in satisfaction of a scientific interest, but a narrative resurrection of a primeval reality, told in satisfaction of deep religious wants, moral cravings, social submissions, assertions, even practical requirements. …Myth is thus a vital ingredient of human civilization; it is not an idle tale, but a hard-worked active force. (Malinowski 19)

There are two kinds of myths: (1) those that aim at explaining the causes of natural phenomena or the nature of governing powers which can all be seen as tentative contributions to knowledge, and (2) heroic or romantic tales that evolve around some human law or custom (Lang 300ff). The second category of myths can be further divided into the sagas of primitive people, the *Märchen* (such as the tales collected by the Grimm Brothers) and the epic poetry and legends of the great civilized races such as the Greeks and the Romans. In this chapter I will restrict myself to a discussion of the second type of myth and its relevance for identity on two levels, namely, cultural and personal, as we are all in need of both a collective life lived in the social group and at the same time an inherent need to strive for personal truth.

Feinstein and Mayo underline the usefulness of myths for the identity of groups and individuals in modern society: "Rituals, like myths, address (1) our urge to comprehend our existence in a meaningful way, (2) our search for a marked pathway as we move from one stage of our lives to the next, (3) our need to establish secure and fulfilling relationships within a human community, and (4) our longing to know our part in the vast wonder of the cosmos" (41). Even though they do not constitute history in the sense of "having really taken place," myths represent "human truths," and as such they link all of us to primordial times. Myths (and the rituals associated with them) inform the human spirit on its journey into the world, but they are also an important way to understand our connection to other people at a time when the welfare of each culture depends on the attitudes and actions of others (Rosenberg xiii).

In this chapter the discussion will center on the archetypal hero myth. The myth of the Zulu hero, Usikulumi, will serve as an illustration of this myth.

Comparative Mythology: A Tool to Discover Universal Patterns (including African Exemplars) and Distinctive Traits in Myths

All authoritative research on myths has shown that the ideas, incidents and plots of the three classes of heroic or romantic tales show remarkable resemblances. Adolf Bastian (1826–1905) called these recurring ideas and themes *Elementarge-danken*, and the particular application of these themes by different ethnic groups, *Völkergedanken* (Campbell 9).

The primary aim of "universal" or "comparative mythology" is to focus on accordances and universal truths in the myths of different cultural groups, to search for *Elementargedanken*.[1] The search for universally applicable "patterns" marks the ritualistic, psychoanalytic, sociological and structuralist approaches to myth.[2] A quick glance at the most influential theories on myths confirms the underlying premise that myths from very distant parts of the world and from very different time zones have very obvious similarities which are variously explained. Müller saw myths as a production of poetical fantasy from prehistoric times, misunderstood by succeeding ages. To Durkheim they were the repositories of allegorical instruction to shape the individual to his group. Sigmund Freud viewed myths as the expression of subconscious wishes, fears and drives. Carl Jung (and his followers, such as Carl Kerenyi, Erich Neumann and Joseph Campbell) thought that myths were the expression of a universal collective unconscious, a group dream that springs from archetypal urges within the depths of the human psyche. Mircea Eliade viewed myths as the essence of religion, conceived from a genuine religious experience; he thought that the sacred experience gives myths their structure and their utility. Because the ancient world contained many different religious ideas and forms, numerous similarities and connections exist from one culture to another.

According to Claude Lévi-Strauss myths are abstract constructions. The structure of all human minds is identical and is revealed by the similar ways in which people solve their problems. Myths are identical products from identical minds, so myths from around the world possess a common structure. They reveal the conflict between opposing forces, and one can discover their meaning by focusing on their underlying structure. Lévi-Strauss constituted the logical structures he identified in myths as evidence for his argument that although different, the savage mind was hardly inferior to the technological rationality of the modern West.[3]

Some scholars doubt whether features of resemblance between indigenous African and ancient Greek and Romans myths exist. Puhvel tells us that similarities between Greek and Native American myths were already noticed in the seventeenth century, that the Orpheus myth in North America formed the subject of two books (3) and that, already in 1724, Bernard de Fontenelle pointed to notable similarities between Greek and Amerindian myths (11). However,

Puhvel is of the opinion that Oedipus-type tales are found only in a continuous band from Europe through the Middle East and South Asia into the Western Pacific, to the exclusion of other native mythologies (i.e., northern Asia, Africa, America, Australia) and that the "average hero legend" is based solely on European, Middle Eastern and South Asian exemplars (3). Bruce Lincoln shows (chap. 4–6) how scholarship on the subject of myth over the course of more than a century tended to privilege Aryan (or Indo-European) examples and discusses the matter of an "Indo-European" descent of language and myth in detail (211ff).[4] However, as I will illustrate below, the myth of Uzikulumi, the Zulu hero, shows a marked resemblance to quite a few classical Roman and Greek hero myths. The obvious similarities between Zulu traditional stories and those of other peoples led Callaway to give the following reason for assembling Zulu nursery tales: "It will, I think, help us to find unsuspected points of contact between the Zulus and other people. ...It will also give them a claim to be reckoned as an integral part of our common humanity, by showing that they have so many thoughts in common with other men, and have retained in their traditional tales so much that resembles the traditional tales of other people" (1). Bryant (670 ff) also noted many strong resemblances between the Grecian and Zulu "mysteries." Golsan found that a myth of the Venda people shows remarkable resemblance to the Oedipus myth (168 ff). The very fact that these similarities, even in detail, are found in such diverse cultures is very significant. It indicates underlying general psychological themes, which are true of humanity the world over, and they have become useful tools in the analysis of the psyche and in the search for identity, as I will demonstrate below.

A secondary dividend of the comparative method is the easy identification of traits that are specific to a particular myth. Such traits can reveal much about the culture of the ethnic groups from which the myth originated and are important for the establishment of their separate identities.[5]

The Archetypal Hero Myth

The archetype of the mythical hero has occupied the ritualist Fitzroy Richard Somerset (fourth Baron Raglan), the psychoanalyst Otto Rank, Sigmund Freud, Carl Gustav Jung and Joseph Campbell, to name but a few. Raglan found that Robin Hood conforms to a type attested to in Oedipus, Theseus, Romulus, Herakles, Perseus, Jason, Bellerophon, Pelops, Asklepios, Dionysos, Apollo, Zeus, Joseph, Moses, Elijah, Watu Gunung (Java), Nyikang (upper Nile), Sigurd-Siegfried, Lleu Llawgyffes (Wales) and Arthur, while Rank's dossier comprises Sargon (of Akkad), Moses, Karna (in the *Mahabharata*), Oedipus, Paris, Telephus, Perseus, Gilgamesh, Cyrus, Tristan, Romulus, Hercules, Jesus, Siegfried and Lohengrin. The pattern involves noble origin; unusual conception; the threat of infanticide, rescue and youthful exile, the exile often involving herding of cattle or sheep; manifesting kingly bearing; return of the hero upon reaching maturity to claim his due; triumph over an obstructionist, such as battle with a three-headed monster during which the hero often proves invulnerable; the father or king's dread becoming justified; marriage to a highborn local; successful reign; but ultimate downfall, exile and mysterious end, often on a hill; disappearance of mortal remains; and a cenotaphic cult at holy sepulchers. Other themes that often occur involve a female who aids and protects the hero, a long journey, theft of an elixir, sacred marriage, and so forth. Puhvel notes that: "The hero is thus a formula-bound bundle of themes..." (Puhvel 16). Neither Raglan nor Rank includes Southern African heroes in their list, but as the tale of the Zulu hero Usikulumi will illustrate, this African hero shows remarkable correspondence to the archetypal hero.

The Zulu Myth of Usikulumi[6] and its Parallels

The name Usikulumi means "the one who talks." This is significant as it probably means that the hero is the one who speaks for everyone.

> Usikulumi's father, the king Uthlokohloko,[7] did not want to have sons for fear that they would depose him. Old women were appointed to kill the sons of the king. The most important theme is present: Usikulumi was of royal descent and there was the threat of infanticide. Usikulumi's mother gave presents to the old women and begged them not to kill him, but to take him to his maternal uncle. This they did. Usikulumi escapes (theme: the hero is saved, as often happens, by the intervention of his mother). He was respected and honored by the boys of his uncle's kraal (village) (theme: the kingly bearing). One day the officers of his father came by and said: "Who are you?" He did not tell them but they took him without doubting, saying: "This child is like our king." They took him to his father (theme: the young hero returns). The king was very angry, and Usikulumi was taken to a great forest (theme: the long journey). The forest was the home of a great, many-headed monster that ate men. Usikulumi was left on a great rock in the middle of the forest. The many-headed monster came out of the water (theme: the obstructionist), but did not kill the young man; it took him and gave him food. The monster also gave him a nation subject to him. He visited his uncle and was received with great joy. He eventually reached his father's kingdom; his father was grieved at his arrival and told his people to take their weapons and kill Usikulumi. He stood in an open space and said: "Hurl your spears at me to your utmost." He stood until the sun set, and they hurled their spears without having the power to kill him (theme: invulnerability). The monster had strengthened him so that he was invulnerable. Usikulumi kills all his father's people and departs with the spoils—he is now king of his own people (theme: father's dread is justified). Then follows the inevitable marriage. Usikulumi courts the daughters of Umzembeni ("Long-toe"). She was, however, a cannibal and had devoured all the men of her country. Her daughters were celebrities among the tribes on account of their beauty, but Umzembeni had even torn off one of her daughters' cheeks, boiled it and eaten it. It was bitter and that was why Umzembeni did not eat her daughters. When Usikulumi arrived, the girls dug a hole in the house and concealed him in it (theme: the hero is aided by a female). He had left his pack of dogs in a bed of reeds. When Umzembeni returned, she could smell human flesh, but

the girls denied that there was anyone. Usikulumi ran away with one of the daughters; they traveled day and night, hoping to escape Uzembeni. She pursued them and they climbed a high tree. She tried to chop down the tree, but was torn to pieces by the dogs. The tree grew again and Uzembeni came to life again until she was finally ground to powder. Usikulumi and the girl escaped and were received joyously by Usikulumi's people.

The legend of Usikulumi has many curious points in common with quite a few Grecian hero myths: Hecuba dreamed that she gave birth to a burning torch, which the seers interpreted as intimating that the child to be born would bring ruin on the city and land of Troy. The infant Paris was sent by Priam to be exposed to the elements on Mount Ida. He was found and adopted by a shepherd. His fatal affair with Helen led to the destruction of Troy.

The Delphic oracle warned Laïus that he would be slain by his own child. He ordered his son Oedipus to be left on the heights of Cithaeron. Again a shepherd played a part in the rescue of the child. He was raised in a royal environment and had the demeanor of a prince. He also killed his father (though unwittingly). Again a monster figured in the form of the sphinx, and Oedipus too became ruler over a nation.

Uranus feared his children, the Titans. Their mother, Gaea, encouraged the youngest, Cronos, to defeat his father, who in turn cursed his son and prophesied that a day would come when he, too, would be supplanted by his children. So Cronos swallowed every son of his that was born until his wife Rhea handed him a stone wrapped in swaddling clothes. Her son, the young Jupiter, having been saved by his mother, was entrusted to the tender care of the Melian nymphs who bore him off to Mount Ida, where a goat acted as nurse. Cronos was attacked by his son, and after a short but terrible encounter he was signally defeated.

The Roman heroes Romulus and Remus also come to mind. Their uncle Amulius feared them and ordered that they be thrown into the Tiber. They, too, were put out to die, were rescued by the she-wolf, grew up as herdsmen, showed signs of leadership and returned to reclaim their grandfather's kingdom.

Myth and Cultural (Ethnic) Identity

The South Africa population consists of many diverse cultures. To illustrate this diversity we need mention only two such cultural groups: On the one hand there are those who consider themselves to be "Afrikaners," the descendants of European colonists, brought up and educated according to Western traditions, and on the other, indigenous black African peoples such as the Zulus or Tswanas with their culture rooted in Africa. These very disparate groups live and work side by side, attend the same sports events and occupy the same lecture rooms at our universities. I believe that mythology has an important role to play as a catalyst in cementing structured coexistence in South Africa, while enhancing the very disparity that could so very easily lead to conflict.

Traditionally the student of European culture studied mythology because it forms such an important aspect of graphic arts and literature.[8] Without knowledge of mythology, thousands of allusions will be lost on the student of English literature.

But myths have much more to offer, and this is borne out by the fact that they have become an extremely popular field of study.[9] The socio-functionalists point out the interrelations between the social order and the myths and rituals that sustain it (Doty 132). Using Kluckhohn's theses as a starting point Doty concludes that "myths and rituals can be studied in terms of their functional ability to provide social solidarity, to transmit cultural values, to provide a firm standpoint in a threatening world, to reduce anxiety, to show relationships between cultural values and particular objects, to explicate origins, and so forth" (Doty 133). According to these socio-functionalists, myths and rituals provide the social cement that binds societies together; they signify culture, social structure and interaction (Doty 137).

At whatever stage of his life a person finds himself or herself, or whatever his or her profession, he or she is limited because of the very fact that he or she is an individual. Through his or her genes he or she belongs to his or her cultural group and derives his or her total being (language, thoughts, etc.) from the society as a whole. Traditions and ceremonies give meaning to the individual's present situation, in terms that do not refer to him or her by name but that apply to him or her in impersonal terms. His or her place within society is established, a society that does not perish like the individual. "By an enlargement of vision to embrace this super-individual, each discovers himself enhanced, enriched, supported, and magnified" (Campbell 383). People who ostracize themselves from society deny themselves the right of "being" in the full sense of the word. Symbols, rites and traditions which are all part of a nation's mythology, celebrate humankind's oneness with the individual group and with humanity as a whole.

Very few young black South Africans know much about their own cultural heritage. The ethos of the black South African student has become one of foreign derivation. These young people have been reared on MacDonald's, American sitcoms and pop music and know precious little about the mythological stories their grandparents used to hear around the fireplace (cf. the discussion of globalization and Americanization by Segers, this volume). Certainly the colonizer is partly to blame for the lack of cultural knowledge and pride among the indigenous peoples of South Africa. Cohen explains the phenomenon as follows:

> Culture becomes politicised when people recognise that ignorance of their culture among others acts to their detriment; that they experience the marginalisation of their culture and their relative powerlessness with respect to the marginalisers. With ignorance of a culture goes the denial of its integrity. Continuous denigration seems to drive people into cultural retreat, where they either make their tradition a covert matter, or appear to desert it in large measure. Western intellectual tradition created its own version of the culture of the colonised which it imposes upon them, and then denigrated, thereby justifying the West's own domination of the colonised as an essentially civilising mission. In so doing they have deprived them of their collective identity. (Cohen 199)[10]

The vibrant rituals and ceremonies of the forefathers, which promoted cooperation and a stronger sense of community have disintegrated and can be seen as part of a general cultural decay.

This lack of interest in cultural heritage has also infiltrated the university curriculum. In a recent paper Dr. Thosago of the University of the North (South Africa) deplores the non-existence of folklore as a recognizable academic discipline in South Africa. According to him folklore has an indispensable usefulness to culture. Classical or ancient culture, which has become very popular in universities throughout the world, should include African culture. Classical studies can no longer afford to maintain privileged values. Comparison and analysis of the cultural treasures of ancient societies will lead to a much more valuable gain: the understanding of human thought across different cultures (Doty 23). The teaching of mythology at the university level centered for many years on a discussion and analysis of myth within its own historical and cultural framework. As fascinating as ancient myths are, they seem totally irrelevant to young people living in South Africa in the twenty-first century. The time has come for South Africans to start telling each other their stories. The myth of the Zulu hero Usikulumi amply illustrates the rich material for comparison between African and ancient European myths. Ancient culture and folklore can and should be utilized at the school and university level to reinforce cultural identity, to cultivate a better understanding among students belonging to different cultural groups and to foster a new appreciation for the cultural heritage of the "other."

The hero myth of Usikulumi demonstrates that the Zulu mind has much in common with the Western mind and that the mythology of the Zulus is as valid and worthy of research as the myths of the ancient Greeks and Romans. The distinctive elements are equally significant and a valuable source of information about Zulu culture. The traditional importance of cattle as indicator of social status is attested to: A young boy, at the bottom of the social ladder, spends his days in the veld looking after the cattle, and the standing of the grown men is determined by the number of cattle they possess. Great value is attached to family relations. We saw that Usikulumi was not sent to just any neighboring king, but to his maternal uncle. The symbolism of the bed of reeds as the source from which society sprung, and the place and image of birth, rebirth and regeneration, is unique in the mythologies of the world. The spear is identified as the traditional weapon. A woman's beauty increases her value since her future husband will have to deliver many head of cattle to her family as "lobola."

Myths are an important source of cultural knowledge, and if such knowledge is shared, it can lead to a greater understanding and tolerance among the peoples of a country.

Individual Experience in a Universal Perspective

An Initiation Ritual

Many influential mythologists have equated the hero myth with an initiation process. Dumézil (126 ff.) suggests that the hero's combat with a many-headed monster is the transformation into myth of an archaic initiation ritual. This initiation does not always belong to the "heroic" type. In Christian mythology St George fights and kills the dragon heroically; other saints achieve the same result without fighting (like Usikulumi).

Freud's (initial) follower, Otto Rank, explains the characteristics of the traditional hero in terms of infantile hostility, childhood fantasies and rebellion against one's father. He identifies the hero with the personal ego that rebels against the domination of the father. These myths fulfill an important role in facilitating the process of terminating childhood dependence and entering into adult life. Through the ordeal that a boy is subjected to before his initiation, he experiences a divine "something," which is the voice of his own true nature whereby he is released from childish dependence on the authority of the parents.

According to Eliade, the ordeals that heroes undergo suggest passage to the beyond, the perilous descent into hell. When such journeys are undertaken by living beings they always form part of an initiation. The hero has a quest: he pursues immortality or some other reward (*Birth* 125). But initiation also implies an existential experience, that is, the experience of ritual death and the revelation of the sacred. This makes the experience metacultural and transhistorical, and the same initiatory patterns continue to be active in culturally heterogeneous societies (*Birth* 131).

An Imaginative Experience

When initiatory patterns have lost their ritual reality, they become literary motifs. According to Eliade, "This is to say that they now deliver their spiritual message on a different plane of human experience, by addressing themselves directly to the imagination" (*Birth* 126).

Paul Saint Yves and Jan de Vries have shown that the ordeals and adventures of the heroes and heroines in folktales (and some fairy tales) are almost always translatable into initiatory terms. Eliade explains these initiatory scenarios as expressions of a psychodrama that answers a deep need in a human being. On the level of her or his imaginative life the reader confronts the ordeals on her or his way to the "other world," while hearing or reading the tales, or even when dreaming (*Birth* 126). The Greeks already knew the power of myths to arouse feelings, to give pleasure, to offer consolation for the difficulties experienced in the present by stirring memory of past adventures (Doty 56).

Nowadays initiatory themes remain alive chiefly in the unconscious, as is confirmed by the initiatory symbolism in works of art. The massive positive public reception of these works proves that modern humankind is still capable of being affected by initiatory scenarios or messages. Reading provides distraction and escape and constitutes one of the characteristic traits of modern humanity. "Modern man satisfies his religious needs by reading books that contain mythological figures camouflaged as contemporary characters and offer initiatory scenarios in the guise of everyday happenings" (Eliade, *Birth* 135). We see ourselves reflected in heroic myths. The presence of initiatory themes in the dreams and imagination of modern humankind proves our unconscious desire to share in the ordeals that regenerate the hero and to identify with the hero. Heroes possess not only our strengths but also our weaknesses. They are not perfect beings, and that is why we can identify with them, learn from their mistakes and feel compassion for them. Heroes make vital choices, and through their ordeal they become wiser, more sensitive beings.

A Spiritual Journey

The hero myth, with the initiation process it implies, is also symbolic of the psychological process every human experiences during her or his lifetime.[11] Eliade relates the hero myth to the symbolism of the center (*Myth* 17). The center is the zone of the sacred, the zone of absolute reality, and all the other symbols of absolute reality are also situated at a center. The road leading to the center is a difficult road, that is, pilgrimage to sacred places, danger-ridden voyages and other experiences of the mythical hero. The hero is in search of his rightful place, in search of his true identity, just as Usikulumi was in search of his role as king and ruler of his people. The hero is seeking the road to the self, to the "center" of his being.

> The road is arduous, fraught with perils, because it is, in fact a rite of the passage from the profane to the sacred, from the ephemeral and illusory to reality and eternity, from death to life, from man to the divinity. Attaining the center is equivalent to a consecration, an initiation; yesterday's profane and illusory existence gives place to a new, to a life that is real, enduring, and effective. (Eliade, *Myth* 18)

According to Jung the process of individuation, which constitutes the ultimate goal of human life, only comes through a series of ordeals of an initiatory type

(Eliade, *Rites* 135). Human life implies crises, ordeals, suffering, loss, a sense of total failure, and the only hope in such circumstances is that of a *rebirth*, a *total regeneration*. Such a purely spiritual birth is found in a deeply felt, genuine, religious conversion. Jesus said, "I tell you the truth, no one can see the kingdom of God unless he is born again"; and when Nicodemus asked Jesus how a man can be reborn when he is old, Jesus answered: "I tell you the truth, no one can enter the kingdom of God unless he is born of water and the Spirit" (John 3:3–5, *New Revised Standard Version*).

In the absence of any deeply religious experience, religion has become "unconscious." It lies buried in the deepest strata of the individual's being. People only become themselves, born into a new, regenerated life, after they have coped with desperately difficult situations. The initiatory scenario functions only on the vital and psychological plane (Eliade, *Birth* 127). By enduring traumas the individual sheds his childlike, unrefined state and is reshaped into a new, more mature being—he receives a new identity and plays a new role. The scarring of the body (e.g., tattooing, blackening of teeth or circumcision), which is part of aboriginal initiation, represents a deeper mark upon the psyche.

Harding gives a slightly altered perspective on the theory of the sacred center (281 ff.):

> If psychological energy is allowed to flow outwards it creates in the outer world, while if it is checked in its outward flowing and turned back towards the center it creates within the individual. The creations produced by the outflowing of energy comprise all of a person's outer activities, work, family, etc. while the inner creation, produced by the inflowing of the energy, is the psychic child which corresponds to Jung's concept of individuality. In the moon religions the inner psychic child, is believed to be immortal because he is beyond the conditioning of this world and exists in a realm different from the external or visible universe. A person who can release his mind from the conditionings of time and place and shift his center away from himself to a more disinterested focal point, is symbolized in the religions of the moon as giving birth to the immortal child or savior.

Harding elaborates on another symbol related to the hero, that of the tree and its fruit (283 ff.) The Babylonian Moon God, Sinn (the young crescent moon), the hero who overcomes his father's enemy, is the fruit of the sacred moon tree. The participant who drinks the juice of the fruit receives the same divine gifts he or she possessed. Dionysus' followers drank the fruit of the vine, which was symbolic of his blood. The wine of the sacrament also represents Christ's blood. Only when the tree of life is fully developed can it produce fruit and bestow immortality through its essence. So, too, the initiates who ate of the Roses of Isis were released from their mortal state.

The drinking of the sacred substance was believed to put the worshipper in touch with the "self," an aspect of the psyche that possesses immutable qualities but which is not the worshipper's personal ego. It is non-personal, partaking of the qualities of the divine self or Atman. It is this non-personal, non-ego, "self" which Jung (of whom Harding is a disciple) calls the "individuality" (Harding 245 ff). The concept takes in more than the conscious side of the psyche and is never fully conscious but remains a potentiality within the human being. Through inner experiences the individuality is progressively delimited. The experiences bring the lost values of the psyche to consciousness, and the human being then becomes more complete. This is a similar experience to the "second birth" in ancient religions that occurred after participation in the various stages of the mystery initiations. "For when a man or woman submits to the laws or principles of his own being and gives up the personal orientation of the ego he gradually defines the limits of his own nature and the individuality crystallizes within him" (246). This exploration of one's own capacities and finding of one's own boundaries occurs during the initiation in the seclusion of a temple or other secluded place where the emotional experience is not hampered by any considerations which must be taken into account in a personal relationship.

Even non-religious people feel the desire for a spiritual transformation, a transmutation, which in other cultures constitutes the very goal of initiation (Eliade, *Rites* 136). This is an indication of humankind's longing to find a positive meaning to death, to accept death as a transition rite to a higher mode of being.

Who then is the hero of the twenty-first century? What is his or her quest? The mystery that needs to be deciphered no longer lies in the animal monster, but in humankind themselves. In order to transcend the human condition and become a protégé of a supernatural being, the individual has to undergo a specialized initiation (Eliade, *Birth* 128). For the Christian, this means a rebirth and new life in the image of God.

Heroes test the limits of human experience. They stand alone and represent the individual's struggle while their behavior initially may seem anti-social.[12] After the ordeal they return and establish a new order or reaffirm the old. "The history of the ways the heroic is defined will be as well the history of the definition of selfhood: active or passive, conquering or receptive, critical toward or accepting of traditional models, and so on…" (Doty 64). The hero's strength of character is as important as his or her great deeds (Rosenberg xii).

Some heroes are allowed to obtain fame for themselves, but the hero myth mostly evolves around the choice between personal achievement or safety and the hero's duty towards his or her fellow human beings (Rosenberg xviii). The war that the hero wages is not always a physical battle. The hero often celebrates a personal, psychological triumph while losing against his physical enemy.

The Modern-day Hero

A society has its own deceased or living heroes: people who personify the ideals and values of their society.[13] Chaka Zulu and Nelson Mandela may well qualify as modern-day heroes who have acquired mythical attributes; that is, they are considered to be so important that they are mythicized (Doty 39). These heroes obtain immortality through their deeds and serve as models for their followers, just as the mythological heroes of Greece or Rome.

The martyrs were the archetypal heroes of the early Christians. They had a quest, suffered hardship; their souls were invulnerable to torture; they became protégés of their supernatural being, Christ, and a cult often originated at their burial place.[14]

Former president Mandela's story has become a reflection of the era of struggle against apartheid. Doty notes that, "The dominant myths of an era reflect its views of behavioral or psychosocial maturity or health, and undergird its models of heroes and heroines" (Doty 64). Not all myths reflect a positive or healthy view of society. The story of the Afrikaner's coming to South Africa as colonizer and attaining political supremacy led a certain radical right-wing group to see themselves as "God's chosen people" to the exclusion of other cultural groups. They have, from their own perspective, acquired a certain identity within South African society as a whole, based on their mythical heritage and tradition.

Another interesting example of South African origin is Danie Theron. He was a hero of the South African War who crawled through enemy lines to bring a message from General de Wet to the beleaguered General Piet Cronje. He later died when seven British scouts surprised him but not before he killed three of the enemy and wounded four. Danie Theron became an icon for the Afrikaner-nationalist, an inspiration for the republican ideal. In February 2003 his remains were secretly removed from his grave at Eikenhof, where he had been buried next to his young wife. It is presumed that a far-right group is responsible for the removal. In a recent newspaper article, Pretorius wonders if Theron will remain the exclusive hero of the Afrikaner, or whether, now that the struggle for an Afrikaner republic is a thing of the past, a shift of focus will perhaps take place, and that Theron might become an inclusive icon with which all cultural groups who have been part of the broader struggle history, can identify.

Conclusion

As I have stated in the introduction to this chapter, every human being leads his or her life on two levels: in an ethnic or cultural group and at the same time on a personal level. On both these levels humankind has a need of a mythology, rites and initiation, which lies at the core of human existence and is a *sine qua non* for the development of social and individual identity.

Our modern societies can be described as "desacralized," devoid of knowledge of their cultural heritage and suffering from a poverty of rituals. The stories of our forefathers are no longer heard, and we have lost our sense of belonging.[15] The people of a country or region can be compared to grains of sand, and the cultural groups within that country, to building blocks. Myths are the mortar that joins the individual grains into separate, solid units, which can be used to build a strong nation. It seems that the lack of "mortar" has led to the disintegration of the "blocks," that is, the cultural groups, each with their own identity.

Psychologically speaking, individuals are in need of rites of passage to help them through life's crises. In Christian churches throughout the world baptism, the Eucharist and confirmation are the fundamental rites of passage intended to aid the believer in his or her spiritual journey towards self-identity. But in many churches these sacraments are mostly performed in a group and the sense of self-identity, the inner life of the person is not always on a par with the status accorded by the congregation. Psychologists the world over recognize the importance of meaningful rites in helping the psyche to regain its equilibrium,[16] and perhaps the time has come to give myth its proper place and to reestablish meaningful rites in our social and personal lives.

Notes

1. Puhvel used the following quotation from Sir William Jones as a central thought on the very first page of his book: "When features of resemblance, too strong to have been accidental, are observable in different systems of polytheism, without fancy or prejudice to color them and improve their likeness, we can scarce help believing, that some connection has immemorially subsisted between the several nations, who have adopted them." (v)

2. It is also widely accepted today that proof of the authenticity of myth—that is, the proof by which it is known as the genuine aboriginal product of a primitive folk—is obtained by "the test of recurrence."

3. On the validity of the myths of so-called primitive societies see also Lincoln (210), Rosenberg (xxi).

4. This view is shared by the well-known mythologists Dumézil, Wikander and de Vries.

5. Segers (this volume) also stresses the usefulness of comparative research in cultural studies in his chapter.

6. I have used Callaway's version of this story (41 ff).

7. Uthlokohloko means the "chief of chiefs."

8. "Mythology is the handmaid of literature." (Bulfinch v).

9. See Doty (xiii ff) for the vast number of publications, CD-ROMs, exhibits, programs and Internet sites.

10. The recent spate of deaths among young boys in initiation schools in South Africa illustrate clearly what can happen when tradition becomes a covert matter.

11. "Concern with the psychology of primitives, with folklore, mythology, and the comparative history of religions opens the eyes to the wide horizons of the human psyche and in addition it gives that indispensable aid we so urgently need for the understanding of unconscious processes." (Jung quoted in Harding ix)
12. Rites of passage always involve isolation, reversion to a raw state, combat and testing (Kirk 19).
13. It is therefore preferable to consider the intervention of suprahuman entities as one of the components of myths rather than deities (Doty 74).
14. St. Jerome's remains at the church of Santa Maria Maggiore were the cause of many miracles.
15. In chapter 1 (this volume) Burger stresses that identity is constructed through narrating because it provides an historic awareness.
16. Bani Shorter, a psychoanalyst, for example, describes the rites of passage five of her patients had to undergo in order to shed their "old self" and regain their identity.

Works Cited

Bryant, Alfred T. *The Zulu People as They Were Before the White Man Came*. Pietermaritzburg: Shuter and Shooter, 1949.

Bulfinch, Thomas. *The Golden Age of Myth and Legend*. London: Harrap, 1919.

Callaway, Henry. *Nursery Tales, Traditions and Histories of the Zulus, in Their Own Words*. Westport, Conn.: Negro UP, 1970.

Campbell, Joseph. *The Hero with a Thousand Faces*. New York: Pantheon Books, 1949.

Cohen, A. P. "Culture as Identity: An Anthropologist's View." *New Literary History* 24 (1993): 195–209.

Cox, George W. *An Introduction to the Science of Comparative Mythology and Folklore*. London: Kegan Paul, 1883.

Detienne, Marcel. *The Masters of Truth in Archaic Greece*. New York: Zone, 1996.

Doty, William G. *Mythography: The Study of Myths and Rituals*. Tuscaloosa and London: U of Alabama P, 2000.

Dumézil, G. *Horace et les Curiaces*. Paris: Gallimard, 1942.

Eliade, Mircea. *Birth and Rebirth*. New York: Harper and Brothers, 1958.

——. *Rites and Symbols of Initiation*. New York: Harper and Row, 1975.

——. *The Myth of the Eternal Return*. 9th paperback printing. Princeton: Princeton UP, 1991.

Feinstein, David, and Peg Eliot Mayo. *Rituals for Living and Dying*. New York: HarperCollins, 1990.

Golsan, Richard J. *Réne Girard and Myth: An Introduction*. New York: Garland, 1993.

Harding, M. E. *Woman's Mysteries*. New York: Bantam Books, 1973.

Kirk, Geoffrey Stephen. *Myth, Its Meaning and Functions in Ancient and Other Cultures*. Cambridge, UK: Cambridge UP, 1970.

Lang, Andrew. *Myth, Ritual and Religion*. London: Longmans, Green, 1901.

Lévi-Strauss, Claude. *The Savage Mind*. Chicago: U of Chicago P, 1966.

Lincoln, Bruce. *Theorizing Myth*. Chicago: U of Chicago P, 1999.

Malinowski, Bronislaw. *Myth in Primitive Psychology*. Westport, Conn.: Negro UP, 1976.

Pretorius, F. "Kan Danie Theron as a Struggle-held herleef…of as eksklusiewe Afrikaner-ikon in vergetelheid versink?" [Can Danie Theron Be Reborn as a Struggle Hero…or Sink into Oblivion as Exclusive Afrikaner Icon?] *Beeld* 27 Feb. 2003: 17.

Puhvel, Jaan. *Comparative Mythology*. Baltimore: Johns Hopkins UP, 1989.

Rosenberg, Donna. *World Mythology: An Anthology of the Great Myths and Epics.* Lincolnwood, Ill.: NTC/Contemporary Publishing Group, 1999.

Shorter, Bani. *An Image Darkly Forming.* London and New York: Routledge, 1988.

Part II

Places and Landscapes

Chapter 6

Land, Space, Identity: The Literary Construction of Space in Three Afrikaans Farm Novels

Hein Viljoen

The ongoing conflicts about land in Zimbabwe and Palestine have again foregrounded the close link between land and identity. Where you live to a large extent determines who you are, and, conversely, people tend to identify with specific spaces and places. The nature of the link between space and identity can vary, however.

The nature of this link as well as the different ways in which it can be expressed in literature is an extremely interesting question. In naturalist literature the central assumption is that space and environment determine the nature of characters and their place in society. In modern novels different, often antagonistic and ambivalent relationships between character and place are thematized.

In this chapter I will analyze the representation and construction of space and identity in three Afrikaans farm novels, viz. *Die meulenaar* (The Miller) (1926) by D.F. Malherbe, *Somer* (Summer) (1935) by C.M. van der Heever and *Die stoetmeester* (1993, literally The Master-Breeder, but translated as *Leap Year*, 1997) by Etienne van Heerden.

The ways in which space and identity are represented and constructed are big issues, and I will confine myself to outlining a few ways to analyze them. After briefly referring to the farm novel and to recent research on the topic of space and identity, I will analyze the relations between space and identity in *Die meulenaar* and use that to sketch out the main traits of the farm novel. Then I will briefly describe the spatial coordinates in *Somer* and draw out some implications of those spaces for identity. Subsequently I will analyze the construction of space and identity in *Leap Year*. The focus will be on the main characters' experience of specific, virtually sacred places and how myth and ritual are used to fill out their identities.

The Farm Novel

Nowadays regional or *Heimat* literature is mostly regarded as a minor popular genre. In South African literature, however, the farm novel, which is a subspecies of the regional novel, has been a dominant subgenre from the beginning. As was suggested in the introduction, the farm is in a sense the archetypal South African form of habitation. It is particularly closely associated with Afrikaner nationalist ideology, as Ampie Coetzee recently again emphasized in his study of the link between land, ideology and identity in the Afrikaans farm novel from a Foucauldian and materialist perspective. In his book, *'n Hele os vir 'n ou broodmes*[1], Coetzee regards the farm novel as an utterance in the discourse about land in South Africa, and he shows how land ownership in particular is closely linked to the ideology and identity of the Afrikaner class of landowners. Land and the threat of losing it through drought or debt play an important role in both *Die meulenaar* and *Somer*. Yet there is more to the link between the farm and identity than class identity, since the author had to find a way of making space meaningful. In *Somer*, as John M. Coetzee argued, this is done by making use of a romantic division between a good, significant space (the farm) and a bad space (the city). This division enables the characters to read the meaning of nature in the end, namely that life and nature are evanescent.

Van Wyk Smith (17) also emphasizes the close link between Afrikaner nationalist ideology and the farm, calling the farm "a capsule of all the racially and culturally exclusive myth and doctrines" that had supported that ideology since 1948. Both *Somer* and *Die meulenaar* are included in Smith's list of works that "thematised the nexus of the 'boer' [farmer] and his 'plaas' [farm] as a timeless icon of national and numinous identity, not only validating an unquestioned right to the land but expressing also the very soul of the Afrikaner's being" (18).

Van Wyk Smith points out the "potent cultural valency" (18) of the farm in any society, calling it "a peculiar combination of nature and nurture, with a high symbolic and emotive surplus value...and sacralized by a host of archetypal cultural and symbolic associations" (18). These include "closeness to the soil, symbiosis with natural forces, hallowed historic myths" and the romantic nationalist association with a particular country. His main argument in the above-quoted article, however, is that the South African farm, which in the context of farm murders since 1994 is associated with insecurity and vulnerability, has always had an ambivalent meaning. He regards it as "an icon of White South Africa's fragile domicility and haunting complicity" (20), and writes that its potency as trope has always depended on memory and on nostalgia "for something always already in the past." It is a "nexus of promise and menace, eden and demon" (20). This ambivalence is a kind of postcolonial unconscious—a vague, repressed unease that the land had been taken away from its original inhabitants, a suppressed history of colonial conquest and occupation.

Van Wyk Smith traces the ambivalent iconology of the farm through diverse South African English texts and encounters three reactions. Against the reactions of honest acknowledgement that he finds in Coetzee's *Boyhood*, or the calculated ignorance of the historical facts in *Too Late the Phalarope* (Paton) he suggests a third, namely a dialectic engagement with the "memory" of the South African farmscape. This implies an engagement with the farmscape as a palimpsest that encodes "conflicting signals of eden and demon, fetish and menace" (24) in itself.

Van Wyk Smith finds this inter alia in *The Story of an African Farm* (1883) by Olive Schreiner—a text that is often regarded as the beginning of South African literature in English. Van Wyk Smith describes it as a "conflictual farmscape" (27) dominated by a solitary koppie (hill) that Waldo, one of the main characters, imagines being a giant's grave. The koppie features centrally in all the main events of the novel and is also explicitly linked to the disturbing presence of a black man that Van Wyk Smith (28) reads as an indication of subliminal primal forces buried in the farm's history. He writes that Schreiner "having powerfully sensed a deep disruptive presence on the farm, leaves the giant buried to re-emerge in several subsequent South African texts" (28).

The further evolution of the subgenre of the farm novel in South Africa can be understood in terms of the different stages postulated by Fowler (see Van Coller). Reflecting an agrarian society it emerged as a formal type in Afrikaans literature during the 1920s and 1930s when the agrarian way of life in South Africa was already giving way under the pressures of urbanization and the market economy. Both *Die meulenaar* and *Somer* represent this phase when the Afrikaner was strongly associated with the farm and with landownership. Next, secondary types of the subgenre developed, turning the original impulse into stereotype and cliché. This happened in the 1940s and 1950s when the farm novel became mostly a popular light genre, exemplified inter alia by the novels of Tryna du Toit in Afrikaans. The secondary forms then underwent a radical ironic revision in the sixties exemplified by E. Leroux's *Sewe dae by die Silbersteins* (translated as *Seven Days at the Silbersteins*, 1964). The revision culminated in the 1990s in a number of novels in which the subgenre is used in a parodic way as a vehicle of criticism of the ideological order of apartheid. Typical parodic Afrikaans novels are Eben Venter's *Foxtrot van die vleiseters* (Foxtrot of the Meat-Eaters, 1993), Etienne van Heerden's *Toorberg* (1986) (translated as *Ancestral Voices*, 1989) and *Die stoetmeester* (1993) and Karel Schoeman's *Hierdie lewe* (This Life, 1993).

Into this phase would fit *The Conservationist* (1974) by Nadine Gordimer, *In the Heart of the Country* (1977) by John M. Coetzee, *The Arrowing of the Cane* by John Conyngham (1986) and, of course, Coetzee's *Disgrace* (1999). All these novels are, in Van Wyk Smith's terms, "resonant expressions" of a discourse interrogating the farm as foundational icon (29), since in all of them the buried giant and the forbidden history of the appropriation of the land re-emerge in the process of imagining alternatives to the traditional history and teleology of the farm.

In *The Conservationist* the hastily buried and re-buried body of a black man repeatedly resurfaces as a kind of return of the repressed in white consciousness. In Van Wyk Smith's analysis Mehring's legal and moral claims to the land are in the end eroded so that the land is restored to its rightful owner, the black man, the buried giant.

In the Heart of the Country enacts for Van Wyk Smith "the despairing liberal white consciousness contemplating its own dissolution" (31). Magda's central concern with a void that needs to be filled culminates in her attempt to bury her father in a porcupine burrow, encapsulating yet reversing "all the ominous engagements between protagonists and buried presences found in earlier novels" (Van Wyk Smith 32). She buries the patriarchy as it were, yet emerges free to tell her story and, in Van Wyk Smith's view, to rejuvenate the farm novel.

In this framework *Disgrace* is for Van Wyk Smith likewise a fundamental re-invention and re-telling of the story of the African farm. In his view the novel enacts the primal white fear of black attackers but is also persistently concerned with the "story of sexual ethics" and "how to negotiate redress for sexual misdemeanour" (33). In this perspective the novel tells of a startlingly different way to negotiate this redress: that of Petrus taking Lurie's daughter as one of his wives and under his protection in order to make amends in a traditional Xhosa way.

There are few similar buried presences in Afrikaans farm novels. One notable exception is Reza de Wet's play *Diepe grond* (literally "deep soil" but a more accurate meaning is "deep waters", 1986). In this play the parents whom Soekie and Frikkie have murdered keep on returning in the demented games their children play while digging for water that would transform the dry and barren farm into an Eden. But this play amply supports Van Wyk Smith's contention that the stories we have been telling about the farm "have always been fraught with tension and contradiction" (34).

The farm is a site where the modalities of space and identity in literature can be studied in a concrete form. It is moreover a site rich in ideological undertones. As a well-known genre that represents the patriarchal order, the farm novel is a highly suitable vehicle for parody and ideological criticism of that order (see Van Coller). Van der Merwe traces the development of the farm novel from "total loyalty" to Afrikaner ideals through "loyal resistance" to "total resistance" during which the farm evolves from "idyllic home", to "locus of a hard but morally sound way of life", turning into "the root of racism and oppression" and becoming, in the novels of the 1980s and in the work of Karel Schoeman, "a place of isolation and loneliness" (165). The farm novel in Afrikaans fiction thus reflects, in his view, "the rise and fall of an ideology associated with the farm—an interconnected system of values in which Christian religion, patriarchy, nationalism, racism, family ties and meaningful labour all play a part" (183).

In the sections that follow I will tease out the ambivalence of the farm, focusing in some detail on the way in which space and identity are constructed and validated in the three farm novels under consideration.

Land, Space and Identity in *Die Meulenaar*

In *Die meulenaar* the farm is under threat from the beginning. The novel is set among the vineyards and mountains of the Western Cape and the plot deals with Oom[2] Tys' struggle for the ownership of the farm Meulkloof (Mill's Cove) despite his many debts and the threat of phylloxera in the vineyards. The plot is complicated by the manipulations of the young attorney, Isak Louw, and his desire for Oom Tys' daughter, Leonore. The miller in the book is Faans, who, as an orphan, was taken into the family at Meulkloof and who operates the water mill on the farm. Faans is somewhat simple-minded but develops a searing love for Leonore, which leads to a jealous confrontation with Louw. In revenge Louw has the mortgage on Meulkloof foreclosed so that the farm has to be sold and Leonore has to abandon her dreams of becoming a concert pianist abroad. The novel ends with her and Oom Tys preparing to lead a simple Christian life in town after the farm has been sold at auction.

Space, the beauties of the region and the changing of the seasons are mostly described by the auctorial narrator. Typically Meulkloof is a space where good, strong, even somewhat primitive figures (like Faans) struggle with nature through the cyclical movement of the seasons. The seasons and nature mostly are in sympathy with the emotions of the characters. Though the idyll is under threat, the farm remains a meaningful space, laden with the memories of happier times. It is a devout place politically under the sign of the *Patriot*—mouthpiece of the so-called First Afrikaans Language Movement of the late nineteenth century. As such it contrasts with the bigger, more open world of Cape Town where people are more liberal and more English-minded (though this contrast is understated). Leonore's visit to Cape Town strengthens her longing for the enchanted world of her ideals abroad, away from the farm that she finds stifling. Oom Tys is a benign and noble patriarch, and the clash between father and son that is typical of many farm novels is absent in this case. Class differences between the white landowners and the jolly colored workers are strong. Though the personal relations are genial and the love stories of the young white and colored people reflect each other, intersecting to a very limited degree, to the modern ear they are embarrassingly patronizing.

The action of the novel is framed by two auctions. The first time selling the farm is avoided by the machinations of Louw, only to be hastened also by his machinations in the end. Oom Tys and Leonore accept the loss of the farm as God's will. The loss of the farm does mean that they lose identity and status, but this is not strongly emphasized. Oom Tys understands his loss as a religious leave-taking of earthly things, and Leonore sets aside her ambition in a spirit of quiet resignation. Faans, however, is devastated by the loss of the mill, because it represents not only his livelihood but also his identity and the possibility of moving out of his state as poor, landless orphan. He strongly identifies with the mill, as the title already indicates, and a substantial part of the novel is devoted to telling his story and revealing his love for Leonore. The problem of what is to become of Faans in the end is resolved when he has a stroke as a result of the blow to the head that Louw and his cronies inflicted on him as punishment for virtually assaulting Louw. This removes the possibility that Faans could become an embarrassment that would threaten the status quo. Poor and without family he cannot aspire to become heir to Meulkloof.

Meulkloof is a contested space—contested not only by the aspirations of different would-be owners like Faans, Louw and Liebermann, the Jew, but also by the forces of nature themselves. A sense of insecurity and loss runs through the whole novel, becoming a sad reality in the end. It is not so much the identity of the settled landowners that occupies the center. Though Oom Tys' and Leonore's stories and memories are important, the novel also is centrally concerned with the dreams of the marginal character, Faans, and his sad end.

Wynand, the main character of Van den Heever's *Somer*, is likewise a landless, marginal character.

Land, Space and Identity in *Somer*

On the face of it, *Somer* is a story of the wheat harvest and of love set in the eastern Free State against a vague backdrop of market forces overseas. Wynand wanders from place to place helping to harvest the wheat crop. He is a romantic who cannot find rest anywhere, always reaching for far-away places and the endlessness of the horizon. Arriving on Oom Tom's farm, love develops between him and the daughter, Linda, while he is exulting in the labor of cutting the corn in the burning heat, in close identification with nature. A hailstorm destroys the harvest of Oom Frans, Oom Tom's brother. The idyll is also disturbed by Hannes, son of one of the neighbors, Oom Faan, who is in love with Linda and jealous of Wyand. In his *Weltschmerz* and experience of rejection, Hannes causes one of Oom Tom's wheat stacks to burn down, seriously injuring himself in the process. With Hannes dead, the harvest completed, the season turning, Wynand has to leave—pursued by the stigma of the fraud that he committed in Johannesburg when trying to buy back the land of his fathers, as he reveals to Linda in the final scene. Linda remains behind in pain, articulating the theme of the novel that life is brief and evanescent. The life force flows through humans and nature alike, indifferently, inexorably (see Van den Heever 80).

In this novel, space is mainly built up by the descriptions of the auctorial narrator, usually placed at the beginning of each chapter. In this respect *Somer* is a typical farm novel, since the narrator describes the farm as a good, idyllic space—religious, mythical, patriarchal yet meaningful through lived experience, through joy in labor, and especially through the sense of the passing away of time and life.

These traits are already clear in the opening passage in which the auctorial narrator also looks through the eyes of Wynand, the wanderer. All the spatial coordinates of this novel are articulated here.

The first impression is of heat, but this is immediately contrasted with coolness. This is an opposition that is used to structure the whole spatial arrangement in the book. A strong contrast is developed throughout between the burning, violent heat of the sun and the calm, cool evenings (see 11) and also between the fields open to the violent sun and the only cooler place on the farm—the garden where there is shade and water. The last shade is, very early on in the novel (6), already associated with death.

Second, the farms are situated in an immense space in which humankind and their structures (like houses) appear insignificant (see also 93, for example). Closely linked to this immensity is a longing for the far horizons, a reaching out for the infinite. On the first page the road is described "as having an eternal yearning for distance, for space" (5, my translation). Space is therefore a vehicle for romantic longing, and a strong contrast between the farm, symbol of stability, and the road, symbol of wandering, is established from the beginning.

Third, space is closely associated with a sense of passing time—of the day, of the season, of life itself. Time and again the characters sigh that everything is passing away, that humankind dies like wheat that is cut. Life comes and inevitably leads to death. This is articulated very strongly in the beginning of Chapter 8. This sentiment reaches its climax in the last chapter where Linda articulates it poignantly: "Farewell. This is the true meaning of life; that in everything that had beauty for you, in everything you set your heart on as if you could never lose it, farewell can already be read" (142, my translation). This also returns in the last words of the book: the novel ends with the deep knowledge that Linda has gained from the events, namely that everything has to pass away (147).

Further, nature and humankind are closely identified. The ripening of life in the wheat echoes the life of humankind and the death of the wheat stools predicts the death of humankind—as happens to Hannes in this novel. The life force acts through humankind and nature equally, bringing to life, causing growth but also maturity and eventually death. Wynand is one of the main articulators of a supreme joy in the hard physical labor of cutting the wheat. Labor is a celebration of the life force and at the same time a conquest of nature, but there is also a strong sense of the capricious fateful power of nature in the book (e.g., 81).

The only spatial coordinate that is missing in the opening chapter is the contrast between light and darkness that the narrator employs elsewhere as an essential spatial coordinate of the novel. In the longing for the infinite and in the celebration of the life force the romantic and vitalistic tendencies of the novel are abundantly clear.

At the same time the auctorial narrator mostly loosely ties his descriptions and meditations to one of the articulating characters—Oom Tom, Hannes, Wynand, in particular, Linda—all of them able to read the message that life flows through everything; that natural things mature, die and pass away (like the wheat) and that humans also grow up and die.

One can discern three levels of characters, three triangles. The first is formed by the three older men: Oom Tom; his brother Oom Frans; and Oom Faan, the outsider with more money who has bought the land of the third brother and is regarded with suspicion: he has designs on their land. The younger generation (Linda, Wynand and Hannes) forms the second triangle, and they are particularly sensitive to the romantic yearning after the infinite, and to the passing of time. The younger ones are susceptible to unnamed yearnings and strange emotions—depths of feeling that the older generation does not seem to have.

As in *Die meulenaar,* space in *Somer* is racially marked space. The social distance between white masters and colored laborers is expressed in the spatial distance between the farmhouse and the laborers' houses and the fact that the laborers are not included in the social gatherings and festivities of the masters. The third triangle in the novel is also a love triangle between the colored laborers Stefaans and April who are competing for the favors of Katryn. Bragging and boasting all the time, they conform to the stereotype of the jolly hotnot.[3]

One can speak of three identities: the settled older generation, believers, trusting in God, struggling with the forces of nature and unknown market-forces; the younger generation, seemingly much less stable, much less self-assured, full of strange yearnings; the laborers, hardly people at all, but rather jolly racial stereotypes, albeit disconcerting in their humorous showing-off and in the dark magical powers ascribed to them (see, for example, the predictions of Oom Malooi about Hannes and Wynand, 46).

Spatial Divisions: The Fields, the House and the Garden

Space in *Somer* is gendered space. The fields and the threshing-floor are male spaces where Linda only ventures to bring coffee. The fields lie open to the merciless forces of nature—the sun, the hail. The small houses, where the women hold sway, are too warm for comfort and their interiors are hardly described. The older women in fact barely play a role in the plot and are virtually invisible, preparing food, warning their men of things that are going wrong.

The farmyard and the garden are in-between spaces where one can socialize and escape from the heat of the day. The garden in particular is an interspace of nature outside the violent sun, a space of coolness, water, and shade. It is here that Wynand recalls the playful days of his youth and remembers it as a lost paradise—an eloquent association. The garden is not gendered or at least not reserved for men (but it is in a sense improper for a young woman to walk in the garden with a stranger as Linda does with Wynand). But the garden is the space where the romantic aspects of the novel—passing away of life, unknown desires, a sense of being caught up—can be read at their clearest. It is also the space where Linda experiences the full maturity of the season and feels the passing of time and of life at its strongest (see the novel's final chapter).

Land, Space and Identity

Again as in *Die meulenaar*, space in *Somer* is space, land under threat. The vagaries of nature, volatile markets and greedy speculators collude to drive the simple and honest farmers from the land with which they closely identify. The threat is that they will lose their inheritance and will have to move to the town or to Johannesburg—the site *par excellence* of iniquity. Without land, they will lose their identity and become flotsam.

The importance of land for identity is equally clear in the case of Wynand. Loss of land in his case also means loss of identity. Wynand's identity as a wanderer is a non-identity: he stands outside the usual matrices in which identity is constructed: he has no family, no heritage, no future; he is always yearning for the faraway horizon; he has no security and no responsibility; and above all, no land. He is stigmatized as a vagabond and people are suspicious of him, accusing him of drinking too much. As such he is obviously not a good marriage prospect for Linda.

The farm is the site of identity, but at the same time the security of this site is under threat. In the end Oom Frans' farm is saved, and the farmers resolve to work the farm out of debt, but their efforts are puny compared to the large forces of nature and the market. Succession by the next generation is also unsure. In all this *Somer* is a kind of elegy for the agrarian life-style that is passing away.

Land, Space and Identity in *Die Stoetmeester* (*Leap Year*)

The third novel I will discuss represents, as I mentioned at the beginning of this chapter, the parodic phase in the development of the subgenre of the farm novel. In the novels from this phase identity and space are still closely linked, though in a different and negative way, and apartheid guilt and fear are dominant themes. *Die stoetmeester* and other such novels, like *Foxtrot van die vleiseters* (Foxtrot of the Meat-Eaters) by Eben Venter, are attempts to tell the story of the farm in a different way. Venter himself ("Skaapboud") has recently written that the traditional leg of lamb served on Sundays in the Karoo has become a symbol of his guilt. In *Die stoetmeester* the dominant theme of guilt is symbolically captured in the figure of the *Caper timidus*—the fainting goat or fall-goat.

The way in which the magical realist space of the imaginary city of Port Cecil and its environs and the identity of its inhabitants are constructed is a fascinating topic. Ritual, politics, remembrance of a tradition and environmental concerns also play an important part in these processes—as do stories. The narrator-focalizer plays a central role in the construction of space and its significance. The book ends in an imaginary resolution of the conflict between white and black—a resolution that seems to be a dead-end one, however.

The first chapter of the novel evokes the central space of Fata Morgana, the estate of the rich settler family, the Butlers, where Sarah Butler is waiting on the stoep (porch) for her dinner guests to arrive. This is the evening, as the narrator says, when everything started.[4] In her meditations several important facets of the farm and the region are evoked—important codes for understanding the novel.

Codes for Understanding the Landscape

Prehistoric is a key word here, but the narrator himself emphasizes the "impassive remoteness, the inscrutability of nature, the indifference in its giving and its taking" (*Leap Year* 2). This indifference of God, of nature, is an important theme that reflects the harsh and unforgiving nature of the region.

In the evening light the landscape seems to soften, but that is an illusion, since Sarah is aware of the presence of death, evoked by the predators creeping from their dens and in the death of the fall-goat slaughtered for dinner.

Sarah smells rain, evoking its magical effect on humans and on nature in this harsh, inhospitable and very dry region. When it rains, people start telling fantastic and magical stories about kudu on the wing and so on. This is an important clue to the magical-realist tone of the novel.

Sarah is conscious of a number of ominous signs. Something is about to happen; nature is in an extraordinary mood. The region as Sarah evokes it is a hard and primeval world with hidden depths. This is exemplified by artifacts from its history in the museum, but most of all by the prehistoric fish, the coelacanth "that represents the primal wisdom of depths so vertiginous that museum visitors shiver at the sight of that primordial snout with its fringe of whiskers" (*Leap Year* 8). Sarah feels the land moving under her feet.

One of the main reasons for this feeling is the fall-goat that the estate is famous for, "A joke of a creature" (*Leap Year* 11). The dominant theme of guilt is symbolically captured in this central artifice of the *Caper timidus*—the fall-goat or fainting goat with an ironic intelligence in its insane yellow eyes. These animals have fear bred so deeply into their genes that they faint and fall prey to any approaching predator, thus allowing other, valuable livestock to escape. The goat also is a figure for the guilt-ridden white landowners, whose guilt is increased by their tampering with the laws of nature.

Right at the beginning of the book the insecurity and guilt of the white settlers are therefore evoked—perhaps ironically—through the eyes of a woman. What we have here is definitely not a rosy-hued typically feminine view. The views of other women—Ayanda Thandani, MaNdlovu—are also clearly articulated in this novel and play an important part in articulating the history of the region and their own identities, but they are all, in a sense, sub-voices of an enigmatic narrator-focalizer.

The Narrator beyond Space and Time

Leap Year opens with a remarkable paragraph:

> Something woke me. It could not have been the night sounds of the port—they are so familiar they form a kind of silence: the sighing of boats at anchor as the incoming tide disturbs their rest; the nightly barking of dogs in the fisherman's quarter; the hiss of steam escaping from the power station at Third Leg; and, if you listen carefully: fins cleaving the ocean depths, comets whistling through the firmament of heaven, the gentle rustle of a rose opening in the garden...(1)

The different "silences" (night sounds) call into being the port city and some of its main parts but do not give us any sense of the spatial relationships between them. They also call into being an extraordinary narrator, who is able to hear fish playing in the deep sea and even comets rushing through space. These sounds situate the city in a very big, cosmic framework. The narrator hears, as it were, the music of the sea and of the spheres, but at the end of the paragraph returns to the intimate and highly significant (symbolic) space of the garden where a rose (equally symbolic) is opening.

Creating space by means of sounds hardly impacting on consciousness (but getting mentioned nonetheless) might be part of the "modern auditory"—the way in which we have become aware of the space-creating power of sound through radio and hi-fi sound production. It is a marker of modernity. Being able to hear the fins of the fish cleaving through the sea is a marker that we are no longer on the realistic surface level of things, but that we are moving into magical-realist space. But note that space and character are closely linked from the beginning: the city comes into being here at the very opening of the novel by means of the things the narrator-character hears.

It is only at the end of Chapter 1 that the reader discovers that the narrator is called Seer Wehmeyer, but the enigma of this narrator is only deepened by his remark that his description of the river at sunset—that it looks like blood and later like oil—is "a prophecy about my own blood, too, and that barely two weeks later I will find myself where I am today" (13).

In Chapter 2 the narrator, from a cosmic perspective, floating on the stream of memory like on the river, visits himself as he is starting his day with the daily ritual of playing with his valuable collection of model steam trains. Seer, in other words, is introducing himself to us. From a need for security that he shares with his sister Sarah, he, at age forty, is still living in his parents' ramshackle old house on the river. Among his books, his records, his collections of poetry and his archive of old legal documents, Seer represents a kind of cynical, life-weary Afrikaner.

Meditating on his own views and his own privileged position, he realizes that his privileges are expressed in terms of space: he cannot live without a variety of spaces that he inhabits with different facets of his being; without spaces where he can be "completely and utterly private" (148), without the aesthetic pleasure of his rose garden.

But as we learn later on, after his nephew, Cawood, has intruded into his world, and Seer has discovered the beauty of a mature male body, he grows disgusted with his way of living, finding it senseless and absurd. He realizes that he has lost the ability to live and that his life motto has been: leave me alone.

Port Cecil: Magical City—and Spatial Hierarchies

The space that is evoked at the beginning is the magical-realist city of Port Cecil, spread along the seven delta arms of the Kei River that flows into the Indian Ocean. The city and the Kei that surrounds it form a very cleverly constructed set of interrelated spaces populated by a number of striking yet typical South Africans. Seamus Butler represents the rich landed British settlers, MaNdlovu and the Thandanis, the Xhosas, and the Wehmeyers, Seer and Sarah (wife of Seamus), the privileged Afrikaners. Through the perspective of the different characters and the way in which they experience their surroundings, a full and rich novelistic world is created. But you will look in vain for Port Cecil on the map of South Africa, for it and the Kei are magical-realist amalgams of the Eastern Cape Province. It is an imaginary city named after Cecil John Rhodes— British arch-imperialist, prime minister of the Cape Colony at the end of the nineteenth century and founder of Rhodesia (now Zimbabwe). The city is an amalgam of elements from the real cities of the Eastern Cape. Port Elizabeth in Algoa Bay is the major harbor city. East London is also a big port city situated in the Buffalo River about 300 kilometers north of Port Elizabeth. The cathedral and the ivy-covered university—Rhodes University—are elements from the old frontier capital of Grahamstown, halfway between Port Elizabeth and East London. The Drostdy that is mentioned stands in Graaff-Reinet, and the Kei River itself actually flows into the Indian Ocean about 70 kilometers north of East London and does not have a delta at all. Since the eighteenth century the

Eastern Cape has been the frontier between the Cape Colony and the Xhosa tribes where nine frontier wars were fought.[5] But both the dryness and harshness of the country are very real.

Like Seer the other central characters, in experiencing their spaces, create an identity for themselves but in the end also realize their own fate. This can be said of all the principal characters, including Ayanda, Zola and MaNdlovu. Seer is also the auctorial narrator who sees with all the characters and who can describe the city and all the other places from a broad bird's-eye view, from a broad unifying perspective that locates everything in space. As such he plays the main role in constructing the spaces of the novel.

Like Seer, the other central characters in the book have specific places that are holy to them. Seer has his parental home but also the graves of his parents as memorial sites. To MaNdlovu the ammunition magazine against the hill is a holy site. We find her visiting this site at the end of Chapter 8. Here place is constructed by her sensory experiences, and the scene ends with her coming into close bodily contact with the soil itself. The magazine, however, is much more than a place where she can come into touch with the land; it is rather a place where she can meet her lost son, Ncincilili. Seamus Butler's memorial site is the little piece of ground in the garden where his father shot himself. Ayanda Thandani's memorial sites are the street where the shape of a policeman who was necklaced in front of her eyes can still be seen—but also an unmarked grave in the cemetery where Seer's parents lie.

Meeting Ayanda in the graveyard illuminates the strange ability of the narrator to stand next to all the characters without them knowing it but also to go back in time—a liberty that he describes as one of his privileges (35). That is why he is able, for example, during this meeting with Ayanda, to see himself from the outside looking as though he "might take fright at his own ghost" and wants to go over to shake his own hand (279). His abilities are explained by the fact that he is probably dead and can see the events from beyond space and time. As a ghost he can travel through time.

Constructing Identities—Symbols, Myths, Heroes, Rituals

Symbolically, the central space of the book is the cathedral square—a contested space when Ayanda's ex-husband, the ambitious taxi-owner named Zola, causes oil to be discovered there. The cathedral was built, it is claimed, on Xhosa ancestral land, and the discovery of oil puts the whole community under high pressure and exacerbates the contest for land between the Xhosa and the white settlers, since land forms an important part of both Xhosa and settler identity. Ritual, politics, remembrance of a tradition and environmental concerns also play an important part in these processes—as do stories. The Xhosa matriarch, MaNdlovu, constantly strives to keep the Xhosa identity intact by insisting on their traditional customs. As part of the project of nation-building she is at the forefront of efforts to lay claim to the land and the oil. Her husband, Talmbongi—the Xhosa praise poet who provides an alternative point of view in the book—refuses to take part in her plans, saying that he does not care about the ground the cathedral stands on, since "My territory is my songs and all who listen to my songs are my people." He questions the assumption that identity should be based on land. She does not, however, recognize the part that telling stories plays in constructing her own identity, since the stories she tells, like the story of her journey with her mother to the city, are also a very important part of her identity: it tells of her mother's suffering and legitimates her claim to the land. The name of her son Ncincilili also points to the constructive power of stories, since it means "I disappear"—it is "the word with which the Kei's imbongis conclude their praise songs" (116). Ncincilili is a story, in other words.

The rituals the people engage in and the heroes they name are also important elements of identity for all the groups in the book. Seer has a daily ritual of playing with his model trains. The annual foxhunt is an important ritual for confirming the masculinity of the settlers. On this occasion the fox flees into the city, so that the hunting party has to traverse all the spaces, ending at the symbolic center, the cathedral where the fox takes refuge. It is on this cathedral square that the confrontation with the township people also takes place on the fateful night of the Leap Year Ball. Many people are killed when nervous soldiers start shooting at the marchers, and this massacre threatens to tear the whole region apart. Some solution, some way to expiate the guilt, has to be found.

Space, Guilt and Sacrifice—the Fall-goat

The solution comes in the form of the ritual sacrifice of a scapegoat—the role that the fall-goat had come to fulfill. The memorial sites, as reminders of guilt, can be regarded as equivalents of the buried giants that Van Wyk Smith pointed out. They represent hidden presences—like that of the coelacanth—that evoke the hidden depths and powers of the region and of its history, but also the hidden psychological abysses in the characters. The main character, Seamus Butler, the breeder of the fall-goat, is the one with the most hidden depths, the one who carries most guilt. He is branded by Africa but carries in his genes a "longing for green hedges, fields of daffodils and lanes winding through the English country side" (50). Seamus compares his own subconscious mind to "a jackal, rancid with wickedness, being wrested from its hole by a bearded terrier in John Lennon glasses [his therapist]" (45). As powerful character he traverses all the spaces in the novel, carrying his guilt and depression with him. He feels he has tampered with the laws of nature by breeding the fall-goat, and he himself closely identifies with the fall-goat, remaining caught in that moment before extinction, that moment before his father shot himself, as his therapist explains to him. In the final analysis, in the darkest corner of his psyche, Seamus discovers that he rejected his son because he too closely identified with his father's suicide. This realization is acted out in a final scene of rejection between the father on horseback and the son in his helicopter (360-1). Thus the old plot element of the struggle between father and son in the farm novel is reactivated. For the legacy in this novel is not the land, but it is guilt that is carried from one generation to the next—it is this dark secret that lurks in the depths under the farm. A perverted image of the important farm novel theme of heredity is presented in the book.

The guilt has to be expiated, however. In this case the fall-goat who is sacrificed to save the Kei from destruction, is Seer himself: he is abducted by masked men and is never seen again. Guilt and sacrifice touch all the characters, as the narrator realizes when he witnesses the final confrontation between Seamus and Cawood: "we are all sacrificial victims, prey to so many things" (360).

The River of Mythical Reconciliation

The book ends in an imaginary resolution of the conflict between white and black when the two women, Sarah and Ayanda, meet each other standing in the river—a resolution that some critics regard as a dead-end, since there is no one to carry their legacy further. But the close identification of both Seer and Sarah with the flowing elemental water offers hope, and the suggestions are that they might turn into fish, surviving the coming flood. One might even say that Seer has at last reached a state of pure identity with the land and with nature. In this state of absolute oneness with nature, he, in the shape of a school of little fish, might symbolically fertilize both women, laying to rest the buried giant.

The imaginary resolution indicates that *Leap Year* is the author's imaginary model of South Africa as a whole at the turning point in its history—the point just before 1994 when the conflict between the different peoples threatened to spin out of control, the point where reconciliation against all odds became possible. It is true that land does constitute communality between the different peoples, but it is rather through myth and ritual, through story and symbolic action, that reconciliation becomes possible. Within the well-known framework of the farm novel Van Heerden has developed a compelling vision of a harsh and unforgiving but magical country. The imaginary resolution at the end can also be regarded as his "answer" to J.M. Coetzee's *Disgrace*.

Leap Year is a fascinating rewriting of the farm novel under the sign of guilt. But looking at the three novels there is one surprising similarity, and that is the central role of the garden. In all three gardens seem to be the heart of the farm, lost paradises all of them. In *Die meulenaar* and *Somer* the garden is still bearing fruit, and fruit plays a significant part in the interactions between men and women. In *Leap Year* the garden bears only roses—it has become a decadent site of nostalgia.

Notes

1. The title can be translated as "Selling a whole ox for an old bread-knife". It refers to unequal trading between the Dutch and the Khoi in the Cape colony in the seventeenth century.
2. Oom literally means "uncle", but is traditionally used in Afrikaans as a respectful form of address for an older man.
3. The jolly hotnot is the stereotypical view of colored persons as noisy, merry (usually under the influence of alcohol), with little sense of responsibility, rarely tempered by superficial feelings of sadness. The word *honot* is derived from *Hottentot*—the name the Dutch gave to the Khoi at the Cape (see van der Merwe, this volume, and Gerwel 33).
4. This is how I would translate the Afrikaans "toe alles begin het." In *Leap Year* it was translated as "on that evening as it all begins" (1).
5. Noël Mostert has recently told the story of the encounter between white and black on this frontier in a fascinating way. He frames this encounter as an important contribution to the making of South Africa and of the modern world, since the Cape of Good Hope "symbolized for many centuries the two great formative frontiers of the modern world: the physical one of the oceanic barrier to the east, and its concomitant one of the mind, of global consciousness" (xv). He regards the Cape's frontier drama as integral to "the confused moral debate about humane conscience and the values of empire" (xvi) of the post-abolitional nineteenth century. To him this moral and political drama and its legacy epitomized by Steve Biko and Nelson Mandela "provided the main formative experience of South Africa" (xviii).

Works Cited

Coetzee, Ampie. *'n Hele os vir 'n ou broodmes: Grond en die plaasnarratief sedert 1595.* [A Whole Ox for an Old Bread Knife: Land and the Farm Narrative since 1595.] Pretoria: Van Schaik, 2000.

Coetzee, John M. "The Farm Novels of C.M. van den Heever." *White Writing.* Sandton, South Africa: Radix, 1988. 82–114.

De Wet, Reza. *Diepe grond.* [Deep waters.] Pretoria: HAUM-Literêr, 1986.

Fowler, Alastair. *Kinds of Literature: An Introduction to the Theory of Genres and Modes.* Oxford, UK: Clarendon Press, 1985.

Gerwel, Jakes. *Literatuur en apartheid. Konsepsies van 'gekleurdes' in die Afrikaanse roman tot 1948.* [Literature and Apartheid. Conceptions of 'coloreds' in the Afrikaans Novel until 1948.] Kasselsvlei, South Africa: Kampen, [1983].

Leroux, Etienne. *Seven Days at the Silbersteins.* Trans. Charles Eglington. Johannesburg: C.N.A., 1964.

Malherbe, D. F. *Die meulenaar.* [The Miller.] Kaapstad: Nasionale Boekhandel, 1967. (Originally published 1926)

Mostert, Noël. *Frontiers. The Epic of South Africa's Creation and the Tragedy of the Xhosa People.* London: Pimlico, 1993.

Suvin, Darko. "Approach to Topoanalysis and to the Paradigmatics of Dramaturgic Space." *Poetics Today* 8.21 (1987): 311–334.

Van Coller, H. P. "Die Afrikaanse plaasroman as ideologiese refleksie van die politieke en sosiale werklikheid in Suid-Afrika." [The Afrikaans Farm Novel as Ideological Reflection of the Political and Social Reality in South Africa.] *Stilet* 7.2 (1995): 22–31, Sept.

Van den Heever, C. M. *Somer.* [Summer.] Pretoria: J.L. van Schaik, 1986. (Originally published 1935)

Van der Merwe, Chris N. "The Farm in Afrikaans Fiction: The History of a Concept." *Strangely Familiar.* Ed. C. N. Van der Merwe. Stellenbosch, South Africa: Content Solutions Online, 2001. 161–186.

Van Heerden, Etienne. *Die stoetmeester.* [The Master Breeder.] Kaapstad, South Africa: Tafelberg, 1993.

———. *Ancestral Voices.* 1989. London and Johannesburg: Penguin Books, 2000.

———. *Leap Year.* Trans. Malcolm Hacksley. London: Penguin, 1997.

Van Wyk Smith, Malvern. "From 'Boereplaas' to Vlakplaas". *Strangely Familiar.* Ed. C. N. van der Merwe. Stellenbosch, South Africa: Content Solutions Online, 2001. 17–36.

Venter, Eben. "Die skaapboud." [The Leg of Lamb.] *Briewe deur die lug.* Ed. Etienne van Heerden. Kaapstad, South Africa: Tafelberg, 2001. 172–175.

Venter, L. S. "Ruimte (epiek)." *Literêre terme en teorieë.* ["Space (narrative)." Literary terms and theories.] Ed. T.T. Cloete. Pretoria: HAUM-literêr, 1992.

Chapter 7

When Outsiders Meet: Boerneef and A. H. M. Scholtz

Chris N. van der Merwe

In Afrikaans literature, the farm has had a symbolic power for many decades. In early fiction, it was a psychological home, a marker of identity for the Afrikaner; in later writing, it is an environment of oppression and racism. The masterly debut of A.H.M. Scholtz, the novel *Vatmaar* (published in 1995, translated into English in 2000 as *A Place Called Vatmaar*), should be read within the context of this tradition of Afrikaans novels and short stories about the farm. *Vatmaar*, according to Gerwel "the first really literary significant novel in Afrikaans by someone who is not a white writer", holds a unique place in the tradition of Afrikaans farm writing (recommendation on the cover of the Afrikaans edition, my translation). In this chapter, I will focus on the "dialogue" between *Vatmaar* and one short story of an earlier Afrikaans author, Boerneef. "Boerneef", which means "country cousin", literally "farmer cousin", was the pseudonym of I. W. van der Merwe, who wrote many nostalgic stories about life on an Afrikaans farm. Boerneef and Scholtz are in many ways very different and yet so similar. In the following analysis, I will discuss some of these differences and similarities and reach some general conclusions about the nature of identity.

Different, and yet similar. Boerneef was a professor in Afrikaans literature; Scholtz was educated only up to grade seven, and not in his mother tongue, Afrikaans. Boerneef was an Afrikaner; Scholtz is classified as "colored". Yet both write in Afrikaans with the same kind of nostalgia about the lost world of their youth. Both Scholtz and Boerneef are romantics, feeling discontented with the world in which they live, searching in their past for a community more harmonious and morally sound. In neither case is the created fictional community without its shortcomings, but in both instances they point the way for modern people towards a more meaningful life.

Boerneef and Scholtz belong to opposite groups: those benefiting from and those suffering through apartheid—and yet, upon close analysis, the borderlines become diffuse. Robert Thornton, in an article entitled "The Potentials of Boundaries in South Africa: Steps Towards a Theory of the Social Edge" remarks that:

> There is no fundamental identity that any South African clings to in common with all, or even most other South Africans. South Africans have multiple identities in multiple contexts, depending on factors of expedience, recruitment and mobilization, and the company one keeps. (150)

In accordance with Max Gluckman, Thornton sees *boundaries* as being at the center of the South African situation. These boundaries are multiple and cross-cutting—for instance, "a Muslim, or a Colored, may span many religious, political, social and cultural contexts" (151). With different criteria for classification, like "race" or "religion" or "language", the dividing lines would every time be different. Each person belongs to various "cultural groups," and each group contains a variety of subgroups.

Differences in identity in South Africa have continually led to conflict, but "South African identities have never polarized sufficiently to permit devastating conflict. It is the very complexity of all possible allegiances, together with the fact that maintaining multiple identities and cross-cutting allegiances has remained possible, that helps to make South Africa uniquely stable and violent at the same time" (152).

Zoë Wicomb, in an article entitled "Shame and Identity: The Case of the Colored in South Africa", also stresses the existence of "multiple belongings" in South Africa, and condemns the rise of the totalizing concept of "coloredness":

> "Multiple belongings" could be seen as an alternative way of viewing a culture where participation in a number of colored micro-communities whose interests conflict and overlap could become a rehearsal of cultural life in the larger South African community where we learn to perform the same kind of negotiations in terms of identity within a lived culture characterized by difference. (105)

In postcolonial theory, much has been made of the dichotomy between the colonizer and the colonized, the Self and the Other, the center and the margin. Yet even in a colonial situation, the divisions are never simply binary. In *The Colonizer and the Colonized* Albert Memmi describes his situation in a colonized country as follows:

> Like all other Tunisians I was treated as a second-class citizen, deprived of political rights, refused admission to most civil service departments, etc. But I was not a Moslem. In a country where so many groups, each jealous of its own physiognomy, lived side by side, this was of considerable importance. The Jewish population identified as much with the colonizers as with the colonized...they passionately endeavoured to identify themselves with the French. (xiii–xiv)

Neither the position of the colonizer nor that of the colonized is uncomplicated. Nikos Papastergiadis, commenting on Stuart Hall's recognition of "the immense diversity and differentiation of the historical and cultural experience of black subjects," remarks:

> The black subject cannot be represented without reference to the dimensions of class, gender, sexuality and ethnicity. Moreover, awareness of the complexity of affiliations which traverse subjectivity necessitates the recognition of the contradictory processes and investments which constitute identity. (123)

In a complex coexistence of a plurality of identities in South Africa, apartheid tried to drastically simplify the situation, using only one criterion, that of race, to classify people—ignoring other differences and similarities; also ignoring the fact that "race" can never be an absolute and "pure" criterion. Races ravel out at the margins. Furthermore, in a situation of continuously shifting identities, apartheid tried to freeze developments and maintain a rigid opposition of Self and the Other, in which the Self could live safely and happily ever after. To give this a moral justification, the concept of "homelands" was developed, where the Others could also live "happily ever after," without bothering the Self.

The prose of Boerneef penetrates this illusory world created by apartheid, where race acted as the only and absolute dividing line. Boerneef's early prose is in many ways "white-centered," focusing on the idealized life of the white farmer families and making caricatures of the colored workers; yet even in his first book, *Boplaas*, he admiringly portrays a colored character, Dirk Ligter, who defies the laws of the farmer and outmatches the policemen who try to catch him. Boerneef is, as it were, on the side of the colored law-breaker.

In his later work, the sympathy with coloreds increases. In *Sketsboek*, the sad fate of the young colored newspaper seller Oupie is told with great compassion. In this chapter, I want to focus on the title story in Boerneef's last collection of short stories, *Teen die helling* (Against the Slope).

The story is set *against the slope*, on the periphery of the city. The setting already suggests the central theme of the story—that of the outsider, the one who does not fit anywhere. The narrator longs for the farm of his youth but realizes that he will not fit in there any more. Neither does he feel at home in the city—therefore, he stays in an in-between space, a suburb, neither farm nor city. The first opposition in the story is thus that of farm and city, with an in-between space inhabited by the outsider. Another opposition suggested in the first paragraphs of the story is that of youth and old age, which partly overlaps with the opposition of city and suburb:

> In hierdie stadswyk aan die onderste helling van die berg knoop stedelinge, veral dié van middelbare leeftyd en ouer, makliker 'n praatjie aan met iemand wat hulle net van sien ken, as die stadsmense wat op die gelykte woon...Die opdraand draai op sy eie manier die rem aan. Dit weet die middeljariges en bedaagdes heel goed, en daarom is hulle soms maar dankie-bly as hulle 'n bietjie kan staan en rus en gesels oor die weer of die politiek of die onmanierlikheid van die hedendaagse jeug.

> In this neighbourhood at the foot of the mountain, wanderers, especially those middle-aged and older, readily start talking to people whom they only know from sight—more readily than city-dwellers who live on the level ground. ...The slope has a way of forcing you to put on the brakes. Middle-aged and elderly people know this all too well, and they are grateful to stop for a while and chat about the weather or politics or the rudeness of the present youth. (Boerneef 459—all translations mine)

Against the slope the Afrikaner narrator befriends two English-speakers, McCorkindale and McAlpine. They are all bound by the ways of the slope, and the connections to different language groups fade in importance. (The fact that their surnames are Scottish might suggest another link between them and the narrator—that of dissociation from "the English." The affiliations become even more complicated—there is a difference in language, but possibly an affinity between Afrikaner and Scottish identity; and a shared view of the ways of the city and the ways of youth.)

Then Andries Harlekyn, a colored, appears against the slope. Initially, the differences between him and the narrator are glaring. Andries Harlekyn seems to conform to all three colored stereotypes mentioned by Jakes Gerwel in his study *Literatuur en Apartheid*:

1. The stereotype of the "jolly Hottentot"—a comic stereotype: somebody superficial, unreliable, drinking too much. Indeed, Andries drinks excessively; he has no permanent work or fixed address, and he is very comical. His surname, "Harlekyn" ("clown") suggests that his basic function is to amuse others. This surname is probably not his own but was given to him by whites who found him entertaining.

2. The stereotype of the colored as dependent child, with the white as parent or guardian. Andries addresses the narrator with great respect: "Good afternoon, Boss. If I had a hat, I would certainly have taken it off. That's how it should be" (Boerneef 460). And when he begs for money, he does so in an extremely humble posture: "Just look how I cup my hands" (462). Andries acts the beggar, and the narrator mercifully provides him with money.

3. Gerwel uses the phrase "I only came with the master" to characterize the third stereotypical presentation of coloreds: the whites are in the center of the story; the coloreds derive their importance only from being in the presence of the white characters. In Boerneef's story, the white man is the narrator, and it is through his eyes that the reader views the world. The narrator is also the central character in the story.

And yet—as the story unfolds, the distance between Andries and the authorial narrator decreases. At this stage it should be mentioned that the story evokes various links between the narrator, the author Boerneef as revealed in his work, and the man Izak van der Merwe, so that it is not possible to make absolute distinctions between the theoretical concepts of the narrator, the implied author and the real author. They are, as it were, various manifestations of the same person; or, in the line of the argument here, multiple identities of one human being—and Andries is related to them all.

Andries grew up on a farm, and he has wandered through the same area that Boerneef portrays with so much nostalgia in his prose and poetry. Like Boerneef, Andries longs for the world of his youth; he talks in a lively manner about matters depicted in Boerneef's prose: working on the farmlands, driving the oxen, being instructed in the message of the Bible. He has a poetic way of expressing himself—he likes the sound of words, and uses them playfully—just like Boerneef in his prose and (later) in his poetry. In the story, he develops from "Hotnot" to poet, as Hein Viljoen has argued (129). No wonder the narrator is attracted to Andries, even though Andries has drunk too much:

> Hy dwing om my kontrei se taal te praat, dié Andries Harlekyn. Andries dwing om my hart week te maak. Vaaljapie ofte nie en almiskie. Met hierdie taal en klinkende name van die ver wêreld sal ou McCorkindale nie hond haar-af maak nie.

> He's talking the language of my region, this Andries Harlekyn. Andries is forcing me to become softhearted. Liquor or no liquor—doesn't matter. Old McCorkindale wouldn't know what to do with this language with the ring of a far-away world. (461)

The dividing lines have moved. The narrator and Andries, white and colored respectively, are now in the same circle, joined by their common love of the farm, their longing for the past, and their vibrant use of the Afrikaans language. In this circle, McCorkindale and McAlpine are out.

At first, Andries's drunkenness is merely comical; later on, his love of liquor is looked at more seriously. It is a cold, rainy evening when the intoxicated Andries struggles up the slope, imagining that he is driving an ox wagon through muddy soil. After exchanging a few words with the narrator, he plods on, singing the Dutch hymn "Ruwe stormen mogen woeden" ("Rough Storms May Rage") at the top of his voice. It becomes clear that the storm outside is symbolic of the storms of life that Andries cannot handle; the imaginary ox wagon struggling through the mud is symbolic of the wearisome journey of life; and Andries's excessive drinking is an escape route that he needs because he cannot cope with life. Like the narrator, he does not fit anywhere—he complains: "Oh, how I long for my far-away world; but I won't fit there any more. I'm too far gone" (461).

The presentation of the drunken colored has by now changed drastically. The narrator has grasped the reason behind Andries's behavior, and as soon as understanding has been reached, the distance between narrator and character shrinks and the stereotype is undermined.

One cannot help remembering that I.W. van der Merwe himself, after losing his second wife to cancer, drank excessively for a while before he became a teetotaler. Andries Harlekyn functions as an alter ego for the writer Boerneef as revealed in his oeuvre and for the man I.W. van der Merwe in his experience of life.

At the conclusion of the story, the portrayal of Andries Harlekyn reaches its deepest and most profound level. Andries, properly under the influence of his "Vaaljapie", mutters to himself:

> "Anries, Anries. Jy moet luister en hoor. Jy wil, maar jy kan nie. Die Here woon hoog. Die Here siet laag. Anries. Ei-en-dee-aar-ee-joe. Hy woon hoog. Hy siet laag...Die Vaaljapie die lê my vas. Maar ek voel onrustig...Meulsrivier se waters is vir ammal te sterk. Agter die dipkraal runnik die donkiehings: 'Maa-ek-het-'n-nuwe-ding-opgetel. Hoe-kort? Te-kort-tekort.' Wanneer blaas die laste basuin?"

> "Anries, Anries. You must listen and heed. You want to, but you can't. The Lord lives high. The Lord sees low. Anries. A-n-d-r-e-u. He lives high. He sees low...The vaal-japie holds me down. But I feel anxious...The waters of the Mill River are too strong for us all. Behind the dipping-pen the donkey brays: 'Ma-a-a-I-picked-up-a-new-thing. How-short? Too-short-too-short.' When will the last trumpet blow?" (463)

The Mill River, too strong for all, mentioned for the second time in the story, is the River of Death, with its mill that nobody can avoid. This interpretation is strengthened by the reference to "the last trumpet." The suggestions of shortcoming, expressed by the onomatopoeic rendering of the donkey's braying, are linked to the concept of the last judgment and indicate fear of inescapable death.

There is no deliverance for Andries, no eternal home waiting. He is not at home, anywhere, neither on the farm nor in the city; life is hard, but death is frightening. From his catechism on the farm he has retained the feelings of guilt but not the experience of salvation. In this respect too, Andries is an alter ego of Boerneef, as revealed in his prose and especially in his poetry—someone desiring to believe simply, as taught in his childhood, but caught up in the doubts of a rationalist age; uneasy on earth, yet threatened by death. How closely they are linked, Boerneef and Andries Harlekyn.

In the last few paragraphs of the story a third person enters the circle of Boerneef and Andries Harlekyn—the grand poet of the Netherlands, Adriaan Roland Holst, quoted by the narrator:

> heb ik ooit wel in een ander lied geloofd
> hier op aard dan de verloren kreet der meeuwen?

> Was there ever another song that I believed in
> than the lost cries of the seagulls here on earth?

> ("Een winteravondval" [A winter sunset], Holst 212—my translation)

The circle of three is complete, and what a surprising circle of soul mates it is. Here, differences of language and social class are of no consequence. The great poet writing in Dutch in the Netherlands; the Afrikaans writer, admiring Dutch poetry and identifying with the feelings expressed; and the drunken colored, staggering against the slopes of Cape Town—they all belong together, paradoxically, by not belonging anywhere. They are misfits fitting together; outsiders who are insiders in this particular circle; all bound by the common experience of being lost on earth.

The author of A.H.M. Scholtz's novel *Vatmaar* could in some ways be part of this circle, but in many ways not. As a matter of fact, the novel could be read as an oppositional dialogue with the prose of Boerneef and with the genre of the traditional Afrikaans plaasroman (farm novel). Where early Afrikaner writers depicted the farm as their spiritual home, Scholtz depicts a village as a spiritual home. Where the plaasroman used to put the Afrikaner in the center, and workers of color as stereotypical figures on the margin, Scholtz portrays Vatmaar as a refuge for people of all races—for the Englishman, Corporal Lewis, as well as his black wife Ruth; and for the black woman, MaKhumalo, and her adopted white son Norman. The heroes and heroines of the book are those who transgress the conventional borders of race—people like the above-mentioned Lewis and his wife, MaKhumalo and her son, and also the colored Aunt Vonnie and her German beloved Heinrich Müller. These are people who have come to realize, as Oom Flip puts it at Ruth's funeral, that "Love knows no boundaries" (41—pages refer to the Afrikaans edition). Love is the binding factor—the erotic love between a man and a woman, and the parental love of a woman towards a child—love that destroys the divisions of race.

Friendship, too, may cross conventional boundaries. Uncle Chai, short for Charlie, is Afrikaans-speaking and classified as "colored"; Corporal Lewis is English and white. Chai is an active member of the "missionary" (read: colored) branch of the Dutch Reformed Church; Lewis refuses to attend their services, except when Chai, as elder, leads the service. Yet, in spite of these differences, Chai shows great compassion with Lewis at the death of Lewis's wife Ruth. Ruth was a faithful member of the Missionary Church, and her burial service was held in the Missionary Church.

The whole community of Vatmaar is present at the service, all sharing in Lewis's sorrow. Chai leads the service, and reads a passage from the Bible emphasizing that God's love includes different kinds of people: "In my Father's house are many mansions". Chai puts this message into practice by reading from the English Bible and conducting the ceremony in English—"out of respect for his friend's language" ("uit respek vir sy vriend se taal," 40). Chai and Lewis cry on each other's shoulder, and embrace each other "as only twins can." They are "twins" not through birth, but through true friendship.

The tolerant Christian community of Vatmaar respects the pre-Christian faith of the Griqua. TaVuurmaak (which means literally "Father make-fire"), one of the oldest people in town, knows and retells the stories of the past. He is proud of his Griqua traditions, stemming from pre-Christian times, and informs the young people about the wisdom of his heathen forebears. When he dies, he is not buried in the Christian way, but according to his Griqua customs, as he requested. In spite of his deviant religious beliefs, TaVuurmaak is respected as founding father in *Vatmaar*, almost as mythological Prometheus (compare his name "Vuurmaak"), without whom the civilization in Vatmaar would never have come into being. The division between Christian and heathen fades away.

Women play a central role in the story of Vatmaar—unlike the plaasromans of Malherbe and C. M. van den Heever, and also the prose of Boerneef, where the set-up is patriarchal. The most prominent character in Scholtz's novel is a woman, Aunt Vonnie, who has lost her beloved in the war and brings up her two daughters admirably on her own. She plays a leading role in the community as well, as can be seen during the deliberations about the buying of a plot for the building of a church (31–32).

It is worthwhile to look closely at the love between Bet and Flip, two other important characters in Vatmaar. For them, there is never the issue of who's the boss? Flip falls madly in love with Bet and believes he belongs to her:

> Bet was now to him beloved, sugar, condensed milk, holy and everything that's nice.
> Since he met her, his life has not been the same. He felt that he belonged to her. God,
> he says as he walks away prayerfully, isn't she pretty? (50)

Bet, on the other hand, has a deep respect for Flip, and follows his instructions. After their first sexual intercourse, he says: "Now we are husband and wife. As if it was a command. And she believed him" (61). Oom Flip and Bet "acknowledge each other's 'Otherness' in an essential way, not only affirming the other's 'I' as an object but affirming the other person as a subject" (du Plooy 164).

As their tale unfolds, it is clear that Bet mostly takes the initiative in important matters. She is cleverer than her husband, yet she never uses her intelligence to make him feel inferior but rather uses it to create a better future for them both. There is no subordinate gender in Vatmaar—men and women work in harmony for the good of the whole community.

The unity of the community of Vatmaar comes to the fore especially at occasions that require all to be involved: funeral ceremonies, the founding of a church, the starting of a soccer club, and the inauguration of a clinic. At such times, it becomes clear:

> The spirit of Vatmaar has always been one of standing together. Not merely neighbors
> together, but all the people together. And with each new enterprise each and every one
> would put his hand in his pocket, even if it was only for a penny on the collection list.
> (294)

The unity of the people is illustrated by the way in which the story of Vatmaar is told. There is not one narrator, but rather a group of narrators, because the story of the town is a communal one. It is quite fitting that the first word in the novel is "Our." The first narrator announces himself as the representative of the people of Vatmaar; he is starting with *their* story. Soon the old patriarch, Ta-Vuurmaak, takes over as storyteller, but when Uncle Chai starts playing a leading role in the narration, TaVuurmaak readily hands the storytelling over to him. Often one narrator's story forms part of another one's story, in a tightly interwoven structure suggesting the organic unity of the people whose stories are told.

This place Vatmaar, providing a shelter for people of all races, for men as well as women, for Christians and non-Christians, seems to have no boundaries at all. Yet that is not the case, and there is a clear dividing line between Vatmaar and the outside world. As it was dangerous, in the traditional plaasroman, for the Afrikaner to leave the farm and go to the city, it is here dangerous to go beyond the safety of Vatmaar. For instance Kaatjie, Aunt Vonnie's daughter, suffers greatly when she goes out to the white community of Du Toitspan to do housework.

The unjust and jealous white woman who employs her causes most of Kaatje's suffering, but there is also a very negative portrayal of the woman who tries to force an abortion on her, someone whose adherence to the Muslim faith is often repeated. There seems to be a wariness of Muslims in the novel. Significantly, when the Muslim woman Mariam Mohammed, chased away by her parents because of her illegitimate child, finds a home with MaKhumalo in Vatmaar, her name is changed to Mary and she adopts the Christian faith. The boundary between Christian and Muslim seems to be retained in the novel.

In general, trouble ensues when the people of Vatmaar enter the white community, or the white people enter Vatmaar. The wise old man, TaVuurmaak, warns the young people of the "Esau nature" of the whites; Flip and Bet both suffer badly through the inhumanity of their white masters; the experience of the people of color seems to indicate that "the whites think more of their dogs than of us" (55). Women of color are often the victims of sexual abuse by the whites and pay dearly when they defy the advances of a white man as Aunt Vonnie discovers when she resists Piet de Bruin.

Whereas the colored was a marginal figure and negatively stereotyped in the old plaasroman, here the racist whites are marginalized and negatively stereotyped, like the dominee (pastor) with whom Chai negotiates about the establishment of a congregation in Vatmaar:

> The dominee was of average length, not too thin, not too fat. He had a head full of thin
> black hair, with yellow-brown eyes. A heavy, thick, broad moustache hung under his
> nose. He was sallow, like the most devoted Afrikaners, people who are proud of having

Africa as their home. "It's only a pity that they want their fatherland only to themselves,
Oom Chai said." (26)

The shallow dominee, so proud of being "white", is extremely patronizing when
dealing with the colored community. There is a blatant discrepancy between his
gospel of universal love and his authoritative, callous treatment of the people of
Vatmaar. Ironically, he assures Vatmaar of the continuous "charity of the
mother church." Chai catches the irony and sighs: "Mother church. What a nice
name..." (27).

In comparison with the conventional plaasroman and also with much of the
prose of Boerneef, the tables are turned in *Vatmaar*—the center and the margin
have changed places. Yet, as in Boerneef's "Teen die helling," there comes a
moment towards the end of *Vatmaar* when the boundary between center and
margin is blurred. This happens at the inauguration of the clinic, to which important whites like the local doctor and the members of the city council of Du
Toitspan have also been invited.

In the plaasroman the comical behavior of the colored workers was often
due to an excessive use of liquor. In contrast, in *Vatmaar* the whites start behav-
ing like normal human beings when they become intoxicated—for example, the
dominee, who "in his drunkenness had an expression in his eyes for the first
time" (301). The whites begin to mix freely with the inhabitants of Vatmaar;
they lose their inhibitions and air of superiority, and see Vatmaar in a different
light: "What a lovely place this Fatma is, says a council member, his face shining
from the meat fat, on his way to his car. Just before he falls over" (303).

All masks have been dropped by now, and conversations become quite
earthy. The grand whites have discovered what Bet has known all along: "People are people, says Sister Bet. Whether he wears a golden chain or clutches his
ball in his trouser pocket" (303).

All borders seem to have vanished now—the outsiders have become insiders in Vatmaar. And yet, no writer, no human being is able to live without any
borderlines—undifferentiated reality would be overwhelming. Scholtz lifts the
barriers of race in his novel but creates a new division, a more moral one: that
between racists and non-racists. The whites, with the help of liquor, have temporarily crossed the border but will most probably return to their previous way
of life outside Vatmaar. The Muslims, too, stay outside.

The novel *Vatmaar* is in many ways engaged in a dialogue of opposition to
the traditional Afrikaans writing on the farm, including the prose of Boerneef.
But in other ways Scholtz's work and that of Boerneef are linked. Both are filled
with nostalgia for a world gone by. The moral values of both authors, despite
differences, are similar in many aspects. Oom Karel, the noble farmer in Boerneef's story "Boplaas", and Aunt Vonnie, the heroine of *Vatmaar*, would have
made an excellent couple—both live in humble submission to God's will and

their charity includes everyone they know. The community spirit in Boerneef's story "Die basaar" (from *Van my kontrei* [About My Country], 1938; see Boerneef 167–174), in spite of the exclusion of coloreds, could in many ways be likened to the community spirit in *Vatmaar*. The white Afrikaner writer and the colored Afrikaans writer, starting out from opposite poles, meet on the borders of their imagined worlds—where Boerneef's narrator discovers a common humanity in Andries Harlekyn, and Scholtz's colored characters celebrate a joint festival with the whites.

Writers are inevitably attracted to borders. They test the validity of conventional divisions; they explore the existence on the other side of the boundaries laid down by society. Yet they can never do away with all boundaries. They could imagine an alternative society with less restrictive patterns. At best, they could dream of a mature society having boundaries continually crossed, allowing free communication among people with various allegiances—all insiders in some circles and outsiders in others, and mostly inhabiting in-between spaces.

No life could be lived without boundaries; there is no freedom without restrictions—a rather hackneyed way to end this chapter. Therefore I will end it instead with a quotation from a more brilliant expression of similar thoughts, in Robert Frost's poem "The Silken Tent". Here the image of a tent is used to depict a woman bound by various cords of love. In the final analysis, the woman is attached to "everything on earth"; but as the wind changes, she becomes conscious, through the various cords, of the variety of her connections. I quote the last seven lines of the sonnet:

> [She]...
> Seems to owe naught to the single cord,
> But strictly held by none, is loosely bound
> By countless silken ties of love and thought
> To everything on earth the compass round,
> And only by one's going slightly taut
>
> In the capriciousness of summer air
> Is of the slightest bondage made aware. (385)

Works Cited

Boerneef. [I.W. van der Merwe] *Versamelde prosa*. [Collected Prose.] Ed. Merwe Scholtz. Kaapstad, South Africa: Tafelberg, 1979.

Du Plooy, Heilna. "A.H.M. Scholtz's novel *Vatmaar*." *Missions of Interdependence*. Ed. G. Stilz. ASNEL Papers 6. Amsterdam and New York: Rodopi, 2002. 157–168.

Frost, Robert. *The Poems of Robert Frost*. New York: The Modern Library, 1946.

Gerwel, J. G. *Literatuur en Apartheid: Konsepsies van 'gekleurdes' in die Afrikaanse roman tot 1948*. [Literature and Apartheid: Conceptions of 'Coloreds' in the Afrikaans Novel until 1948.] Kasselsvlei, South Africa: Kampen, [1983].

Holst, A. Roland. *Verzamelde gedichten*. [Collected Poems.] The Hague: Bert Bakker; Bussum: C.A.J. van Dishoeck, 1971.

Memmi, Albert. *The Colonizer and the Colonized*. Boston: Beacon Press, 1967. (Originally published 1957)

Papastergiadis, Nikos. *Dialogues in the Diasporas: Essays and Conversations on Cultural Identity*. London: Rivers Oram Press, 1998.

Scholtz, A. H. M. *Vatmaar*. Kaapstad, South Africa: Kwela Boeke, 1995.

———. *A Place Called Vatmaar*. Cape Town: Kwela Books, 2000.

Thornton, Robert. "The Potentials of Boundaries in South Africa: Steps Towards a Theory of the Social Edge." *Postcolonial Identities in Africa*. Eds. R. Werbner & T. Ranger. London: Zed Books, 1996. 136–161.

Viljoen, Hein. "Taalhandelinge in 'Teen die helling' van Boerneef." ["Speech Acts in 'Against the slope' by Boerneef."] *Woorde as dade. Taalhandelinge en Letterkunde*. Eds. H.P. van Coller and G. J. van Jaarsveld. Durban and Pretoria: Butterworth, 1984. 117–134.

Wicomb, Zoë. "Shame and Identity: The Case of the Colored in South Africa." *Writing South Africa: Literature, Apartheid, and Democracy, 1970–1995*. Eds. David Attridge & Rosemary Jolly. Cambridge, UK: Cambridge UP, 1998. 91–107.

Chapter 8

Civilization and Wilderness: Colonial Spatial Binaries and the Construction of Contemporary South African Identity in André Brink's An Instant in the Wind and Kirby van der Merwe's Klapperhaar slaap nooit stil nie (One Can Never Sleep Quietly on a Coir Mattress)

Louise Viljoen

Space, Identity and (Afrikaans) Narrative

The transformation of South African society since the advent of democratic rule in 1994 has focused the attention on the ways in which identity is constructed in a multicultural society. In this chapter I will argue that (Afrikaans) narrative is one of the areas in which issues around the construction of identity in South Africa have been worked out in the past and that this process is still continuing. Although it has been said that gender, class, race and sexuality are the most frequently cited axes of identity, oppression and resistance (Blunt & Rose 6), readings of Afrikaans literature alert one to the fact that other factors like language, ethnicity, religion and space also come into play in the (re-)construction of identity. Apart from the fact that space is one of the basic elements of any narrative, Afrikaans narrative seems to be especially preoccupied with space in the broadest sense of the word because it is part of a literature that originated against the background of a history of colonization and decolonization. This history involved the settlement of land, the conflict with indigenous peoples arising from this, the allocation of different spaces on the basis of race, class and gender and the discord arising from those allocations. This history also led to postcolonial reconsiderations of the relationship with South African space on the part of Afrikaans authors. Both the Afrikaans language and literature have close links with this history of colonization and decolonization because Afrikaans is a language that developed from the Dutch spoken by the first European settlers at the Cape (Ponelis 99–120). Although the language came to be associated with the oppressive ideology of apartheid, it was also the language of the struggle against apartheid because more than half of the South Africans who use Afrikaans as first language are colored people

who were excluded by the racist basis of Afrikaner nationalism. Afrikaans literature has the same ambivalent status: even though it was partly co-opted by the
political agenda of Afrikaner nationalism in the first part of the twentieth century, the counter-hegemonic strain in Afrikaans literature became the dominant
one from the 1960s onwards.

Because of its close involvement with these historical processes, Afrikaans
literature emphasized the transformation of space to *place* through naming, mapping, description, storytelling and mythologizing from its early stages on. This
does not only happen in the early texts in which European settlers and their
descendants place themselves in South African space, but also in the texts in
which descendants of the indigenous peoples of South Africa contest the way in
which space was appropriated by settlers. The focus on space also manifests in a
substantial number of texts as a preoccupation with *land* and the ownership of
land (see Coetzee, *'n Hele os*). The notion of space also features in Afrikaans
literature that examines the concept of a *country*, often against the background of
statements and questions about national identity. Afrikaans literary texts also
work with the notion of space as *landscape*, which is an aestheticized space that
resonates in specific philosophical and artistic traditions. Although the importance of space has been acknowledged in discussions of early Afrikaans literature (see A. Coetzee, *Marxisme* and J.M. Coetzee, *Doubling*), race, class and
ethnicity were the factors that predominated in research into Afrikaans literary
texts thus far. Race was the focal point in studies like Gerwel's *Literatuur en
apartheid*, February's *Mind Your Colour*, the collection of essays *Ras en Literatuur*
edited by Malan and Gardner's *Impaired Vision*; class was the focal point in studies like Coetzee's *Marxisme en die Afrikaanse letterkunde* and De Jong\h's *'n Ander
Afrikaanse letterkunde*. In this chapter identity will be seen as a construction based
on the complex interplay of a variety of elements; the focus will be on the
interaction of spatial elements with race, class, gender and sexuality in two
Afrikaans novels because they offer revealing insights into the way in which
issues of identity are worked out through the manipulation of narrative space.

Two Afrikaans Novels

The first of these novels is André Brink's *An Instant in the Wind* that was published in the heyday of apartheid: the Afrikaans version, entitled *'n Oomblik in die
wind*, was published in 1975 and its English version in 1976. Although this novel
by an established white Afrikaans writer was based on the Australian (hi)story of
Mrs. Fraser (also used by Patrick White in *A Fringe of Leaves*), the narrative about
the relationship between a colored slave and a white woman set in eighteenth-
century South Africa can be read as a comment on apartheid South Africa and
presents its reader with a vision of an ideal society free from the restrictions of
race and class.

The second novel, entitled *Klapperhaar slaap nooit stil nie* (a title that literally means One Can Never Sleep Quietly on a Coir Mattress), is a first novel by the colored Afrikaans writer Kirby van der Merwe, published in post-apartheid South Africa in 1997. Before the democratization of South Africa colored writers writing in Afrikaans found it intimidatingly difficult to gain entrance into the Afrikaans literary system. Although a few colored poets writing in Afrikaans (S.V. Petersen, Adam Small and P.J. Philander) were included in the canon of Afrikaans literature from the late fifties onwards, access to established publishers remained difficult for colored writers. Circumstances have changed with the creation of the publishing house Kwela Books in the early nineties and the publication of novels by colored writers like A.H.M. Scholtz, S.P. Benjamin, Karel Benjamin, E.K.M. Dido and Kirby van der Merwe. Unlike Brink's novel that has a historical setting but reflects on matters of identity in apartheid South Africa, van der Merwe's novel is set in and reflects on the processes shaping identity in post-apartheid South Africa.

Before elucidating the basis for comparison with Brink's novel, the use of the term "colored" must be explained. This term is a highly contentious one because of its associations with the history of oppression and racism in South Africa (see February vii). It has been pointed out that there was a tendency to construct "colouredness as a category midway between black and white" and that it "was given institutional expression in the ambiguous position accorded coloured people in the racial policies of United Party segregation, Verwoerdian apartheid and Botha's tricameralism" (Erasmus 18). This is perhaps most clearly demonstrated by the Nationalist Government's Population Registration Act of 1950 in which a "colored" person was defined negatively as "not a White person or a Black." For these reasons the term "colored" is contested by colored writers and academics in the field of Afrikaans literature who find it racist and offensive (see February, Smith et al., Willemse, Gardner and Willemse et al.). Within the context of the struggle against apartheid these writers and academics chose to call themselves "black" as a sign of solidarity with the political struggle. Since the beginning of democratic rule in South Africa in 1994, the question of colored identities and their relationship to black identities have increasingly come under discussion. Zoë Wicomb writes about colored identity in her article "Shame and Identity: The Case of the Coloured in South Africa" and comments on the

> resurgence of the term *Coloured*, once more capitalised, without its old prefix of *so-called* and without the disavowing scare quotes earned during the period of revolutionary struggle when it was replaced by the word *black*, indicating both a rejection of apartheid nomenclature as well as inclusion in the national liberation movement. Such adoption of different names at various historical junctures shows perhaps the difficulty which the term 'coloured' has in taking on a fixed meaning. (93)

The matter of colored identities in South Africa is also taken up in the collection of essays entitled *Coloured by History, Shaped by Place*, edited by Zimitri Erasmus. In the introduction Erasmus notes that the discourse of the struggle years during which colored people adopted the term "black" as "an inclusive political identity marking" did not acknowledge "the specificity of colored experience or the heterogeneity and locatedness of blackness" (18–19). She argues for a re-imagination of colored identities that will move beyond the notion of "mixed race" identities that are still based on racist notions of purity and authenticity, seeing them as "cultural identities comprising detailed bodies of knowledge, specific cultural practices, memories, rituals and modes of being" (21). In the light of these arguments and because it enables one to point out certain specificities and nuances, I will use the term "colored" instead of "black" when referring to the writer Kirby van der Merwe as well as some of the characters in both these novels.

A comparison between these two novels brings to light the complex interactions of race, gender and class with space in the construction of South African identities. Both these novels deconstruct the spatial binary that opposes wilderness to civilization and the racialization of those spaces in order to envision the transformation of South African cultural identity during different phases of South African history. Brink's novel was published during the apartheid years and used a historical setting to comment on the restrictions on race, class and gender inhibiting the construction of identity in South African society. Van der Merwe's novel was published in post-apartheid South Africa and reflects on the processes shaping the construction of identity during the years following the beginnings of the new political dispensation in 1994. A comparative reading of these two novels also demonstrates the way in which the issues concerning the role of race and gender in the construction of identity changed with the advent of a new political dispensation. Van der Merwe's novel almost reads like a re-working of or answer to Brink's novel: Brink's novel used the relationship between a colored slave and a white woman in the eighteenth century to comment on the way in which these identities should interact in an idealized post-apartheid South Africa; van der Merwe's novel uses the relationship between a colored woman and several white men to comment on the complexity of the interactions between colored and white identities in the realities of post-apartheid South Africa.

Space, Race and Gender in André Brink's An Instant in the Wind

The narrator in Brink's novel uses invented historical documents, purportedly dating from the mid-eighteenth century at the Cape (Jolly 31), as the basis for his story about the relationship between a runaway slave Adam Mantoor and a white woman Elizabeth Larsson. According to the narrator, he wants to scrape "the crust of history" off the documents, not "simply to retell it but to utterly expose it and to set it in motion again" (15). From this it becomes clear that he wants to reveal the relevance of the historical events for contemporary South African society.

The narrator's reconstruction of events "begins" when an expedition into the South African interior, conducted by the Swedish explorer Larsson and his Cape-born wife Elizabeth ends in disaster. After their guide commits suicide, the accompanying Hottentots desert the expedition and Larsson disappears into the bush, Adam Mantoor approaches Elizabeth. He is a slave who has escaped from Robben Island to which he was banished after being convicted for lifting his hand against his master. He has been living in the freedom of the interior for several years and has shadowed their expedition for some time. The novel then tells the story of their circuitous return journey to the Cape and the love affair that develops between them. The first part of the journey ends when they reach the coast and spend an idyllic summer living in a cave above a beach. Despite the fact that they are aware of the problems awaiting them in the Cape, they resume their return journey through the hazardous semi-desert called the Karoo. Elizabeth hopes to convince the colonial society at the Cape to grant Adam his freedom as a reward for saving her life and to accept their relationship. The final passages in the novel suggest that she failed to achieve this: instead of being fetched by Elizabeth on the beach where he waits for her, Adam is picked up by soldiers. This indicates that the constraints imposed by race and class in colonial South Africa crushed their hope of being together as husband and wife (the fictionalized historical document with which the novel begins confirms this by mentioning that Elizabeth married an elderly neighbor after her return to the Cape).

One of the most important structural devices in the text is the spatial binary governing colonial settlement, expansion and exploration, in this case the opposition between the colonial settlement at the Cape and the unexplored interior of South Africa. Critics have shown that this binary evokes others, like the opposition between civilization and lack of civilization, between the Cape with its European settlement and Africa, between culture and nature (Massyn 51n) and between the attachment to community and the fantasy of being free from community (Massyn 46). To emphasize this opposition the narrative almost excessively uses the word "wilderness" for the interior, suggesting that it is an uninhabited space. The idea of the interior as an uninhabited space is emphasized by Brink's use of phrases like the "wild and empty land" (Brink 15), "indestructible, wild, fierce landscape" (57) and references to "the inhospitable landscape and the endless space" (104). These phrases and images are not only used by the arch-colonizer and arch-explorer Larsson (he is the very image of the scientist-explorer described by Pratt in *Imperial Eyes*), but also by the narrator and the characters Adam and Elizabeth when they are given the chance to narrate and focalize the events. Even a critic like Hassal falls into the trap of seeing the landscape of the interior as an empty space when he comments that Brink's representation of the landscape conveys "his passionate attachment to it and his grief for its fall from unpeopled magnificence" (13). This reminds one of J.M. Coetzee's comment that South African literature representing the South African landscape as empty can be seen as a "failure of the historical imagination" to acknowledge the presence of the indigenous inhabitants of the land (*White Writing* 9).

The text then goes on to play upon another binary governing colonial thought, namely the one that associates the white person with civilization and the colored or black with the lack of civilization. This is also the case with the way in which the identities of Adam and Elizabeth are constructed. Elizabeth's race (white) and class (she is the daughter of a reasonably well-to-do Dutch official) immediately affiliate her with the Dutch settlement at the Cape. On the other hand, Adam's race (he is colored because he is descended from Hottentots and slaves from Java and Africa) and his class (he is a slave) link him to the lack of civilization implied by the wilderness. Despite the dangers this may hold for the author's political project, it seems as though the narrator wants to "naturalize" the affiliation between race, class and a specific space by suggesting that there is a natural bond between the colored slave Adam and the "wilderness" described in the narrative. Because of the five years he spent in the interior before encountering Elizabeth, he acquired knowledge of the land that helps them survive their journey to the Cape. The narrative suggests that this is not only a rational or experiential knowledge, but that it is also based on some "natural" ability to feel the land and experience it with his senses. At one point Adam scornfully contrasts the abstract knowledge contained in the maps of the interior that Elizabeth wants to use with his own concrete experience of the land: "*My* land I've seen with my eyes and heard with my ears and grasped with my hands. I eat it and drink it. I know it isn't something out *there*—it's *here*" (*Instant in the Wind* 33—my emphasis).

On more than one occasion in the novel Adam forcefully tries to communicate to Elizabeth this instinctive knowledge that will allow her to "feel" the land rather than know it rationally (Brink 118–123; 197). The most notable of these moments occurs during their short season in the beach paradise. Adam forces her to go with him to a small island close to the coast, not knowing whether they will be washed away by the incoming tide or not, the idea being that they will have an almost mystical and immediate experience of the sea in the moment of extreme fear or danger. "Listen to the sea. ...That's what we've come for," he says (121). The intensity of this experience of immediacy is heightened by also making it a moment of sexual union, albeit that Adam forces himself on Elizabeth. Although a certain kind of reading of the novel interprets this as a moment of intense self-realization and freedom from colonial restrictions (Massyn 45), it can also be read as implying that there exists a natural bond between the identity-constituting categories of race (the colored), class (the slave), space (the wilderness) and a certain kind of sexuality (instinctive and uninhibited).

His slave master also articulates the "naturalness" of Adam's bond with the land when he tells Adam that he was "bred for this land. Malgas for strength, Javanese for intelligence; Hottentot for endurance. You see? You belong here" (78; see also the passage on 35). Although Adam reacts angrily to this, the narrator and controlling intelligence in the narrative seem to comply with this insidious view by stressing Adam's instinctive bond with the land, implying that identity is a biological essence rather than a cultural construction.

The contrast between Adam and the Swedish explorer Larsson is also constructed in such a way that it emphasizes Adam's natural bond with the wilderness. Elizabeth feels that he looks like a "clown in the wilderness" (19; see also 86) when she sees him for the first time and he is wearing clothes that he stole from her husband. She seems to feel that the trappings of civilization are inappropriate to him who fits so "naturally" in the wilderness. Her civilized explorer-husband Larsson, on the other hand, is made to look clownish by the wilderness, in life (the incident with the lion) as in death. When they discover his remains in the veld, the "first they noticed was the pathetic gaiety of small torn patches of clothing fluttering from the dead branches and the long white thorns—next, the black, three-cornered hat, its proud plume broken and dishevelled" (57). The European Larsson does not "belong" in the wilderness and succumbs to it; the man of mixed racial descent Adam "belongs" in the wilderness rather than in the sumptuous clothing of civilization—thus maintaining the binaries of colonial thought.

One could also argue that Brink's representation of Adam as the natural inhabitant of the wilderness perpetuates the age-old and culturally specific notions of the "wild man" and its derivative, the "noble savage". Hayden White writes that the wild man became transformed from an object of loathing and fear into an object of open envy and admiration by the end of the Middle Ages, thus becoming "the ideal or model of a free humanity, his presumed attributes made the essence of a lost humanity, and his idealized image used as justification for rebellion against civilization itself" (168). According to White's argument, the concept of the noble savage emerged from this not to elevate the idea of the native but rather to demote the idea of nobility; he notes that it was used by eighteenth-century writers like Diderot and Rousseau to attack "the European social system of privilege, inherited power, and political oppression" rather than to redeem the savage (191). Although it is clear that Brink also writes his novel to attack the system of privilege, inherited power and political suppression prevalent in South Africa at the time he was writing his novel, one has to question the wisdom of displacing European concepts like that of the wild man and the noble savage on to his colored character Adam.

In all fairness to the author one must note that the tendency towards a biological construction of Adam's identity is undercut by other strains in the narrative that expose the so-called "naturalness" of his bond with the land. Despite his instinctive understanding of the wilderness, Adam insists that he, too, is of the Cape and that he wants to return there, even though he knows that it will mean imprisonment and possibly execution. Statements like the following by Adam deconstruct the notion that he is a natural child of the wilderness: "I did not choose the wilderness because I wanted to. I simply had to. And by now I've learned to stay alive, to survive like an animal. But I'm not an animal. I'm a human being" (91; see also 22). His reminiscences about the Cape (such as his upbringing as a slave, the incident that led to his imprisonment on Robben Island, his escape) also counter the essentialist construction of his identity by filling it out with localities and specifics. The idea of the colored slave Adam as one of the "authentic" inhabitants of the land, instinctively at home in the wilderness and bred for this land, is furthermore deconstructed by his encounters with indigenous people who demonstrate the limits of his capacity to survive in the interior (as in the case of the old woman who helps him survive a snake bite and the Bushman who finds water for him in a dry river-bed where he lies on the verge of expiring).

In keeping with the colonial tendency to feminize colonized landscapes and colonized subjects like the slave Adam, the narrative suggests the possibility of gendering the "wilderness" as female. This is confirmed by the fact that although the white woman Elizabeth is associated with civilized Cape society as Adam's opposite, she feels confined in her surroundings and hankers after the wilderness. The sense of adventure that makes her go on the expedition with Larsson, her affinity for storms (20, 38) and the feeling of reckless freedom she experiences when climbing the mountains around Cape Town (25) can all be seen as indications of a "natural" potential to be one with the wilderness. In one instance it is even implied that this affinity has something to do with her gender. Adam's comment "Woman: you, wilderness in which to lose oneself" (92), seems to be an (anachronistic) echo of the Freudian notion of "woman as the dark continent." This is reinforced by an earlier moment in which Elizabeth implores the explorer Larsson, who is to become her husband: "Here I am, explore me. Don't you see? I am a prisoner here" (41).

Elizabeth's notion of herself as wild and unexplored territory contrasts with her mother's opinion that the idea of "a woman in the interior" is "madness" (64; see also 181). The narrative suggests that it is this "madness" in the eyes of society that enables Elisabeth to have a meaningful relationship with Adam across the divides created by colonial notions of race and class. Using the terminology of society's discourse, she regains her "sanity" when they return to the Cape and she is unable to honor her promise to protect Adam. The novel implies that being regarded as abnormal or mad is preferable to being socially acceptable in a racist, classist and patriarchal society—a clear reference to the apartheid society in which the novel was written.

The novel's attempt at visualizing an ideal space for South African society is strongest in the passages describing Adam and Elizabeth's stay in their beach paradise before resuming their journey back to the harsh realities of Cape society. There is a deliberate attempt to represent this biblical Eden, complete with naked Adam, woman and snake, as a space in which identity is to a great extent a *tabula rasa*: race, class, gender and sexuality seem to represent no restrictions to fulfillment of the self. Built into this representation of an ideal space are, however, also the gender hierarchies generated by the biblical representation of Eden: Adam is the hunter, Elizabeth gathers fruit and shells; he leads, she follows; when they find a snake she finds it beautiful, he kills it because it is dangerous; he takes possession of her sexually, she acquiesces (121; see also the description of their first sexual encounter on page 108). The description of the way in which Adam forces himself on Elizabeth during the incident on the island comes dangerously close to idealizing what could almost be interpreted as a rape scene:

> Instinctively she closes her legs, but he forces her down again, prying her thighs apart with his knee, hurting her. She begins to cry, no longer understanding what is happening. He seems possessed, ramming into her. She goes on struggling as if he were a stranger overpowering her. But in the very act of crying and struggling against him, she discovers, shockingly, blindingly, that she is no longer fighting him but actually clinging to him. (121)

If this is to be read as the author's metaphor for an ideal South Africa in which the restrictions governing class and race have been overcome, one cannot but deduce that he has not succeeded in visualizing a space in which gender inequalities have been resolved. The attempt at "un-gendering" space by representing it as a biblical Eden does not succeed in emptying gender categories of their harmful cultural contents.

In contrast to this picture of the ideal space, the narrative presents the reader with a concentrated image of its opposite. When Adam and Elizabeth come upon a farmstead on their way back to the Cape, they are forced back into the position of master and slave that they have abandoned in the wilderness. Elizabeth is taken into the house by the farmer and his wife, and Adam must go round the back with the other slaves and servants. It is made abundantly clear that this farmstead is the threshold between the wilderness and Cape society, especially when it is revealed as a racist, classist and patriarchal space in which the slaves are treated as inhuman and Elizabeth is expected to sleep with the farmer who also abuses his wife. Though they succeed in fleeing, it becomes clear that this incident represents the space to which Elizabeth will submit when she abandons Adam at the end of the novel.

The novel ends with a passage in which the narrator imagines what Adam would have thought as the soldiers came to fetch him on the beach where he was waiting for Elizabeth: "Come, he would think, breathless in the wind. The land which happened inside us no one can take away from us again, not even ourselves. But God, such a long journey ahead for you and me. Not a question of imagination, but of faith" (250). Adam's imagined words refer back to those with which the narrator concludes the introduction to the novel in which he states his intention to "imagine" a novel on the basis of historical documents:

> To travel through that long landscape and back, back to the high mountain above the town of a thousand houses exposed to the sea and the wind. Back through that wild and empty land—*who are you? who am I?*—without knowing what to expect, when all the instruments have been destroyed by the wind and all the journals abandoned to the wind, when nothing else remains but to continue. It is not a question of imagination, but of faith. (15)

The final words of the novel may be interpreted as an admission on the part of the narrator that his attempt to visualize a politically free South Africa was flawed and that the road ahead would require faith, rather than the narrative imagination displayed in the novel. That these are also the sentiments of the author is suggested by the dedication of the novel to Brink's fellow dissident and Afrikaner, the poet Breyten Breytenbach, with the following words: "For Breyten such a long journey ahead for you and me." The fact that the first democratic elections in South African took place nineteen years after this novel was first published in Afrikaans in 1975 proves that Brink was prudent to think in terms of a "long journey ahead" at the time.

Space, Race and Gender in Kirby van der Merwe's Klapperhaar slaap nooit stil nie

Kirby van der Merwe's novel *Klapperhaar slaap nooit stil nie* (One Can Never Sleep Quietly on a Coir Mattress) is also predicated upon the binary opposition between civilization and wilderness—in this case the civilized Cape, which is the domain of the whites, and the wild interior, which is the domain of those who are colored or black. Whereas Brink's novel encompasses a wide geographical space and opposes the colonial settlement at the Cape to the wilderness in the interior of South Africa, van der Merwe's novel plays within a much smaller geographical range by opposing the white suburbs of Cape Town to the city's colored and black townships, a division that was made official by apartheid's

Group Areas Act and which has been largely maintained in post-apartheid South Africa. The author evokes the memory of a colonial attempt in 1659 and 1660 to plant a hedge of wild almond trees and build forts with Dutch names like "Keert de koe" ("Stop the Cow"), "Houd den bul" ("Hold the Bull"), "Kijckuijt" ("Be on the Lookout") and "Ruiterwacht" ("Horseguard") to protect the colonial settlement against attacks from the outside and to stop their cattle from being stolen by the Hottentots (Böeseken, *Nuusbode* 17; Böeseken, "Die koms" 34). This fence between the white colonizers and the indigenous peoples becomes a metaphor for the barriers that divide people of different races and classes into separate spaces. *Klapperhaar slaap nooit stil nie* seems to imply that crossing these (spatial) barriers is an important feature in the construction of identities in post-apartheid South Africa.

The protagonist in *Klapperhaar slaap nooit stil nie* is a young colored woman named Kinta Januarie. Even though she grew up in poverty-stricken circumstances, she manages to go to university and to become a successful lawyer. The life she has built for herself apart from her family is disturbed when she hears that the father she has never known is lying on his deathbed in a Cape Town hospital. She starts visiting him night after night and meets two white men at his bedside. One is a retired policeman called Hans Brink, who grew up with her father on the farm where Hans was the son of the landowner and Kinta's father the son of the housekeeper. She grows attached to this man who can be said to represent the old racist order: she visits him in his flat to listen to the stories he tells about her father and even entertains the idea of taking him into her home when she sees the way in which he neglects himself.

The other white man Kinta Januarie meets at her father's bedside is the young doctor Gustav van As. Although Gustav seems to be falling in love with her, she resists his advances. Because she knows so little about her father, she starts writing down her childhood memories as well as the stories Hans Brink tells her about her father—she does this "to flesh out the skeleton of (her) past" ("Om die geraamte van my verlede op dié manier stadig maar seker vleis te gee." All translations my own.) (74).

This constitutes a curious paradox: on the one hand she tries to escape her past by hiding from her family in her upwardly mobile lifestyle, but on the other hand she has the need to know about her past. Her father's sickbed and eventual death force her to confront her family, namely her opportunistic half-brother Abe who has started his own church and her sister Mymoena who lives with her boyfriend, a gangster called Kat, in one of the colored townships on the Cape Flats (142–143). On more than one occasion she takes Gustav with her when she has to visit her family in the townships because of her father's illness and death. He also accompanies her to the gathering after the funeral at her sister's house from where he is lured away by Kat and his friends to run some gangster errands for them. They try to kill him and leave him on a deserted beach where fishermen find him. During his recuperation Kinta takes him into her house that she has previously jealously guarded against any intrusions by outsiders.

Whereas Brink's historical novel tried to visualize an ideal space in which the negative effects of race, class and gender divisions would be absent, van der Merwe's novel charts the spaces affecting the construction of identity in a transforming post-apartheid South Africa. The story of Kinta's journey through life and her struggle with identity can be read in terms of two opposing spaces: the colored townships on the Cape Flats ("die Vlakte") to which people of color were relegated by the apartheid system and the spaces in which white people were allowed to live and work. When she starts writing up the stories she hears about her father, she remembers the spatial detail of her fatherless childhood. Among these memories are those of living in a one-room shack in someone's backyard with her mother, brother and sister (24–26). The novel's title refers to the coir hair mattress on which she had to sleep with her brother and sister; the fact that the title says that one can never sleep quietly on a coir hair mattress, hints at the lack of privacy and the possibility of sexual abuse in such circumstances (36, 39–40). Her obsession with hygiene stems from this time in her life when she had to endure dirt, fleas and unpalatable smells.

Another space that she recollects from her childhood is the white neighborhood in which her mother worked as a housekeeper: she remembers them nervously hurrying through the streets because of the animosity projected by the white people and the growling dogs (20–21). She also vividly recalls accompanying her mother when she was employed as a seasonal worker, picking peas on a farm. The dismal working conditions make Kinta remember the space of this farm as a "green hell": "Today I know, hell is green; hell is a vividly green place" ("Vandag weet ek, die hel is groen; die hel is 'n heldergroen plek"), she writes (87).

Kinta leaves the marginalized spaces of her childhood when she enters university, has an affair with one of her white university professors and moves in with him in his house in a white neighborhood (80). After he leaves South Africa to teach in America and she has become a successful lawyer, she buys the house (133), recreating it to be the complete opposite of the spaces in which she spent her childhood. She transforms it into "a sugar white wonder" ("'n suikerwit wonder") (23) that is "light and dry like a bleached sheet" ("lig en droog soos 'n blouselgebleikte laken") (133). She compares her journey from the colored townships on the Cape Flats to the white neighborhood with crossing the line demarcated by the colonial hedge of wild almond trees:

Hoe het sy die Vlakte ontsnap? Oor die heining gekom? Die laning van bitteramandels. Die aluinwaters van die Liesbeeck? Eenvoudig, dink sy, ek het die toegangsfooi betaal. Een pond vleis, nie 'n druppel bloed meer of minder nie. (79)

How did she escape the Cape Flats? How did she get over the fence? Over the hedge of bitter almond trees? The alum waters of the Liesbeeck River? Easily, she thinks, I paid the entrance fee. One pound of flesh, not a drop of blood more or less. (my translation)

It is clear that the crossing of this barrier between the erstwhile spatial opposites is no uncomplicated matter. The fact that Kinta cannot completely leave or forget the spaces of her childhood becomes physically manifest when her father becomes ill and dies and she is forced to take up contact with her family again. Each time that she returns to the spaces of her childhood, she takes one or both of the white men with her. These journeys to what is for them the "other" side of the race and class barrier are in some ways the exact opposite of her own journey years before. She takes Hans Brink back into the colored townships, which he has previously only entered to act against rioting students when he was a policeman during the years of the struggle against apartheid. When he attends Adriaan's funeral with Kinta, he wonders what she would say if she knew that he had batoned rioting students in the very same church during the struggle years (159).

It is especially Gustav's journeys to the other side of the barrier that kept him apart from colored South Africans that become important rites of passage. Kinta takes him with her when she goes to call on the woman called Ouma (Grandmother), who was actually her philandering father's first wife but who helped raise her as a child. Ouma lives in a derelict farmhouse near Cape Town in which several families squat (14). Kinta comments on the irony of the fact that Ouma now lives in this old Cape-Dutch Homestead on a farm they once visited together when she was a child (19). On that occasion they could only look at the well-kept house from a distance because they were not even allowed on the stoep (porch) of the house (19). Because the South African farm is often seen as representative of a history in which colored and black people were denied land ownership and land rights, this is indeed an ironical moment. The depiction of the farmhouse taken over by squatters can be read as a comment on the shifts of power in post-apartheid South Africa. It is interesting to note that both the white men in Kinta's life, Hans and Gustav, have negative memories of the farms on which they grew up. Hans Brink remembers the farm where he grew up as a strongly patriarchal space over which his father ruled like a violent despot. It was because of this that he left the farm to become a policeman who ironically perpetuated the cycle of patriarchal violence he was exposed to as a child. Gustav remembers the screaming of pigs about to be slaughtered in the slaughterhouse on the farm where he grew up (191–192). In this way van der

Merwe adds his voice to those of other Afrikaans authors like Etienne Leroux, Etienne van Heerden, Koos Prinsloo, Alexander Strachan and Eben Venter who have parodied the genre of the farm novel in order to criticize the social order it represented.

On another occasion Kinta takes Gustav to her sister's house in a colored township, thus introducing him into a space he has never experienced before. Her sister's gangster boyfriend takes Gustav to a township shebeen (the local name for a bar) (144) and to him this experience represents a "new world" ("nuwe wêreld") (144) that fascinates and scares him in the same way that the gangster Kat does. The latter has tattoos all over his body and face, three golden rings in each ear and golden letters spelling his name set in his front teeth (156). He evokes the same kind of fear and fascination that Gustav felt for the East when he was a child (155), a moment in the narrative that equates the white South African's relationship with the colored or black South African with the relationship between the West and East that Said theorized in *Orientalism* (1978). This experience must be read against the background of Gustav's idealization of life in the colored townships, especially the stereotype of the warm and affectionate extended family that contrasts with his own experience of an uncaring nuclear family (76–77).

Gustav also buys into other stereotypes and myths about the coloreds: he refers to their traditional foods and wants to see the Cape Coon Carnival that takes place on the second of January of each year (78–9). Kinta warns him not to idealize township life (77) and resists the notion that his touristic notions about the coloreds represent an authentic version of reality. Although she does not want to go to the Coon Carnival with him, the narrative itself does not resist representing the carnival and "makes" her attend it with Gustav. She opposes the idea that her own identity as a colored can be equated with touristic stereotypes, seeing them as constructions conveniently used by others to categorize the coloreds as "excessive clowns" ("uitspattige hansworse") (78), thus confirming their feelings of superiority.

Writing about "The Case of the Coloured in South Africa", Zoë Wicomb takes the same kind of position as the fictional character Kinta when she argues *against* "fabricating a totalizing colouredness" and *for*

> 'multiple belongings' (that) could be seen as an alternative way of viewing a culture where participation in a number of coloured micro-communities whose interests conflict and overlap could become a rehearsal of cultural life in the larger South African community where we learn to perform the same kind of negotiations in terms of identity within a lived culture characterized by difference. (105)

At one point in *Klapperhaar slaap nooit stil nie* Kinta thinks of Gustav: "A week, a day in the townships and he will have had enough for the rest of his life. That will cure him" ("'n Week, 'n dag vir hom in die townships en hy't genoeg gehad vir die res van sy lewe. Dit sal hom regruk") (79). The near-fatal outcome of Gustav's introduction into township life when Kat's gangster friends almost kill him seems to prove Kinta's point. It is only after he completes this rite of passage that Kinta takes him into her house to live with her while he recuperates. Gustav's journey into the spaces of the townships seems to be the reverse of Kinta's journey out of the townships years before.

The novel ends with a description of Kinta and Gustav climbing Table Mountain; the final moment in the novel shows them sitting on a narrow ledge on the mountain, as it is getting darker. Gustav does not know how they will be able to get off the ledge, but Kinta, who is an experienced mountain climber, seems sure that she will be able to lead the way. Read against the background of what has gone before, this moment in which the colored woman leads the white man safely through dangerous terrain has clear symbolic overtones. The similarities but also the contrast with Brink's novel, in which a colored man leads a white woman through the wilderness of the South African interior, are striking.

Conclusion

Both these novels are concerned with the way in which spaces, both physical and metaphorical, impact on the construction of South African identity. Van der Merwe's novel almost reads like a reworking of, or an answer to Brink's novel. *An Instant in the Wind* uses the relationship between a colored slave and a white woman in the eighteenth century to comment on the way in which colored and white identities should interact in an idealized post-apartheid South Africa, finally conceding that it is not a workable idea by devising a tragic ending for the narrative. *Klapperhaar slaap nooit stil nie* uses the relationship between a colored woman and several white men to comment on the complexity of the interactions between colored and white identities in the realities of post-apartheid South Africa. The way in which the novel conceives of its heroine Kinta Januarie's identity reminds one of Erasmus' comment that colored identities should not be seen in terms of mixed race identities but rather as cultural identities comprising "detailed bodies of knowledge, specific cultural practices, memories, rituals and modes of being" (21). In the final analysis one can say that van der Merwe's novel is more inclined than Brink's to emphasize the specificities of South African identities and less prone to fall into the trap of honoring colonial discourse's interpretation of the binary opposition between the spaces of wilderness and civilization, reserving the former for coloreds and/or women and the latter for whites.

Works Cited

Blunt, Alison & Rose, Gillian, eds. "Introduction: Women's Colonial and Postcolonial Geographies." *Writing Women and Space. Colonial and Postcolonial Geographies.* New York and London: Guilford, 1994. 1–28.

Böeseken, A. J. "Die koms van die blankes onder Van Riebeeck." ["The Arrival of Whites under Van Riebeeck."] *500 jaar Suid-Afrikaanse geskiedenis.* Ed. C. F. J. Muller. Pretoria and Kaapstad, South Africa: Academica, 1980

———. *Die nuusbode.* Kaapstad, South Africa: Nasou, 1966.

Brink, André. *An Instant in the Wind.* London: Fontana/Flamingo Paperbacks, 1983. (Originally published 1976)

Coetzee, Ampie. *Marxisme en die Afrikaanse letterkunde.* [Marxism and Afrikaans Literature.] Bellville, South Africa: Universiteit van Wes-Kaapland, 1988.

———. *'n Hele os vir 'n ou broodmes: Grond en die plaasnarratief sedert 1595.* [A Whole Ox for an old Bread Knife: Land and the Farm Narrative since 1595.] Pretoria: Van Schaik, 2000.

Coetzee, J. M. *Doubling the Point: Essays and Interviews.* Ed. David Attwell. Cambridge, Mass. and London, UK: Harvard UP, 1992.

———. *White Writing: On the Culture of Letters in South Africa.* New Haven and London: Yale UP, 1988.

De Jong, Marianne. *'n Ander Afrikaanse letterkunde: Marxistiese en sosiaalgerigte teksopvattings in Afrikaans.* [Another Afrikaans Literature: Marxist and Socially Conscious Notions of the Text in Afrikaans.] Pretoria: RGN, 1989.

Erasmus, Zimitri, ed. "Re-imagining Coloured Identities in Post-Apartheid South Africa." *Coloured by History, Shaped by Place: New Perspectives on Coloured Identities in Cape Town.* Cape Town: Kwela Books; Maroelana: SA History Online, 2002.

February, V. A. *Mind Your Colour: the 'Coloured' Stereotype in South African Literature.* London: Kegan Paul International, 1981.

Gardner, Judy H. *Impaired Vision: Portraits of Black Women in the Afrikaans Novel 1948–1988.* Amsterdam: Vrije Universiteit UP, 1991.

Gerwel, G. J. *Literatuur en apartheid: Konsepsies van 'gekleurdes' in die Afrikaanse roman tot 1948.* [Literature and Apartheid: Conceptions of 'Coloreds' in the Afrikaans Novel until 1948.] Kasselsvlei, South Africa: Kampen, 1983.

Hassal, A. J. "The Making of a Colonial Myth: The Mrs. Fraser Story in Patrick White's *A Fringe of Leaves* and André Brink's *An Instant in the Wind.*" *Ariel* 18.3 (1978): 3–27.

Jolly, Rosemary. *Colonization, Violence and Narration in White South African Writing: André Brink, Breyten Breytenbach and J. M. Coetzee.* Athens: Ohio UP; Johannesburg: Witwatersrand UP, 1996.

Malan, Charles, ed. *Ras en literatuur.* [Race and Literature.] Pinetown, South Africa: Burgess, 1987.

Massyn, Peter-John. "Droom en werklikheid: 'n Oomblik in die wind as simboliese daad." ["Dream and Reality: *An Instant in the Wind* as Symbolic Deed."] *Stilet* 4.2 (1992): 37–53.

Ponelis, Fritz. *The Development of Afrikaans.* Frankfurt: Peter Lang, 1993.

Pratt, Mary Louise. *Imperial Eyes: Travel Writing and Transculturation.* London and New York: Routledge, 1992.

Said, Edward W. *Orientalism.* London: Penguin Books, 1991. (Originally published 1978)

Smith, Julian F., Alwyn Van Gensen & Hein Willemse. *Swart Afrikaanse skrywers: Verslag van 'n simposium gehou by die Universiteit van Wes-Kaapland, Bellville op 26–27 April 1985.* [Black South African Writers: Report of a Symposium held at the University of the Western Cape, Bellville on 26-27 April 1985]. Bellville, South Africa: UWK Drukkery, 1985.

Van der Merwe, Kirby. *Klapperhaar slaap nooit stil nie.* [One Can Never Sleep Quietly on a Coir Mattress.] Kaapstad, South Africa: Kwela Boeke, 1999.

White, Hayden. *Tropics of Discourse.* Baltimore: The Johns Hopkins UP, 1978.

Wicomb, Zoë. "Shame and Identity: The Case of the Coloured in South Africa." *Writing South Africa: Literature, Apartheid, Democracy, 1970–1995.* Eds. Derek Attridge & Rosemary Jolly. Cambridge, UK: Cambridge UP, 1998. 91–107.

Willemse, Hein. "The black Afrikaans Writer: A Continuing Dichotomy." *TriQuarterly* 69 (1987): 237–247. Spring/Summer.

Willemse, Hein, Marion Hatting, Steward Van Wyk & Pieter Conradie. *Die reis van Paternoster. 'n Verslag van die tweede swart Afrikaanse skrywersimposium gehou op Paternoster vanaf 29 September tot 1 Oktober 1995.* [The Journey to Paternoster: Report on the Second Black Writers' Symposium held at Paternoster from 29 September to 1 October 1995.] Bellville, South Africa: UWK Drukkery, 1995.

Part III

Cultural Identity

Chapter 9

The Construction of "Colored" Space and Identity in Dido's 'n Stringetjie blou krale (A String of Blue Beads)

Minnie Lewis

Literature has been an important part of *constructing* the so-called nation of so-called Coloreds... (Raiskin 207, my emphasis)

I have chosen to focus on E.K.M. Dido's acclaimed contribution to Afrikaans literature, her novel *'n Stringetjie blou krale*[1] (A String of Blue Beads) (2000), to highlight the concept of space and identity and the construction thereof within the frame of reference of the "colored" person. The primary motivation for this choice is that at present Dido is one of the most promising new voices of "color"[2] in the Afrikaans literary arena. Hers is the voice of a woman whose life and work portray a keen understanding of the search, finding and constructing of her own space and identity.

In this gripping book by Dido the reader is brought face-to-face with the harsh reality of racism and the intricate work of constructing a livable space and convincing identities for the "constructed hybrid,"[3] Nomsa/Nancy. The novel moves between opposing cultures and into different spaces at different moments. This movement undoubtedly influences the identities of Nomsa/Nancy but also illustrates the state of flux of the concept of identity as the reader becomes aware of how Nomsa/Nancy weaves between, joins, denies and embraces various identities. Nomsa/Nancy moves between, away from and back into different spaces and identities in her search of who she is and where she belongs. This reminds me of Erasmus' second pillar[4] in her exposition on identity where she argues that "coloured identities are distinguished not merely by the fact of *borrowing per se*, but by *cultural borrowing* and *creation* under the very specific conditions of creolization" (Erasmus 16, my emphasis).

In this chapter I will take a close look at those spaces occupied by Nomsa/Nancy, the main character, at different moments in her life as well as the various identities embraced and produced by her in the "in-between" spaces she occupies.

The politics of location brings forward a whole host of identifications and associations around concepts of place, placement, displacement; location, dislocation; memberment, dis-memberment; citizenship, alienness; boundaries, barriers, transpositions; peripheries, cores and centers. It is about positionality in geographic, historical, social, economic, educational terms. It is also about relationality and the ways in which one is able to access, mediate or reposition oneself, or pass into other spaces given certain circumstances. (Boyce-Davies *Black Women*, 153)

Space and Identity of the "Colored" Person as Constructed in Dido's Book

The "colored" people of South Africa boast a colorful and diverse past. Theirs is a past that has been extensively researched and been an insatiable topic of discussion and debate. Their diversity is found in their "belonging" to various groupings, their "mixture" is more than one of race—and yet they have an authentic identity. This is illustrated by Venter where he indicates that:

> From where do the Coloured people of South Africa come—who were their progenitors? Opinions differ and the question itself may even lead to an emotional political discussion. ...For many years a formidable and polyglot array of "experts"—qualified or otherwise—have sought to clarify the issue. ...What is true is that few communities in the world can claim origins as disparate, widespread and complex as the South African Cape Colored. ...In fact, the average Coloured, whether we meet him in the country or the town, *is* South African. What else could he possibly be? (Venter 13)

Later in this chapter, these aspects of diversity and complexity as illustrated in Venter's quote above will be examined by way of an analysis of Dido's *'n Stringetjie blou krale* (A String of Blue Beads). It is hoped that a close look at the life of Nomsa/Nancy, the female "colored" and her construction of space and identity, will highlight the various issues surrounding the concepts of space and identity that will be dealt with in the first half of this chapter.

Nomsa/Nancy and the Spaces She Occupies

> Dis eenvoudige klein krale. Gare wat seker eens op 'n tyd wit was en nou swarterig en smetterig lyk, is as rygstring gebruik. Iets kriewel in my gedagtes. Iets wat ek wil-wil onthou...

> They are ordinary small beads. Thread that once must have been white but now seems black and grimy was used as threading. Something stirs in my thoughts. Something I want to remember... (Dido 21, all translations mine)

This book by Dido tells the story of a woman (Nomsa/Nancy) who grows up in a kraal in one of the laagers in Transkei.[5] At the age of about nine, she leaves the kraal with the blessing and insistence of her biological mother, to live with a "colored" family in the town in order to receive an education. Siena, her adoptive mother, has her classified as "colored" so that she is able to attend the "colored" school. She is taught Afrikaans and the mannerisms and cultural practices of the "colored" people. As time goes by she becomes more and more "colored," to the detriment of her black roots. Siena and Jan, along with Nomsa/Nancy, move to Cape Town.[6] Here she becomes a nursing sister, marries Bennie, becomes a mother herself and almost completely forgets her black past. Then she is haunted by nightmares that she cannot decipher, and eventually this leads to the breakdown of her family and forces her to revisit her past and embrace it as part of that which she has become. After a trip to the Transkei and a visit, as urged by Sisi Radebe (the sangoma[7]), to the graves of her mothers and her family in the kraal, she is able to find "wholeness."

At a key moment in her adult life, Nomsa/Nancy realizes that unless she physically "displaces" herself by going back to the kraal, the laager of her (biological) parents, she will never find her "place" or herself (her identity). Furthermore, she realizes that until she comes to terms with her losses and both physically and mentally finds that place of acceptance and forgiveness, she will never know peace, some sort of wholeness or a true identity.

Nomsa/Nancy and Geographical Space

Ek het agter die huis gaan sit en skielik geweet dié wêreld is baie ver van die laere af. (Dido 78)

I went and sat at the back of the house and suddenly knew that this world was very far from the laagers.

This referral to her two worlds[8] being "worlds" apart not only reflects the physical, geographical space or distance, but also, and more so, she is referring to the manner in which these opposing spaces differ from each other.

She finds herself caught between varying spaces and their influences on her identity, her very being and sanity. She realizes that if she is to continue her life in the space of colored Nancy, to survive and live a fulfilled life, and also move beyond these spaces to grow as an individual, she needs to retrace her steps, recover the beads she lost in her travels between various spaces occupied by her throughout her life. She discovers that she needs to go right back to her life as a child in the laager in the Transkei and pick up all the beads of her life she discarded as she grew into other spaces and identity, divorced from her roots.

The traumatic aspect of displacement in Nomsa/Nancy's life is most evident in the presence of the nightmares. It is in this realm, with the help of Sisi Radebe, that she realizes the impact the various moments and spaces of displacement have had on her life. She has given up so much of herself and known spaces, voluntarily and involuntarily, and has had to deal with the dislocation and alienation these moments of displacement have brought about in her life. This displacement is experienced as a mixture of physical, geographical space and the emotional and ideological aspects that afford meaning to those physical locations.

Memory of and Attachment to the Geographical Space. In Nomsa/Nancy's case her moves between spaces are by and large spatial, but the symbolic spaces she has had to loosen herself from, others she has had to embrace, and those she has had to integrate in her construction of livable space and identity, are significant here.

It is interesting to note that Dido's book starts with the memory of and the attachment to geographical space. There is the immediate introduction to a reconstructed space of the main character Nomsa/Nancy, by way of the nightmare:

> "Help! Asseblief, enigiemand! Help my!" My stem is al skor geroep en gepleit. Maar daar is niemand. Ek en die naamlose dreigende gevaar is alleen op die klipperige heuwel met die geil doringbome. ...Met 'n sug van verligting draai ek na hom en klou aan hom vas. Dit was toe net 'n droom! (Dido 7-8)

> "Help! Please anybody! Help me!" My voice is hoarse because of the shouting and begging. But there is nobody. The nameless, threatening danger and I are alone on the stony hill with the lush thorn-trees (acacias). ...With a sigh of relief I turn and cling to him. It was only a dream!

The reader learns that these nightmares have been occurring in her (Nancy's) life for some months. This dreamed space is vitally important to Nomsa/Nancy in her quest for re-discovering her past, an integral part of her identity, and a forgotten and often suppressed part of who she is. This suppression of the black aspect of her identity happened willfully as well as at the hands of her biological and adoptive mother, in which instance she had no say.

> Dis hoe ek Nancy Hendriks geword het. Sonder my toestemming. Sonder my ma's se wete of toestemming. Teen die einde van my eerste jaar in die dorp was ek 'n bruin mens. Ek was te behep met die nuwe "ek". Ek wou soos die bruin mense wees en alles vergeet van my lewe in die kraal en van die mense in die laer. (Dido 91, 95)

> That's how I became Nancy Hendriks. Without my consent. Without my mother's knowledge or consent. By the end of my first year in the town I was a "colored" person. I was much too concerned about the new "me". I wanted to be like the colored people and wanted to forget about my life in the kraal and about the people in the laager.

These are but two examples of the manner in which Nomsa/Nancy's suppression of her "blackness" takes place both with and without her consent.

Nomsa/Nancy's memory of her past spaces, as a child in the kraal with her laager people, had been distorted by her transition. Those geographical spaces she had occupied had been recreated by her memory, and by and large had been made to be something to be ashamed of, something to be denied. But this is exactly the problem for Nomsa/Nancy, for although memory recreates the geographical spaces occupied by her, it does not erase them from her lived experience. The willfully suppressed spaces and parts of her identity surface in her nightmares as a space where these aspects are addressed and integration sought. Not until she revisits this space of memory and acknowledges the attachment to geographical space with the help of the sangoma, Sisi Radebe, and undertakes a physical journey back to the kraal of her biological family, will she be able to meaningfully move in and between the various other spaces she occupies.

When she returns from her trip to the Transkei, a trip during which she rediscovers past spaces, past identities, she experiences some kind of wholeness. This wholeness comes from acknowledging her past, embracing it and incorporating it into which she has become. The nightmares cease and she dreams a peaceful, non-threatening dream as an indication that her journey to and through old, familiar but forgotten and forsaken identities and spaces has been successful.

Symbolic Space—Center versus Periphery. Nomsa/Nancy moves from the far-off fringes of the periphery to that which she feels is center, only to find that it is a different margin. She experiences the margin as being somewhat closer to the center. The move is from being Nomsa on the periphery, as a black child in the laager, to Nancy Hendriks, the "colored" child of Jan and Siena Hendriks and later the wife of Bennie Karelse. This move by Nomsa/Nancy indicates the gradual differences within the periphery.

Much like the opposing nature of the center and periphery is the life of Nomsa/Nancy as black and "colored" person. The space of her life in the kraal and that of the town is very far removed from each other, and to avoid the constant dialogue between these two opposing spaces she finds herself in, she suppresses the space of the kraal and embraces the life of "colored" Nancy, and tries to push "black" Nomsa to the periphery. But it is quite evident by the persistent nightmares she experiences as a grown woman that the dialogue between the center and periphery is always present by the very nature of their existence and opposing natures. Nomsa/Nancy finds herself not truly belonging to either the center or the periphery, but rather the space opened by the dialogue between the two.

Nomsa/Nancy and Liminal Space. The main character in the book, Nomsa/Nancy, is placed within this "in-between"[9] space after her transition and transformation as a child from black Nomsa to colored Nancy. She is no longer black, but neither is she truly "colored." Nomsa/Nancy has moved from being black Nomsa to colored Nancy, and in order to be Nancy she has to suppress Nomsa's identity. Initially this suppression is almost impossible, for all evident identity markers indicate her blackness. She is unable to speak and even understand the "strange" language, Afrikaans, that the people in the town speak. When Joyce McKerry, the daughter of Siena's neighbor, tries to make her acquaintance, her lack of understanding Afrikaans or being able to speak it becomes evident:

> "Tjank as jy wil tjank!" het sy op my geskree. Hierdie keer het sy haar woorde met handgebare opgevolg, en ek kon raai dis omtrent wat sy gesê het. Ek het net my kop geskud en niks gesê nie. Dit was duidelik dat sy nie my taal kon praat nie en ek het nie geweet hoe om vir haar met my hande te verduidelik... (Dido 57)

> "Cry if you want to cry!" she shouted at me. This time hand signals accompanied her words and I guessed that was about what she said. I shook my head and said nothing. It was obvious that she could not speak my language and I did not know how to show her with my hands...

When her mothers[10] leave her with Siena, this space, between the center and the periphery, or rather between periphery and center of a different margin, that she occupies is illuminated. She is left with people whose language she is unable to understand or speak, whose cultural tradition is in stark contrast to that which she is used to.[11]

Nomsa/Nancy occupies this space that is viewed by Erasmus as a rather fragile space to occupy. The fragility of this space lies in the fact that it does not belong to either of the opposing spaces of center or periphery. Because of her transition from black Nomsa to colored Nancy, she no longer fits into the space of her "blackness," but by the same token, she does not really fit into that of "coloredness" either. When Nomsa/Nancy visits the kraal with her colored mother, Siena, her move away from the margin she occupied as Nomsa to the liminal space occupied by Nancy, is clear:

> Ek was bly om weer in die laer en in ons kraal te wees, maar nie oor dieselfde rede as antie Siena nie. Ek wou net by almal met my voorkoms spog. En ek het. Nog meer toe my susters nie hul oë van my linte kon wegdraai nie...ek het nie in die hutte gegaan nie...Die binnekant van die hut was vir my te donker en kaal. (Dido 85)

> I was glad to be in the laager and in our kraal again, but not for the same reason as auntie Siena. I wanted to boast with my appearance. And I did. Even more so when my sisters could not take their eyes off my ribbons...I did not go into the huts...The inside of the hut was much too dark and cold for me.

Nomsa/Nancy has moved from one (racially) defined group to another.

Nomsa/Nancy is thrust into this "in-between" space as a child, but at the tender age of nine she does not comprehend the intricacies of occupying a space so removed from that which she is used to or being introduced to in the form of the colored identity. The moment she is speechless, when she arrives in town to live with Siena and Jan, can be viewed as a "liminal moment," but because of her tender age, she immediately embraces the colored identity to replace the black identity she has had to shed. It is only after her nightmares as a grown woman that she really ventures into the liminal space. This time she is unable to flee this daunting space, because her wholeness hinges on her finding her place, her identity, within this liminal space. There is no other space to flee to, because she no longer belongs to either the center of the colored margin she occupied as Nancy, or the margin occupied by black Nomsa. It is in this undefined and creative space that she experiences freedom and a true sense of self. In this space Nomsa/Nancy's identity is not defined by being black Nomsa or colored Nancy, or Siena and Jan's daughter, or Bennie's ex-wife, or Jean and Vicky's mother; here she is who she has chosen to be—Nancy Nomsa Karelse.

Construction of Identity and Evident Identity Markers in Dido's Book

As indicated previously, identity markers have much to with tangible aspects of everyday life. These markers indicate certain aspects concerning our identity that are visible to others and ourselves that do not necessarily reflect the "real" person, but can, as is the case with Nomsa/Nancy, be fabricated and constructed. These identity markers and other aspects concerning the construction and problematic nature of identity will be looked at in subsequent paragraphs.

The Dilemma of Colored Identity: Nancy—the Constructed Hybrid.

When Nomsa's biological mother decides that she is to be educated outside the laager, she sets in motion the *de*construction of Nomsa's black identity and eventual transformation to Nancy, the "colored." Initially Nomsa is not keen to live in the town, separated from her mothers and siblings and the space(s) in which she has grown up, but as the transition becomes more and more real to her and she starts embracing this new self, colored Nancy, she casts aside "black, Xhosa" Nomsa. The dilemma surrounding her new colored identity is that she is still classed among those within the boundaries of the margin, but now no longer black, and yet not "white enough" either. This dilemma is even more real for Nancy as she does not really belong to either this marginal space of the colored or that of the black Nomsa.

One of the most illustrative examples of Nancy's dilemma as a "constructed" hybrid is when Bennie, her husband, learns that she is black by birth, Nomsa Hlabathi from a kraal in a laager in the Transkei. Her journey toward wholeness requires that she tell her husband about her black past, because in doing so she will no longer be denying the "black" part of her identity but will be including it into whom she has become, colored Nancy. At first Bennie is filled with disbelief and markedly shocked at her revelation. He points to the identity markers[12] that, according to him, set her apart from blacks, but this does not alter the truth about her, that a part of her is and will always be black Nomsa. Bennie becomes extremely rude and violent with Nomsa/Nancy as the reality of her words, that she is black by birth, sinks in:

> "Loop net uit my lewe uit, Nancy. Ek wil jou nooit weer sien nie. Gaan bly tussen jou mense in die squatter camp in Crossroads. Jy hoort daar. Verdwyn net uit my lewe en uit my kinders se lewe uit. Dink jy miskien hulle sal 'n swart ma wil hê?"...Wat ek

gedink het 'n troefkaart is, besorg my 'n klap wat my sterretjies voor my oë laat sien. My kop ruk agteroor en kap hard teen die deur. (Dido 152, 156)

"Walk out of my life Nancy. I never want to see you again. Go and live amongst your people in the squatter camp in Crossroads. You belong there. Just disappear out of my life and out of the lives of my children. Do you think they would want a black mother?"…What I thought to be my ace, turned out to ensure a slap that made me see stars. My head jerks backwards and bangs against the door.

"I…I'm still the same person Bennie" ("Ek…ek is nog dieselfde mens, Bennie") (Dido 148) and "I was born a black person and only later became 'colored,' but it does not really matter, I'm still the same person" ("Ek is as swart mens gebore en het eers later 'n Kleurling geword. Maar dit maak mos nie saak nie, ek is nog dieselfde mens") (Dido 154).

Nomsa/Nancy's resolve that she is still the same person is ironic. She may still outwardly be the "constructed" colored, but her wholeness hinges on the fact that she should accept who she was and incorporate it into which she has become, to experience peace of mind and some kind of wholeness.

Marginality: Within the Margin of Colored Identity.

Coloured cultural production has always been precarious and marginal, making it difficult to claim and mark space powerfully. (Erasmus, *Coloured by History* 22)

Nomsa/Nancy finds herself not truly belonging to either her "colored" or her "black" family. Neither is she able to claim a distinct identity, for hers is constructed and marked by disparity. She is both Nomsa Hlabathi and Nancy Karelse, separated by race and culture, but also uniquely one. This is a most difficult position she finds herself in, for as Erasmus indicates concerning the colored identity, it means denying one part of your existence in order to embrace another. Nomsa/Nancy denies her "blackness" to embrace her "coloredness," and this eventually leads to a fragmented wholeness of not belonging to either the culture or identity she has separated herself from, or that which she has embraced as Nancy. In both she finds herself at a margin, never quite belonging to the center but always part of the periphery. Within her colored identity Nomsa/Nancy experiences marginalization and is herself guilty of perpetuating "internal" marginalization. This internal marginalization by Nomsa/Nancy is evident at the birth of her son Jean and her initial rejection of him because he appeared "less than Colored."[13] This marginalization is again noted in Bennie, her husband, whose racism is aimed at some of those who share a marginal position with him, and this is most noticeable in his treatment of Nomsa/Nancy when he learns of her black roots.

Nomsa/Nancy and "Colored" Female Identity.
Nomsa/Nancy is a striking example of the complex nature of the "colored" female identity. As discussed previously, the colored identity is one that can be seen as "identity in jeopardy,"

and more so is the case of Nomsa/Nancy's identity as a colored female. In Nomsa/Nancy's case the aspect of her female identity is complicated by the fact that she is a woman from two cultures, both which subject their women to "double marginalization," and here she has to bear the brunt of both. As a grown woman, battling the debilitating effects of nightmares, she cannot loosen herself from the black female identity of the kraal, no more than she can divorce herself from the colored female identity, imposed on and embraced by her, for the sake of education. Nancy, although a marginalized woman, also marginalizes other women on the grounds of their black identity, even her kraal mothers, by not keeping in contact with them. In distancing herself from them, both physically and emotionally, she is denying her black female identity and affirming to herself, and everybody else, that she is a colored female. As a colored woman, doubly marginalized, she also personifies a double emancipation in that she breaks through the boundaries of race and gender marginalization and survives to tell her story.

When Nancy/Nomsa accepts that Bennie no longer wants her as part of his life, when she faces the fact that she needs to revisit her past and past spaces and when she moves into the unknown of the liminal space, her emancipation becomes evident. Her acceptance of the fact that Bennie wants to move on with his life without her and that she needs to (re)build a life for herself without him is the first sign of her newfound independence. By telling Bennie the truth about her past, she has not only freed herself to embrace her suppressed past but has also liberated herself from a man who, to a great extent, measures his love for her on outward appearances and is unable to get past his racial prejudices to embrace her for who she really is. Her thoughts at the end of the book highlight the importance and value of her newfound independence and self-worth:

> Met elke tree wat ek verder van Bennie af gaan, weet ek dat ek van my onlangse verlede af wegstap. My meer as twintig jaar se verlede. Hoe verder ek stap, hoe ligter raak my tred by die besef dat Bennie geen meer houvas op my het nie. Ons deel die kinders. Dis al...Net—nooit weer sal ek toelaat dat hy my minderwaardig laat voel of my emosioneel ontwrig nie. (Dido 240)

> With every step further away from Bennie I realize that I am walking away from my recent past. My more than twenty years' past. The further I walk the lighter my step becomes by the knowledge that Bennie no longer has a hold on me. We only share the children. That's all...Only—never again will I allow him to make me feel inferior or upset me emotionally.

She has become the woman she wants to and needs to be and she does not need to be dependent on anybody, least of all Bennie, to be that woman.

Nomsa/Nancy and the Identity Markers She Encounters: Names and Name-giving.

...the dynamic of 'naming' becomes a primary colonising process because it appropriates, defines, captures the place in language. (Ashcroft et al., *Reader* 392)

A name, whatever it may be, is probably one of the most fundamental keys in establishing and "understanding" one's identity. Without doubt this concept of naming, in the life of the main character in *'n Stringetjie blou krale*, is one that features most prominently throughout. As a young child in the laager, Nomsa has her mother's maiden name as surname, because her father has not yet paid the lobola in full. She is denied his surname on grounds of traditional rules, and in a sense a part of her identity is not integrated because of this. As a young child, "adopted"[14] by Siena and Jan, her names are changed in order to fit in and identify more closely with the colored community. Initially she is known as Nomsa Hlabati, and only once her father has paid the outstanding amount for lobola would she be able to "get her Mayekiso-surname," but this name eludes her, because her biological father dies a premature death due to an accident at the mines in the north. With her "adoption," and with the aid of a few lies by Siena, her adoptive mother, she becomes Nancy Hendriks:

> Dis hoe ek Nancy Hendricks geword het. Sonder my toestemming. Sonder my ma's se wete of toestemming. Teen die einde van my eerste jaar in die dorp was ek 'n bruin mens...Ek was Nancy Hendricks en my wettige ouers was Jan en Siena Hendricks. (Dido 90)

> That's how I became Nancy Hendriks. Without my consent. Without my mother's knowing about it or consenting to it. By the end of my first year in town I was a Colored person...I was Nancy Hendriks and my lawful parents were Jan and Siena Hendriks.

Not only did her name change on that particular day, but also the "names" she used to call her adoptive parents. They went from being "sisi" (sister) and "bhuti" (brother) to being "antie" (auntie) and "oom" (uncle), and finally on the said day of her adoption, they became "ma" (mom) and "pa" (dad). This change of name also signals a significant moment in Nomsa/Nancy's life, because in the wink of an eye, she goes from being a Xhosa to a colored with the following words uttered by Siena: "You are now our child, which makes you a Colored. You are a Colored person. But in front of your mothers you must call me sisi Siena" ("Jy is nou ons kind, wat jou Kleurling maak. Jy's 'n bruin mens. Maar voor jou ma-goed moet jy vir my sisi Siena sê") (Dido 91).

Another interesting issue here is the fact that the threatening presence in Nomsa/Nancy's nightmares is nameless. "The nameless threatening danger and myself are alone on the stony hill.... The nameless thing is right there..." ("Ek en die naamlose dreigende gevaar is alleen op die klipperige heuwel.... Die naamlose ding is by my...") (Dido 7–8). It is only when she, with the help of Mama Radebe, identifies and acknowledges the significance and importance of the "nameless threat" and the "voice" speaking Xhosa that Nomsa/Nancy begins on her journey to wellness and wholeness.

Clothing. Clothing is another identity marker of importance in this novel. As a child in the kraal Nomsa is content with the code of dressing stipulated for women. Her mothers wore skirts down to their ankles, while young girls wore much shorter skirts. Scarves to cover their bald heads were also worn, and to Nomsa/Nancy underwear was unheard of in the kraal. Their clothing distinguished them from other black cultures. But later the clothing of her kraal's people becomes a thing of shame to her when her mothers visit her in the town, wearing nothing to cover their breasts. As the child of Siena and Jan, Nancy is always "well dressed" by Siena and learns to take great pride in her appearance. She loves beautiful clothes and dressing up, and this remains part of who she is as she grows up. It is also during stressful times in her life that the ravages thereof are evident because of her lack of dressing up. One such occasion is when she becomes depressed after the birth of her son, Jean. She walks around the house all day in a gown, not combing her hair or dressing herself or the children. Without her characteristic clothing, Nomsa/Nancy is in a sense without identity. Her domestic help cooks and takes care of the children. Lena, her domestic, constantly nags her during this time to take a bath and dress up, which she eventually does.

The aspect of clothing once again comes to the fore in the book when Bennie, at that stage Nancy's divorced husband, invites her to a function at his work and insists that she wear something in "African style" (Dido 222). The invitation is purely from a selfish motive, namely, to help him get a promotion. But it gives Nomsa/Nancy the opportunity to show Bennie that she has managed to integrate her identities and is comfortable with whom she is; she need not impress people, as he still does, with appearances.

> Ek ervaar 'n blydskap dat al die mense wat my Xhosa hoor praat en my klere bewonder, my aanvaar soos ek is. (Dido 224)

> I experience a joy that all those people who hear me speaking Xhosa and admire my attire, accept me as I am.

Language. Languages play a major role in the life of Nomsa/Nancy. As a child in the kraal she speaks Xhosa, her mother tongue, fluently and has no knowledge or use of any other language. It is only when she moves to town and becomes a colored person that the need arises to be able to understand and also speak Afrikaans. This identity marker, alongside others, sets her apart from her Xhosa family and friends and opens the door for an education and a whole new identity to her. Not only is knowledge of Afrikaans a prerequisite for her new colored identity, but the way in which it is spoken is also important.[15]

The spaces occupied also influence the use of the language. Nomsa/Nancy experiences it as a child before the magistrate the day she officially becomes Nancy. Another instance when she experiences the influence of space on language is when she meets Joyce again in Cape Town and comments that: "Joyce's manner of speaking was almost as big a shock to me as my parents' home. What happened to the Afrikaans that she taught me as a child? I wondered" ("Joyce se manier van praat het my amper net so 'n groot skok as my ouers se blyplek gegee. Waarheen het die Afrikaans gevlieg wat sy my as kind geleer het? Het ek gewonder") (Dido 109).

The fact that the voice in the nightmare speaks Xhosa enhances the importance of language as an identity marker in Dido's novel. "Buyela ekhaya. Come back home…" ("Buyela ekhaya. Kom terug huis toe…") (Dido 8). It enhances the notion that no aspect of one's identity can truly be erased. It can be forgotten and denied, as Nomsa/Nancy's life illustrates, but total erasure is not as easy.

Skin Color. Nomsa/Nancy is fair-skinned even though she is black/Xhosa by birth. The fact of her being fair-skinned dispels the myth that people can successfully be classed by the color of their skin. In the book the importance of skin color in society is illustrated by the fact that Nomsa/Nancy has no trouble fitting in with her colored family, as she is even more fair-skinned than her adoptive mother. When Siena, her adoptive mother, takes her to the magistrate's office to legally adopt her, she does not allow Nomsa/Nancy to say a word but wants the magistrate to make his decision on Nomsa/Nancy's skin color. Because Nomsa/Nancy has a fair skin, it makes the transition from black Nomsa to colored Nancy easier than it would have been if she had a very dark complexion.

It is interesting that Nomsa/Nancy mentions that her biological mother was fair-skinned but very much a "pure"[16] Xhosa. She mentions that, because her biological mother was so fair-skinned, she often suffered the ridicule of other black people who suggested that she had "white blood."

When Nomsa/Nancy tells her husband that she is Xhosa/black by birth he retorts that she is not black but very fair-skinned. He cannot believe that Nomsa/Nancy who looks so obviously colored and speaks Afrikaans so fluently is black. "Hoe kan jy 'n darkie wees as jy gladde hare en 'n ligte vel het? En wat van jou spraak?…Al die swart mense is nie swart van kleur nie…" (Dido 149–150). ("How can you be a 'darkie' if you have sleek hair and a fair skin? And what about your accent?…Not all black people have a dark complexion…"). Bennie does not realize that her "blackness" is not a mere matter of skin color.

He is one of many characters in the book who pay much attention to the color of people's skin to determine their racial identity. Nomsa/Nancy's colleagues at the Training College, and especially her colored colleagues, accept her as colored because she appears to be colored, but when it becomes known that she can speak Xhosa fluently she is nicknamed "kafferpoppie/KP."[17]

Hair and Hair Texture.

Hairstyling and texturising were (and still are) key beautification practises in the making of womanhood among young coloured women. (Erasmus, *Coloured by History* 13)

Hair texture is significant throughout the novel[18]. As a young child in the laager, Nomsa/Nancy is subjected to the cultural practice of having her hair shaved as a female member of her family. When she arrives in the town, she is both surprised and annoyed at the practice of the colored women who wear their hair long and styled, unlike that which she is used to in the laager. Nomsa/Nancy's surprise and annoyance is evident in the following statement:

Elke keer as haar hare in haar oë geval het, het sy haar nek wild eenkant toe geruk en die hare woes in die ander rigting geswaai. As sy goeie gewoontes soos my mense s'n geken het, het sy haar hare nes myne bles gehou... (Dido 56).

Every time her hair fell into her eyes, she would shake her head to the side and her hair would wildly move in the opposite direction. If she had good habits like my people, she would shave her head and keep it bald like mine...

The importance of hair, its texture, length and the care taken with it, becomes most evident in Nomsa/Nancy's life once she becomes a colored. Once she is used to and excited about her growing hair and its grooming, it becomes an important issue in her colored life. Her hair becomes one of the physical markers that set her apart from Nomsa, apart from her laager life and biological mothers. As she grows up, her hair remains one of the vivid identity markers in her life.

Another interesting aspect concerning hair as an identity marker is her mother Siena's reaction when she meets Bennie. She is most disgusted by his "mop of hair."[19] Siena, like many colored women, tends to place a lot of emphasis on hair and its texture. So when she meets Bennie and sees his Afro, all she sees is that he does not have sleek hair.

The importance of hair and hair texture for Siena is also evident from the care she takes in growing and "sleeking" Nomsa/Nancy's hair. Then there is Nomsa/Nancy's son Jean, whose hair is kept very short to hide the kink[20] in his hair. She also pulls out her hair during her nightmares, and this act is significant, given that her life started out as part of a culture in which women had no hair on their heads. It is also her hair that appears to lack life and luster when she is tormented by the nightmares, put on medication and cast out of the lives of her husband and children.

The importance of hair as an identity marker in Nomsa/Nancy's life once again comes to the fore after she has undertaken a trip back to the laager where she grew up and revisits her mothers' graves. Upon her arrival at her (adoptive) parents' home, the first thing she hears from her mother is that her hair needs attention. "En kyk hoe lyk jou kop! Net môre loop jy hêrdresser toe" (Dido 201). ("And look at your hair! Tomorrow you are going to the hairdresser.")

There are many more instances in the book where hair and hair texture are clear identity markers, but unfortunately they cannot all be discussed in this chapter.

Conclusion

The search for and (re)construction of identity(ies) are important because they become the process(es) by which one begins to understand who you are.

In her quest for wholeness Nomsa/Nancy has to recover a discarded past, accept a fragmented present and embrace a future with a some kind of new-found wholeness yet knowing that the spaces and identities she presently cherishes will eventually also change. In Nomsa/Nancy's search for and construction of space and identity we find that her life has come full circle.

The symbolism of the full circle in Nomsa/Nancy's life is introduced by the title of the book, and this motif runs right through the book. A string of beads played a very important role in Nomsa/Nancy's life in the kraal, for this was the method her own biological mother used to keep track of her children's ages. Similar beads around the sangoma's neck jolt the past to the foreground in Nomsa/Nancy's memory and bring her world tumbling down around her, but at the same time the string of beads offers her some peace when sisi (sister) Radebe (the sangoma) gives her a string to wear. The string of beads around sisi Radebe's neck mesmerizes her and sets in motion her journey into the past and her return as an enriched person. A string of beads has no clear beginning or end, and it symbolizes a sense of completeness; so too, only when Nomsa/Nancy's life has gone full circle, to the Transkei and back, does she experience a sense of completeness. The point of complete wholeness, or absolute completion, is never reached, but a sense thereof is experienced in the quest to attain that "completeness" and "wholeness." As the circle symbolizes a sense of completeness and wholeness, it also indicates a recurrent movement, a never-ending state of flux, always in motion, never static.

Another aspect from Nomsa/Nancy's black past that underpins the circle motif is the circular formation of the huts in the kraal and the kraals forming the laager into which Nomsa/Nancy was born. This circular formation offers protection from the outside world and encloses the inhabitant, creating a sense of oneness, a sense of belonging. It is only after having come full circle that Nomsa/Nancy is able to face the future, forgiven, having accepted her past and being proud of who she has become.

The final paragraph of *'n Stringetjie blou krale* beautifully threads together the various intriguing aspects that have formed part of the full circle Nomsa/Nancy's life has traveled to establish a sense of self and place and also highlights the symbol of the circle, signaling some sort of wholeness and completion:

> My hande gaan onwillekeurig na die string blou krale om my nek wat ek nou pal dra, en ek klem dit vas. Dankie, Mama. Dankie, Mam'omkhulu, vir die geleentheid wat julle my in die lewe gegee het. Ek, Nancy Nomsa Karelse, gaan saam met my kinders en Ma en Pa sonder geheime die toekoms in. Ek weet waar ek vandaan kom—en dit maak my sterk. (Dido 240)

> My hands go involuntarily to the string of blue beads that I always wear around my neck now, and I clasp it tight. Thank you Mama. Thank you Mam'omkulu (big mother), for the opportunity you gave to me in life. I, Nancy Nomsa Karelse, am moving into the future with my children and mother and father without secrets. I know where I come from—and that makes me strong. (My translation)

Notes

1. All translations into English are my own.
2. I refer here specifically to "writers of color" from the decade 1990–2000.
3. I speak about a "constructed hybrid" due to the fact that Nancy is born (black) Nomsa, but transformed by various steps to become the "colored" Nancy. She is therefore hybrid by construction.
4. Erasmus identifies four pillars to her argument concerning colored identities; here I'm thinking of the second one as found in *Coloured by History*.
5. Kraal: a number of huts built in circular form that houses a specific clan/family. The kraal is usually maintained by the women and headed by a male. A number of these kraals would be located in fairly close proximity to each other and would form part of a specific laager.

    Laager: a laager is usually circular in form, comprising a number of kraals. Different clans would have their own kraals in a different laager.

    Transkei: this was one of the so-called independent TBVC states under the governance of South Africa until 1976 when it became independent. The TBVC states included Transkei, Bohuputatswana, Venda and Ciskei. Today the Transkei is once again incorporated into South Africa and forms part of the Eastern Cape Province.
6. This move of the Nomsa/Nancy and her adoptive family is necessitated by the fact that financial difficulties in the Transkei, after becoming independent in 1976 forced many, white and black alike, to move to the big towns. The lack of work later forced Nancy's parents to also move to the Cape Flats. In the book Dido deals with this aspect very aptly (101–112).
7. A sangoma is one who specializes in traditional medicine and healing.
8. With reference here to the world of the kraal and laager she has previously lived in and the town where she now lives with her adoptive parents.
9. This "in-between" state of the liminal space is viewed here as that space beyond the center and periphery. It is not a space caught between the opposing spaces of center and periphery but one that is beyond the margins of both these aspects.

10. Nomsa had two (black) mothers—her biological mother (Mama Omncinci, who was her father's second wife), and the other Mam'omkhulu, who was her father's first wife. In their cultural tradition both these women are accepted as mothers.

11. Examples include: In the kraal children do not answer/talk back to their elders; in the town she witnesses Joyce talking back to her mother. The townsfolk buy wood rather than going out in search of it. The females also wear their hair long and are not bald like the women of her kraal.

12. He refers to her hair and her skin color as well as her good command of Afrikaans and no obvious black accent.

13. Jean is dark-skinned and his hair is not sleek.

14. I use the word "adopted" here in the sense that they took Nomsa as their own after her mother(s) left her in Jan and Siena's care to secure an education for her, but it was without their consent, or Nomsa's for that matter, that they changed her name.

15. Here it must be understood that Afrikaans, once seen as an important marker of Afrikaner-ism, is also a language spoken by black and colored South Africans. During the apartheid re-gime, Afrikaans was the medium of instruction in many schools for blacks and coloreds. Af-rikaans is the native language of the majority of the Cape colored people. The Afrikaans spoken by coloreds on the Cape Flats can be described as dialect of Afrikaans and is often referred to as "Cape Afrikaans." There are distinct differences, especially in the pronuncia-tion of words, between this Afrikaans and that which was termed as "Standard Afrikaans." This standard form of Afrikaans is spoken by the majority of white Afrikaans-speaking South Africans and is the form used in business, schooling, churches, politics, and so on. The Afrikaans that Nomsa/Nancy was taught in the Transkei is not the "Cape Afrikaans" she hears Joyce speaks when she arrives in Cape Town, but rather something closer to "standard" Afrikaans.

16. "Purity" with regards to race is debatable but is used for the sake of argument here.

17. "Kafferpoppie/KP" means "black doll" (Dido 136)

18. In the colored community much emphasis is placed on hair and hair texture. People are viewed according to their having sleek, curly or kinky hair ("kroes hare").

19. At the time of meeting Nancy's mother, Bennie was sporting an Afro, the fashionable hair-style at that time.

20. Kinky hair ("kroes hare") refers to hair texture that is usually thick, curly and frizzy.

Works Cited

Ashcroft, Bill *Post-Colonial Transformation*. London: Routledge, 2001.

———, Gareth Griffin, and Helen Tiffin, eds. *The Post-Colonial Studies Reader*. London: Routledge, 1995.

———, Gareth Griffiths, and Helen Tiffin. *The Empire Writes Back: Theory and Practice in Post-colonial Literatures*. 1989. London: Routledge, 1999.

Attridge, David. et al. *Writing South Africa: Literature, Apartheid and Democracy* 1970–1995. Cam-bridge, UK: Cambridge UP, 1998.

Boyce-Davies, C. "Finding Some Space." *Black South African Women Writers. A Current Bibliography of African Affairs* 19.1 (1986–1987): 31–45.

———. *Black Women, Writing and Identity: Migration of the Subject*. London: Routledge, 1994.

De Beauvoir, Simone. "Woman and the Other." *Literature in the Modern World*. Ed. D. Walder Oxford, UK: Oxford UP, 1990. 305–310.

Dido, E. K. M. *'n Stringetjie blou krale*. [A String of Blue Beads.] Cape Town: Kwela Books, 2000.

Du Plooy, Heilna. "An Overview of Afrikaans Narrative Texts Published between 1990–2000." *Stilet* 23 (2001): 14–31. 2 June.

Erasmus, Zimitri. "Hair politics." *Senses of Culture: South African Culture Studies.* Eds. Sarah Nuttall and Cheryll-Ann Michael. Cape Town: Oxford UP, 380–392.

——. *Coloured by History, Shaped by Place: New Perspectives on Coloured Identities in Cape Town.* Cape Town: Kwela Books, SA History Online, 2001.

Hall, S. "Cultural Identity and Diaspora." *Contemporary Postcolonial Theory. A Reader.* New York: Arnold, 1996. 110–121.

Holquist, M. *Dialogism: Bakhtin and his World.* London: Routledge, 1990.

Lotman, Jurij. *Universe of the Mind. A Semiotic Theory of Culture.* Bloomington: Indiana UP, 1990.

Minha-ha, Trinh T. "No Master Territories." *The Post-Colonial Studies Reader.* Eds. Bill Ashcroft, Gareth Griffiths, and Helen Tiffin. London and New York: Routledge, 1995. 215–218.

——. "Writing Postcoloniality and Feminism." *The Post-Colonial Studies Reader.* 264–268.

——. "Woman, Native Other." *Writing Postcoloniality and Feminism.* Bloomington: Indiana UP, 1989.

Mongia, P. *Contemporary Postcolonial Theory.* A Reader. New York: Arnold, 1996.

Nuttall, Sarah, and Cheryll-Ann Micheal, eds. *Senses of Culture: South African Culture Studies.* Cape Town: Oxford UP, 2000.

Phillips, R. *Mapping Men and Empire.* London: Routledge, 1997.

Raiskin, J. *Snow on the Cane Fields.* Minneapolis: U of Minnesota P, 1996.

Venter, A. J. *Coloured. A Profile of Two Million South Africans.* Cape Town: Human & Rousseau, 1974.

Viljoen, Hein. "Marginalia on Marginality." *AlterNation* 5.2 (1998): 10–22.

Walder, D., ed. *Literature in the Modern World.* Oxford: Oxford UP, 1990.

Wicomb, Zoë. "Shame and Identity: The Case of the Coloured in SA." *Writing South Africa. Literature, Apartheid and Democracy 1970–1995.* Cambridge, UK: Cambridge UP, 1998. 91–107.

Willemse, Hein. *Dialogie in die Afrikaanse Letterkunde met die Toepassing op Geselekteerde Swart Afrikaanse Skrywers.* [Dialogism in Afrikaans Literature with an Application to Selected Black Afrikaans Writers.] Ph.D. thesis. Bellville, South Africa: University of the Western Cape, 1995.

Chapter 10

The Underestimated Strength of Cultural Identity: The Search for Cultural Specificity between Localizing and Globalizing Tendencies

Rien T. Segers

A Nursery Rhyme for Scholars and Students

At the annual meetings of the World Bank and the International Monetary Fund in Washington in September 1999, Wole Soyinka, the Nigerian writer and Nobel laureate, said:

> Culture is a matrix of infinite possibilities and choices...from which we can extract arguments and strategies for the degradation or ennoblement of our species, for its enslavement or liberation, for the suppression of its productive potential or its enchantment, for the stagnation of social existence or its renewal.

Soyinka's words will function as a background against which I would like to introduce the concept of cultural identity. I think there are at least two reasons for devoting a chapter to questions concerning cultural identity.

The first reason can be found in the immense popularity of the concept of cultural identity itself. The scholarly, journalistic and popular press is filled with references to the field of cultural identity and its related themes, national and corporate identity. One often feels as if one is encountering a huge container concept that has lost its specific meaning due to overuse. The task of scholarship is to look at the specificity of semantics, especially if it concerns such an important social concept. That's exactly what I am trying to achieve here: looking for the lost semantics of the concept of cultural identity and framing it within its natural context.

The second reason has to do with demonstrating the validity of the concept of cultural identity. I strongly believe that insight into cultural identity will result in a deeper insight into a number of contemporary integration processes, such as those of the European Union, the "new" South Africa and the "new" Germany. However different these processes might be, the fundamental problem is the differentiation between insiders and outsiders, which is an essential element of my conception of cultural identity. Let us focus briefly on a simple but intriguing nursery rhyme:

The Germans live in Germany; the Romans live in Rome,
The Turkeys live in Turkey; but the English live at home.

We could ask a number of questions here, such as: Which nation invented this nursery rhyme? When was it invented? To what extent is it justified?

It is the last question that will be the specific focus of this chapter. In other words, the focus will be on the question as to the situation that cultures and nations find themselves in today. Should this situation be characterized by the concept localization or by the concept of globalization? Is it correct to define localization (as some do) as a predominantly nineteenth-century concept and globalization as a predominantly late twentieth-century concept?

These are simple questions but they have complicated answers. I shall explain and deconstruct the current great millennium myth, which implies a belief that the structure of contemporary society or even of "the world" can only be characterized by the concept of globalization: globalization as a mythical construction of the post-industrial society.

There is a caveat here: this chapter denotes a specific set of *Western* assumptions concerning concepts such as culture, nation and cultural identity. I shall mainly concentrate on cultural identity here, since this concept is not only in vogue in many scholarly circles around the globe, but also because this concept determines to a great extent other concepts that are of crucial importance to the discourse of our time, namely, globalization, localization, multiculturalism, ethnicity, nation-state, ideology, and so on. Insight into cultural identity implies at the same time a partial insight into all those tricky container concepts.

My guiding principle is the systemic theory of culture (Even-Zohar, Luhmann, Maturana, Varela; for a bibliography see, for example, Tötösy de Zepetnek; for a recent critical analysis see Sevänen). This theory considers culture as a system consisting of a number of subsystems, such as economic, educational, religious, technological and artistic subsystems. Each subsystem is based on all activities as performed by participants, people active within that subsystem. This means that a systemic approach is interested in all the "actions," in all the "activities" as performed by any participant within a particular subsystem.

Culture: An Attempt at Definition

Before its anthropological incarnation, culture predominantly meant refinement. The nineteenth-century humanist Matthew Arnold, for instance, considered culture as a study of perfection, an inward condition of the mind and spirit. He regarded cultured people as drawing ever nearer to "the beautiful" and "the graceful." Culture, in his view was the best that has been thought and said. This conception of culture still remains very much in vogue today among scholars as well as among the general public.

Cultural anthropologists have reworked this accepted concept of culture to apply it not only to a learned and sophisticated few, but also to *all* human beings. As Clifford Geertz notes: "Culture…is not just an ornament of human existence, but…an essential condition for it…There is no such a thing as a human nature independent of culture" (12). This implies that as human beings we are *all* cultured. Culture in this sense has become a value-free concept as opposed to the value-laden Arnoldian concept.

The question of whether this concept of culture is needed seems to be justified, since there are so many other words seemingly describing more or less the same anthropological concept, such as a set of norms, value systems, behavior pattern, rituals and traditions. The organizational psychologist Edgar H. Schein (10–11) correctly answers this question, as described below. He argues that, unlike all the other words mentioned above, the concept of culture adds two relevant critical notions.

First, there is the implication of *structural stability* in a community or group of people. Cultural elements are elements that are not only shared but are also stable and "deep," which means less conscious, less tangible and less visible. Cultural elements also bind together into a coherent whole; they reveal a certain pattern at a deeper, invisible level.

Second, culture denotes the accumulated *shared learning* of a given group, covering behavioral, emotional and cognitive elements of the group members' total psychological functioning. Schein (10) correctly observes: "For shared learning to occur, there must be a history of shared experience, which in turn implies some stability of members in the group."

The implications of the view set out above are that culture is constructive in nature. Culture is not a set of innate or ontological characteristics with a static nature but rather a set containing a great number of actions performed by those who participate in that (sub)culture. These actions are performed on the basis of more or less conventional schemes.

My understanding of culture is influenced by Geert Hofstede's (5) ideas about it. I subscribe to his view because his definition unites three important elements: the decisive value of culture, the importance of cultural relativism and the constructed character of culture.

Hofstede (5) distinguishes two meanings of the word culture. There is culture$_1$, which refers to civilization, a refinement of the mind, which can be found in education, art and literature. This is not a description of culture I would like to refer to. I shall select Hofstede's culture$_2$ which

> deals with much more fundamental human processes than culture one; it deals with the things that hurt. Culture$_2$ is always a collective phenomenon, because it is at least partly

shared with people who live or lived within the same social environment, which is
where it was learned. It is the *collective programming of the mind which distinguishes the members
of one group or category of people from another.* (5, my emphasis).

According to Hofstede, culture is learned, not inherited. It derives from your
social environment, not from your genes. He distinguishes culture from human
nature based on the following reasoning: as a human being you can feel fear,
anger, love, joy, sadness, et cetera. All these feelings are part of human nature.
However, the way in which these feelings are expressed is modified by culture.
Culture is the software of the mind. It is also distinguished from the personality
of an individual. The latter is described as a unique personal set of mental programs an individual does not share with any other human being. Hofstede's description of "personality" is somewhat naive, but his concept of culture is
extremely useful.

An example of this is the Monica Lewinsky scandal in the United States, or
perhaps we should say the Clinton scandal. In many cultures, no wife, children
or even an entire nation wants the husband, father or political leader to engage
in adultery, perjury or bribery. It does not fit the image one constructs of a husband, a father or a president. Even the suspicion of adultery, perjury or bribery
gives rise to the same human feelings of anger, sadness and disgust in many cultures. It would result in the same headlines in the media and in the same criticism from the media in most cultures, since this is the level of human nature:
violation of confidence, a central human value in most cultures. But the way
those feelings of violation of confidence are expressed is culturally bound, is
dependent on "the programming of the mind" in that particular culture.

The programming of the Dutch political mind in this respect would be such
that a Dutch political leader in a similar position to Mr. Clinton would have re-
signed immediately on his or her own initiative, not necessarily out of respect
for the people of the country or for his or her relatives but out of fear of the
Dutch House of Representatives. It would mean the definitive end of a political
career. After a year of silence the fallen Dutch leader would become Chairman
of the Association of Cheese Makers or Tulip Growers and he would be out of
public sight forever. The programming of the Dutch mind is still heavily Calvinist.

The programming of the Japanese political mind is completely different. A
Japanese political leader in similar circumstances would step down immediately
out of shame, since he would think that he had lost face. At the press conference he would bow very deeply, apologize and take all responsibility, even for
things he cannot be held responsible for. Recently, a new phenomenon has
been added to this traditional program: the leader must cry. After a year of silence, the Japanese political leader re-enters politics through the back door of
the Lower House, where he could direct his faction again and significantly influ-

ence Japanese politics as if nothing has happened. The programming of the Japanese mind is heavily based on the Japanese version of Buddhism.

Hofstede has a systemic (*in sensu* Niklas Luhmann) conception of culture. He does not see culture as a vast unspecified domain but rather as an entity consisting of different levels that are interrelated. At the same time, a person always belongs to a number of the following levels, or indicators of identity, for instance: a national level according to one's country; a regional/ethnic/religious/linguistic affiliation; a gender level; a generation level; a social class level; an organizational or corporate level for those who are employed. The implication is that it is impossible to speak about "the" identity of a person or of a group; it may vary according to circumstances.

Hofstede (13) undertook a large-scale intercultural research project that revealed the following five dimensions, on the basis of which cultures can be classified:

1. Social inequality, including the relationship with authority;
2. The relationship between the individual and the group;
3. Concepts of masculinity and femininity; the social implications of having been born as a boy or a girl;
4. Ways of dealing with uncertainty, relating to the control of aggression and the expression of emotions;
5. A long-term orientation in life versus a short-term orientation.

Hofstede's conception of culture has a number of advantages. In his conception, culture is an ever-changing entity—not a static one; culture is learned, not inherited; there are no criteria on the basis of which culture A is "intrinsically" better than culture B (with a few exceptions such as a culture that deliberately and seriously violates human rights); "culture" is a mental construction rather than the innate property of a certain community. This implies that Hofstede's view of culture is more useful with respect to its application in actual research than many other definitions of culture that base themselves on ontological or essentialist conceptions.

What Is Cultural Identity? Just Another Container Concept?

A weak aspect of Hofstede's book, however, is that the very concept of cultural identity is not used. This concept is needed to discuss questions whenever two cultures come into contact with each other or (on an academic level) are compared with each other. A key question, such as "How can the distinctiveness or the specificity of this culture be determined?" is in fact a question concerning the cultural identity of a particular community. The extent, to which a certain culture can be said to have distinctive and common traits, can only be determined on a comparative basis. As the American sociologists Jepperson and Swidler (368) recently stated: "The essential strategy for making the invisible visible is *of course* comparative research. And that is exactly why disciplines which have a comparative basis should take the lead in research in this domain" (my emphasis).

A description of cultural identity is clearly linked to other important concepts such as ethnicity, nation and nation-state. I here take the guidelines given by Adrian Hastings to define those terms. Hastings (3) considers ethnicity to be denotative of a group of people with a shared cultural identity and spoken language. He correctly considers ethnicity to be the major distinctive element in a pre-national society, but ethnicity, he adds, "may survive as a strong subdivision with a loyalty of its own within established nations."

Hastings (3) defines a nation as "a far more self-conscious community than an ethnicity. Formed from one or more ethnicities, and normally identified by a literature of its own, it possesses or claims the right to political identity and autonomy as a people, together with the control of specific territory, comparable to that of biblical Israel and of other independent entities in a world thought of as one of nation-states." This clears the way for a description of a nation-state:

> [A] state which identifies itself in terms of one specific nation whose people are not seen simply as "subjects" of the sovereign but as a horizontally bonded society to whom the state in a sense belongs. There is thus an identity of character between state and people. ...In [the state], ideally, there is basic equivalence between the borders and character of the political unit upon the one hand and a self-conscious cultural community on the other. In most cases this is a dream as much as a reality. Most nation-states in fact include groups of people who do not belong to its core culture or feel themselves to be part of a nation so defined. Nevertheless almost all modern states act on the bland assumption that they are nation-states. (Hastings 3)

Books discussing the cultural identity of a particular nation or nation-state often refer to certain "special features," "characteristics" and "traits" of that nation-state or its people. Often these observations are principally based on impressions, introspections, myths and, last but not least, jokes rather than on factual evidence or empirical research. Obviously, I do not want to deny, for instance, that the thousands of jokes concerning national and cultural stereotypes may highlight particular aspects of the cultural identity of a particular community or nation, but they are just indicators and no more than that.

For instance, consider the following two jokes. The first originated in New York, the second in Tokyo.

> In a New York hotel, American and Japanese engineers meet for the first time and introduce themselves. Obviously the American goes first: "Hello, my name is John, John Smith. Nice to meet you. I am an electrical engineer and—by the way—at the moment

I am working for Kodak." After two minutes of silence the Japanese says: "Hello, I am Toyota and my name is nobody."

This joke may serve as an indicator of the American self-image as individualistic, self-confident and successful. The joke also implicitly constructs an image in which Japanese professionals are not individuals and are neither self-confident nor successful.

Obviously, the Japanese in their turn have a pagoda full of jokes about Americans, such as this one.

An American and Japanese meet each other on a safari trip in Kruger Park. They take a walk together, somewhat outside the safe tourist path. All of a sudden a hungry-looking lion confronts them. The American immediately starts running. But the Japanese does not move and carefully opens his black leather briefcase in order to take out a pair of running shoes. Looking back at the Japanese, the American starts shouting: "Come on, run for your life, leave those running shoes behind; you don't have a chance anyhow to run faster than the lion does." The Japanese thinks, waits a bit and says politely: "The one I have to outrun is not the lion, but you."

This joke may serve as an indicator of the Japanese self-image as smart, civilized and competitive, whereas the American is seen as impulsive, thoughtless and pushy.

These jokes not only demonstrate the well-known fact handed down to us by social psychology that the image of a neighboring people is constructed as a negative counterpart of one's own image, on the basis of which the in-group people can identify themselves more easily with their own self-image (Fink 453), but the jokes should also show that the construction of cultural identity involves at least two parts: the in-group and the out group, the perception of oneself and the perception of the other (*Selbstwahrnehmung* and *Fremdwahrnehmung*). The Japanese looks at the American from a Japanese perspective and vice versa. Here we enter the interesting domain of stereotyping: In our times, therefore, it is of great importance to have an adequate, well-balanced insight into the cultural identity of a particular nation. A distorted view can significantly hamper good understanding and adequate communication with citizens of that nation. Very often political conflicts and wars find their deep origin in distorted visions of one's own and the foreign identity.

In a collection of essays, Ernest Gellner asks that serious attention be paid to cultural identity:

[It] is not a delusion, excogitated by muddled romantics, disseminated by irresponsible extremists, and used by egotistical privileged classes to befuddle the masses, and to hide their true interests from them. Its appeal is rooted in the real conditions of modern life, and cannot be conjured away, either by sheer good will and the preaching of a spirit of universal brotherhood, or by the incarceration of the extremists. We have to understand those roots, and live with their fruits, whether we like them or not. (*Encounters* 45)

Much scholarly research and journalistic writing about cultural identity take as their point of departure well-established stereotypes, which sometimes do not exceed the level of the type of jokes mentioned above. These writings are normally based on an ontological and static belief in the specificity of a certain community: the Afrikaner as a tough racist, the Japanese as the company warrior, the American as the super-individualist, the Englishman as the gentleman, the Italian as the unreliable business partner, et cetera. Stereotypes have a longer and stronger life than one might expect; in many cases they construct a rather one-sided and over-generalized image.

What alternative can we offer that would make it possible to overcome the old essentialist approach to identity and to bypass the new extreme relativism which says that identity escapes every attempt at definition?

In order to understand the roots of cultural identity we need to understand the semantics of this very concept. Here, we don't have to go through the work of Sigmund Freud, George Herbert Mead, Erik Eriksson, Talcott Parsons, Jürgen Habermas and others to come up with a well-grounded description of identity. William Bloom offers an elegant summary of current thinking, concluding that

> identification is an inherent and unconscious behavioural imperative in all individuals. Individuals actively seek to identify in order to achieve psychological security, and they actively seek to maintain, protect and bolster identity in order to maintain and enhance this psychological security which is a *sine qua non* of personality stability and emotional well-being. This imperative works from infancy through adulthood and old age. Moreover, identifications can be shared, with the result that individuals who share the same identification will tend to act in concert in order to protect or enhance their shared identity. (53)

These are words that one can easily agree with, but the problem arises when we try to describe somebody's personal identity or the cultural identity of a particular people. Talking about personal and cultural identity can be tricky, especially if wishful thinking, stereotypes and a strong belief in the overstressed uniqueness of a particular person or country are the only guidelines.

For the concept of cultural identity this implies that the cultural identity of a particular group or people is only partly determined by national identity. Cultural identity is a broader concept than national identity. In this respect I subscribe to E. J. Hobsbawm's view; he emphasizes that belonging to a particular state "is only one way in which people describe their identity among many others which they use for this purpose, as occasion demands" (182). Whether it is justified to conclude on the basis of that argument that the power of nationalism is receding around the globe, as Hobsbawm does, is another matter—it seems to be wishful thinking. The struggle between localization and nationalization on the one hand and globalization on the other is not yet decided. Based on recent political developments in some parts of the world, however, on the wars, fighting and severe ongoing discussions, my forecast would differ from that of Hobsbawm. I shall return to this point in the next section.

Often, cultural identity is seen as a range of characteristics that are unique to a particular culture and "innate" to a specific people. The Japanese scholarly tradition of *Nihonjinron* (Studies about Japaneseness) is a typical example of this approach (for a critical survey see, for example, Dale, Yoshino and Segers, *Sleutelboek*).

But in other cultures, too, many examples of this type of thinking can be found, and in many cases not only practiced long ago. For example, in South Africa the history of the Great Trek is heavily mythologized with the Voortrekker Monument in Pretoria as its grand icon. The Trek is but one episode from the history of the Afrikaners, who were often mythologized as God's chosen people. At his coming to power as prime minister in 1948 the Afrikaner patriot D. F. Malan essentialized this way of thinking when he said: "The last hundred years have witnessed a miracle behind which must lie a divine plan. Indeed, the history of the Afrikaner reveals a will and a determination which makes one feel that Afrikanerdom is not the work of men but the creation of God" (quoted in Sparks 31).

Another view suggests that cultural identity has a structuralist character, where a particular culture is seen as consisting of a set of characteristics that are all interrelated, more or less independently of the people who "produce" that culture.

The alternative for the conception of identity as a set of unique or structural characteristics is the idea of identity as a *construction*. Within such a constructive framework, the cultural identity of a particular nation or of a certain ethnic group within that nation can be attached to three factors: (1) the statistics concerning that nation or group at a given time in history, (2) the programming of the mind within a particular community on the basis of which the cultural identity of the in-group is being constructed, (3) the way in which people from outside conduct a process of selection, interpretation and evaluation concerning the specificity of the in-group; in other words, the outside image of the cultural identity of a foreign nation or group. The relationship between these three elements is a dynamic one. Ideally, the (scholarly) construction of identity should be based on *all three* factors. (For a more extensive explanation see Segers, "Research".)

What are statistics with respect to cultural identity? They are "facts," figures that can be found in statistical handbooks concerning a particular country or ethnic group and which determine to a great extent the programming of the mind of a given society, and vice versa. For instance, they list the total number of citizens of a country, the size of the country, the gross national product, average income, percentage of unemployment, the number of museums, the number of books produced, and so forth.

Since we do not have direct access to the way in which individuals' minds are programmed, we have to resort to visible indicators thereof. We have to look at the style of conduct and communication in a particular community, to use Gellner's (*Nations*, 92) more pragmatically oriented definition of culture. This style of conduct and the communication of the citizens of a state or the members of a particular ethnic group form their visible cultural identity. This visible cultural identity can be suppressed or thematized by opinion leaders (individuals and institutions) within that particular community. It is impossible to talk about cultural identity without taking into consideration which spokespeople are defining it and along which lines this happens.

Obviously, the thematization of a particular identity by opinion leaders within a nation-state does not necessarily imply that this proclaimed identity also exists in the hearts and minds of the people within a nation-state. A campaign does not automatically transform a cultural situation of great diversity that has existed for many generations. For instance, the present campaign of proclaiming a South African product or company "Proudly South African" cannot construct one cultural identity in South Africa, not now and not in the foreseeable future, since the groups within that country have distinctly different historical roots, languages, religions and educations. Institutions such as "national" sports (e.g., soccer, rugby, and cricket) may have better results in the gradual construction of one nation than superimposed, extremely expensive campaigns by the government.

The third element of the identity triangle consists of the constructions made by people, usually opinion leaders or important institutions from outside, concerning the conduct and communication of the people inside.

It would be somewhat misleading to think that the idea of considering national or cultural identity as a construction originated in systems theory (from Ludwig von Bertalanffy to Niklas Luhmann). Scholars working outside this domain have arrived at more or less the same conclusion. An interesting example is Benedict Anderson, who coined the term "imagined community." In an attempt to define the concept of nation, he states: "it is an imagined political community—and imagined as both inherently limited and sovereign. It is *imagined* because the members of even the smallest nation will never know most of their fellow-members, meet them, or even hear of them, yet in the minds of each lives the image of their communion" (15). I am not saying that Anderson's imagination is equivalent to Luhmann's construction. The similarity is to be sought in the emphasis on the mental processing of a particular object.

To consider cultural identity as a construction means that it is a mental conception that may vary according to the constructor, the time and place of construction. This implies that it is impossible to speak about "the" cultural identity of a community. In theory there are as many cultural identities of a given community as there are times, places and people that construct those identities. This should not prevent scholars, however, from the necessary task of describing and systematizing the common characteristics based on those several existing identities. Moreover, in reality we are usually confronted with only one *dominant* construction of the cultural identity of a particular country.

The most recent development concerning the concept of cultural identity has been the addition of the prefix "post" as an attempt to resolve the paradox between globalization and nationalization. The term "post-national identity" was coined by Dewandre and Lenoble. It implies the paradox between the necessity of the construction of one political European identity based on the development of the European Union as against the promotion of the cultural distinctiveness of the several European nations and regions, one political identity versus many distinctive cultural identities, all living under the same roof of a house called "post-national identity." This concept of post-national identity seems rather utopian, prompted by wishful thinking "from Brussels with love." (For more extensive criticism see Picht; for an extensive discussion on European cultural identity see the essays in Segers and Viehoff.)

There is, however, yet another caveat to be considered, one that in particular applies to cross-cultural or comparative studies concerning cultural identity. Richard Handler has formulated the following reasonable objection in this respect: "Identity has become a salient scholarly and cultural construct in mid-twentieth century, particularly in social-scientific scholarship in the United States. Its prominence in that context, however, does not mean that the concept can be applied unthinkingly to other places and times" (27).

Western notions of collective identity are grounded in individualist metaphors. Attributes of boundedness, continuity, uniqueness, and homogeneity that are ascribed to human beings are ascribed to social groups as well. This leads Handler (33) to the following conclusion: "Thus it seems to me that if other cultures imagine personhood and human activity in terms other than those we use, we should not expect them to rely on Western individualistic assumptions in describing social collectivities."

Clifford Geertz (24–25) tells an anecdote that reveals a completely different approach to boundaries and the essence of a community. It concerns the Balinese state, where the rulers did not compete for boundaries (territory) but for the allegiance of men:

The Dutch, who wanted...to get the boundary between two petty princedoms straight once and for all, called in the princes concerned and asked them where indeed the borders lay. Both agreed that the border of princedom A lay at the farthest point from which a man could still see the swamps, and the border of princedom B lay at the point from which a man could still see the sea. Had they, then, never fought over the land between, from which one could see neither swamp nor sea? "Mijnheer," one of the old princes replied, "we had much better reason to fight with one another than these shabby hills."

Cultural Identity under Pressure from Globalization? Concerning the Vitality of the Local

The scholarly focus on cultural identity is confronted with two serious objections. First of all, there is the fear that research into the specificity of a particular culture invokes nationalistic tendencies. Research into cultural identity could reinforce "old-fashioned nationalism," based on the fact that it could result in determining the "unique" characteristics of a certain community or people.

I am not so sure that this objection is justified. The outcome of a research project is strongly dependent on the status of the research methodology employed. If the methodology is based on an ontological understanding of the innate characteristics of a particular culture, the research results will reveal the full colors of this metaphysical basis. However, if the methodology is based on the idea that cultural identity should be defined by the triangle of characteristics explained above, then the danger of stressing the innate uniqueness of a culture is absent. In addition, the fact that we consider cultural identity to be a construction rather than a "given" adds to the rejection of the imminent danger involved.

A second objection that is leveled against the concept of cultural identity concerns the idea that the current globalization tendency in the world will destroy most parts of the specificity of a particular "local" culture. It is the famous adage concerning the big unknown world becoming a small familiar village. From a superficial point of view, the village theory looks good and it has strong advocates, starting with its guru Marshall McLuhan. But let us take a more refined look at the globalization problem.

If we examine the interrelations between cultures now, at the beginning of a new millennium, we can perceive two contradictory but strong tendencies:

> [O]n the one hand, there is the search for cultural authenticity, the return to origins, the need to preserve minor languages, pride in particularisms, admiration for cultural self-sufficiency and maintenance of national traditions; on the other hand, we find the spread of a uniform world culture, the emergence of supranational myths and the adoption of similar lifestyles in widely different settings. Modern technological societies have generated a transnational, composite, mass culture with its own language whose linguistic imprint is already universally evident. (Organisation for Economic Co-operation and Development [OECD], *One School* 16)

This paradox between localization and globalization can be found in many parts of the world and in many different ways. Concerning European unification, for example, Philip Schlesinger (325) aptly described this paradox as follows:

> On the one hand, the difficult search for a transcendent unity by the E[uropean] C[ommunity]—one which must recognise component differences—throws the nation-state into question from above, arguably contributing to crises of national identity. The political and economic developments in the integration process, however, are out of phase with the cultural: what European identity *might be* still remains an open question. On the other hand, the ethno-nationalist awakenings in the former communist bloc and current developments within western Europe—whether neo-nationalist separatisms or racist nationalisms—tend to reaffirm the principle of the nation-state as a locus of identity and of political control.

Schlesinger correctly points a finger at the ultimate paradox of the last decade of the twentieth century: the clash between the indigenous, inner culture of a particular community on the one hand and the global outer culture of a certain constructed *ensemble* of a number of communities. On a programmatic level, this paradox goes under different catchwords and slogans, including localization or nationalization versus globalization, "small is beautiful" versus "big is necessary and inevitable," individual responsibility versus centralist efficiency, and so on. On a pragmatic level, these slogans relate to conflicts at several distinctive levels: between an individual and his or her direct working environment (say, a university department), between a department and a new faculty structure, between the faculty and the development of a new government system, between a national government and the regulations of a supra-national institution.

The paradox between localization and globalization has appeared under a great number of different labels. William Butler Yeats long ago said that our world is caught between the two eternities of race and soul, with race reflecting the tribal past, and soul anticipating the cosmopolitan future.

Closer to the present, Benjamin Barber (21) labeled the two sides of this paradox "Jihad" and "McWorld," respectively.

The Jihad trend, named after the Islamic fundamentalist movement, stands for extreme localization: the Balkanization of nation-states in which culture is pitted against culture, people against people, and tribe against tribe. It is a movement against interdependence, against integrated markets, against modernity and against modern globalizing technological developments.

On the other side, McWorld, according to Barber, paints the future in shimmering pastels, "a busy portrait of onrushing economic, technological and ecological forces that demand integration and uniformity and that mesmerize peoples everywhere with fast music, fast computers, and fast food—MTV, Macintosh and McDonalds—pressing nations into one homogeneous global theme park, one McWorld tied together by communications, information, entertainment, and commerce" (31). Barber notices that the Jihad tendency pursues a bloody politics of identity, while McWorld strives for a bloodless economics of profit.

With regard to the latter movement (McWorld), Barber sums up in a black observation:

> Music, video, theatre, books and theme parks—the new churches of a commercial civilisation in which malls are the public squares and suburbs the neighbourless neighbourhoods—are all constructed as image exports creating a common world taste around common logos, advertising slogans, stars, songs, brand names, jingles and trade marks. Hard power yields to soft, while ideology is transmuted into a kind of videology that works through sound bites and film clips. Videology is fuzzier and less dogmatic than traditional political ideology; it may as a consequence be far more successful in instilling the novel values required for global markets to succeed. (25)

It is clear that Barber holds an extremely negative view of a future in which localization and globalization will go hand in hand and reinforce each other constantly. But is it all that dark? Need it be all that pessimistic? Let us first consider what is really understood by globalization, this fashionable container concept.

Arjun Appadurai (6–7) has suggested that globalization consists of five dimensions, five cultural flows that cross each other at various levels in many parts of the world:

> Firstly, there are *ethnoscapes* produced by flows of people: tourists, immigrants, refugees, exiles and guestworkers. Secondly, there are *technoscapes*, the machinery and plant flows produced by multinational and national corporations and government agencies. Thirdly, there are *finanscapes*, produced by the rapid flows of money in the currency stock exchanges. Fourthly, there are *mediascapes*, the repertoires of images and information, the flows which are produced and distributed by newspapers, magazines, television and film. Fifthly, there are *ideoscapes*, linked to flows of images which are associated with state or counterstate movement ideologies which are comprised of elements of the Western Enlightenment world-view—images of democracy, freedom, welfare, rights, etc.

It is tempting to speculate on the question: What will be the strongest force in the near future: localization or globalization, Jihad or McWorld? Obviously, the question is too complex to be answered in a few pages. In any case, both tendencies, with their completely opposite aims, exist in the same place and at the same time. It is difficult, however, as has been tried in a number of publications, to come up with convincing arguments implying that the globalization tendency will be a much stronger force than the localization tendency in the near future.

The well-known Japanese economist and consultant Kenichi Ohmae could be mentioned as a representative of the globalization movement. His recent book *The End of the Nation State: The Rise of Regional Economies* became a "global" academic best seller. In this book Ohmae advocates the theory that nation-states have already lost their role as meaningful participants in the global economy of today's borderless world. What are the arguments for his theory? He comes up with four reasons, which I shall give in his own words:

> First of all, the uncomfortable truth is that, in terms of the global economy, nation states have become little more than bit actors. They may originally have been, in their mercantilist phase, independent, powerfully efficient engines of wealth creation. More recently, however, as the downward-ratcheting logic of electoral politics has placed a death grip on their economies, they have become—first and foremost—remarkably inefficient engines of wealth distribution.
>
> Secondly, and more to the point, the nation state is increasingly a nostalgic fiction. It makes even less sense today, for example, than it did a few years ago to speak of Italy or Russia or China as a single economic unit. Each is a motley combination of territories with vastly different needs and vastly different abilities to contribute.
>
> Third, when you look closely at the goods and services now produced and traded around the world, as well as the companies responsible for them, it is no easy matter to attach to them an accurate national label. Is an automobile sold under an American marque really a U.S. product when a large percentage of its components comes from abroad?
>
> Finally, when economic activity aggressively wears a national label these days, that tag is usually present neither for the sake of accuracy nor out of concern for the economic well-being of individual consumers. It is there primarily as a mini-flag of cheap nationalism—that is, as a jingoistic celebration of nationhood that places far more value on emotion-grabbing symbols than on real, concrete improvements in quality of life. (207–8)

Another example frequently used to prove the supremacy of globalization is what has come to be called "Americanization." Many scholars and journalists go so far as to suggest that those two concepts are synonymous. The term "Americanization" means the spreading of American culture (or what is regarded as such) into all corners of the world: Hollywood films, American TV soaps, American bestsellers, American cars, Americanized food, and so forth.

There are two main problems with substituting globalization with Americanization. First of all, one could question the extent to which the elements just mentioned really are representative of the culture of the United States. It is altogether possible that in constructing these art forms, parts of the value system and some of the artistic norms of the so-called non-American global periphery were seriously involved. As far as I know, no serious research has yet tackled this or similarly structured questions.

Second, it should be stated that the reception of these so-called American cultural products might be different according to the specificity of the receiving culture. Important conventions that make up that specificity structure the direction and the depth of Americanization. I would venture the hypothesis that Americanization has been carried out differently in South Africa than in the Europe or in Asia.

Ralf Dahrendorf may be introduced as a representative of the localization theory. After his fine analysis of the future of the nation-state, he remarks:

> Auf absehbare Zeit wird der Nationalstaat der Rahmen individueller Rechte und die Aktionseinheit der internationalen Beziehungen bleiben. Das gilt auch in und für Europa. Der Nationalstaat wird hier und da angenagt und angekratzt, bleibt aber in seinem Kern durch neuere Entwicklungen unberührt. Er ist auch der Raum, in dem Menschen Zugehörigkeitsgefühle empfinden können. Einstweilen haben wir noch nichts besseres erfunden als den heterogenen Nationalstaat. (760)

> In the near future the nation-state will function as the background for individual rights and as the actor for international relations. That is also true in and for Europe. The nation-state is somewhat threatened and somewhat damaged in some places, but essentially it is not touched by recent developments. The nation-state is also the space within which people can experience feelings of belonging. So far we have not invented something better than the heterogeneous nation-state. (My translation.)

To phrase this in other well-known German words: "Europa ist ein Kopfgeburt und die Regionen sprechen das Herz an." (Europe is just a mental construction, but it is the regions which are close to the heart.)

Thus, localization and globalization are two sides of the same coin. On the one hand we can observe that "nationalism is back today with a vengeance all over the world" (Radhakrishnan 83), from Canada to India, from the former USSR to Iraq, from Japan to South Africa. For the time being, I am one of those who believe that nationalization or localization will dominate globalization, at least for the foreseeable future, and not only outside western Europe as some critics want us to believe, but also to a considerable extent in the countries that belong to the key group members of the European Union. In this context Helmut Dubiel (896) points out new forms of German nationalism, but similar tendencies are alive and well in many other countries of the European Union.

On the other hand, we can see the severe impact of the five cultural flows of globalization (the flows of people, technology, finances, media and ideas). Globalization will persist as an extremely strong tendency and its strength may even increase. But in the decades to come the nationalization tendency will be able to adopt and adapt many global trends. Globalization will be nationalized to a great extent.

Let me add here that the threat to the nation, to nationalization or localization, does not primarily consists of globalization tendencies, but rather the threat comes also from within the nation itself. We could think here of the splitting-up of rather well-established nation-states, such as Canada, Belgium, Spain, or of former countries such as the USSR, Czechoslovakia and Yugoslavia. In a way, we could add paradoxically the unification of Germany, where the following joke could be heard shortly after the unification: an East German says to a West German: "We are one people now!" The West German replies: "We too!"

Understanding the complicated paradox contained within localization versus globalization is an object that is highly interesting and rewarding for a number of scholarly disciplines. Understanding this paradox, however, can only be achieved through the central concept of cultural identity. This very concept represents the ultimate reason for the serious conflicts between the smaller community and the larger constructed *ensemble,* or between two or more smaller communities.

When applying the concept of cultural identity, another fallacy should be deconstructed, namely, that of the old opposition between the West and "the rest." This opposition is in many cases the hidden, invisible basis upon which many theories are being based. This fallacy of cultural imperialism considers—consciously or not—the West (which often just means the United States) to be the center and "the rest" to be the periphery. Localizing movements are performed in the periphery; globalizing trends are realized in the center, such as the new economy and successful and appealing TV programs.

In order to avoid cultural imperialism, a more realistic model of regions should replace the simplistic center-periphery oppositional geography. Sinclair, Jacka and Cunningham (301) present a more realistic scenario—that of creolization.

Instead of the image of "the West" at the center dominating the peripheral "Third World" with an outward flow of cultural products, we see the world as divided into a number of regions, each of which have their own internal dynamics as well as their global ties. Although primarily based on geographic realities, these regions are also defined by common cultural, linguistic, and historical connections that transcend physical space. Such a dynamic, regionalist view of the world helps us to analyze in a more nuanced way the intricate and multidirectional flows of television across the globe.

By emphasizing the importance of the regionalist point of view questions concerning postcolonialism could also be dealt with in a more adequate way. Postcolonial identity consists in many cases of two opposite tendencies: identification with as well as separation from colonial conventions and institutions. This can be seen, for instance, in South Africa, where a number of "colonial" institutions (such as the parliamentary, judicial and educational system) are maintained, but where at the same time strong opposition exists against the mental programming of those who were in power within those institutions during the apartheid era. When a regionalist point of view is chosen, then such a situation is not seen as a contradiction, a mistake or on the contrary as a positive development but is just described as a situation of postcolonial identity with similar developments in the region in which—in this case—South Africa is situated. Obviously, postcolonial identity may result in very different socio-political contexts: from the Zimbabwe reverse-apartheid hardliners to the Proudly South African approach.

We could now ask why there is this focus on culture and cultural identity. In a moment of unsophisticated generalization, one could say that half the Library of Congress consists of books that more or less deal with this very topic. But there are at least two reasons that make it necessary to concentrate systematically on these topics and to reinterpret them according to ever-changing social circumstances.

The scholarly reason is, as we have seen, that "culture" is still too often conceived of as an ontological concept, which leads directly to unjustified claims of superiority, dominance and ultimately atrocious wars. These wars and other evil developments immediately lose their *raison d'être* and their justification if culture is seen within a systemic and constructivist context.

The second reason is based on the socio-political relevance of the concept of culture around the turn of the millennium. A recent book by Samuel P. Huntington, an academic bestseller in the United States since September 11, 2001, convincingly argues for the central role that cultures play now and will play in the upcoming decades. His general thesis is that the communist world collapsed in the late 1980s, which meant the end of the Cold War, the end of a world divided by ideological, political and/or economic principles.

Obviously, the end of the Cold War does not mean either eternal or temporary peace, as some utopian voices said right after the fall of the Iron Curtain in 1989. Another distinction quickly arose: the cultural distinction. This implies "that culture and cultural identities, which at the broadest level are civilizational identities, are shaping the patterns of cohesion, disintegration, and conflict in the post-Cold War world. ...The most important groupings of states are no longer the three blocs of the Cold War but rather the world's...major civilizations" (Huntington 20–21).

Huntington distinguishes nine different cultures: Western, Latin American, African, Islamic, Sinic, Hindu, Orthodox, Buddhist and Japanese. We can, of course, disagree with Huntington about the number of civilizations he distinguishes or about his definition of each civilization. This boils down to questions such as why Japan is recognized as a distinct civilization and Korea is not? Is it justifiable to define "African civilization" as sub-Saharan including the country of South Africa? Regarding this question, Huntington sums up some of the problems himself:

> The north of the African continent and its east coast belong to Islamic civilization. Historically, Ethiopia constituted a civilization of its own. Elsewhere European imperialism and settlements brought elements of Western civilization. In South Africa Dutch, French, and then English settlers created a multifragmented European culture. Most significantly, European imperialism brought Christianity to most of the continent south

of the Sahara. Throughout Africa tribal identities are pervasive and intense, but Africans are also increasingly developing a sense of African identity, and conceivably sub-Saharan Africa could cohere into a distinct civilisation, with South Africa possibly being its core state. (47)

Whatever the justification for the number and specificity of the several civilizations may be, the message is clear: the most important distinctions between peoples are no longer ideological, political or economic but cultural. To quote Huntington once more: "In this new world the most pervasive, important, and dangerous conflicts will not be between social classes, rich and poor, or other economically defined groups, but between peoples belonging to different cultural entities" (28). And Vaclav Havel stated along the same lines: "Cultural conflicts are increasing and are more dangerous today than at any time in history."

Conclusion: The Cultural Turn

Looking at the contemporary world, be it a region, a nation-state or an ethnic group within that nation, implies looking at a complicated wrestling game between globalization and localization. In order to understand the fact that in many cases localization will be the winner, we should pay attention to a neglected force: the importance of the cultural factor which is like a home crowd, always in favor of the local wrestler. Whereas the globalization tendency is a force that is mainly driven by technological and economic flows in one form or another, the localization tendency is based on cultural identity. In many cultures globalizing tendencies are being localized to a certain degree, as we have seen above. To what extent? That depends on the strength of a particular cultural identity.

The fact that cultural identity is the decisive factor in constructing the specificity of a certain society could be called the "Cultural Turn." This means, among other things, that contemporary political and social developments, and also economic and technological developments, whether they have a global or rather a local nature, can only be understood via the concept of cultural identity as it has been defined above. Without an interest in and an understanding of the major differences and the striking similarities between cultures, no adequate construction can be made of modern civilizations or of groups of people within those civilizations.

In most parts of today's world, cultural borders no longer coincide with national borders; cultural diversity within one nation-state is more the rule than the exception. To give just one example, until the late 1960s, the Netherlands was a state with hardly any ethnic diversity, a rather homogeneous state despite its international history, like many others in western Europe at that time. Yet on January 1, 1991, the four largest cities in the country (Amsterdam, Rotterdam, The Hague and Utrecht) had a total population of almost two million. Of those two million people, more than 400,000 (21%) were people of non-Dutch descent (mainly Turks, Moroccans and people of Surinam and Netherlands Antilles ethnic origins) (OECD, *Trends* 71).

All over the world, a growing number of very serious political and ethnic conflicts have arisen, originating in an imbalance in the relationships among the three cultural factors in the triangle explained above. The nature of this imbalance may vary from place to place: it may be a wrong, one-sided selection of the material statistics, an inadequate and too strong self-image or a distorted look at the foreign partner. The nature of the imbalance may be different, but the result is always the same: cultural relativism gives way to cultural absolutism.

It goes without saying that the current political situation in many parts of the world implies that the study of culture and of cultural identity has become an important item for scholarship. Issues related to culture and cultural identity seem to be and will stay *the* issues of the coming decades of the new millennium. The "cultural turn" will continue to bare its teeth. In one of its many reports now more than fifteen years ago, the OECD (*Education* 43) wrote:

> Awareness of an ethnic or regional identity, or of a minority status, can be hidden for many decades by the myth of national unity and identity, of ethnic homogeneity, of mass culture or planetary culture. It can also be hidden by an analysis in terms of social groups or the evocation of proletarian internationalism. Today, ethnic or racial claims, nationalist or regionalist movements, and movements for independence or autonomy, have broken up communities which were merely a facade.

This process of breaking up seemingly homogeneous communities and the consequent struggle for identity will undoubtedly continue for a number of years in many parts of the world. To study this process from a cultural point of view offers as many challenges as possibilities for cultural studies in the years to come.

I have been trying to demonstrate in this chapter that the "English" in the following English nursery rhyme can be substituted by any other nation or any ethnic group living in a particular nation:

> The Germans live in Germany, the Romans live in Rome,
> The Turkeys live in Turkey; but the English live at home.

As Hofstede (235) observed:

> Everybody looks at the world from behind the windows of a cultural home and everybody prefers to act as if people from other countries have something special about them (a national character) but home is normal. Unfortunately, there is no normal position in cultural matters. This is an uncomfortable message, as uncomfortable as Galileo Galilei's claim in the seventeenth century that the Earth is not the centre of the Universe.

To conclude with a variation on Hobsbawm (183), the owl of Minerva that brings wisdom flies out at dusk. It is a good sign that it is now circling around cultural identity.

Works Cited

Anderson, Benedict. *Imagined Communities: Reflections on the Origin and Spread of Nationalism*. London: Verso, 1983.

Appadurai, Arjun. "Disjuncture and Difference in the Global Cultural Economy." *Culture, Nationalism, Globalization and Modernity*. Ed. Mike Featherstone, London: Sage, 1990. 295–310.

Barber, Benjamin. "Jihad vs. McWorld." *The Globalization Reader*. Eds. Frank J. Lechner and John Boli. Malden, Mass. and Oxford, UK: Blackwell, 2000. 21–26.

Bloom, William. *Personal Identity, National Identity and International Relations*. Cambridge, UK: Cambridge UP, 1990.

Dahrendorf, Ralf. "Die Zukunft des Nationalstaates." [The Future of the Nation-state.] *Merkur. Zeitschrift für Europäisches Denken* 48.9/10 (1994): 751–761.

Dale, Peter. *The Myth of Japanese Uniqueness*. London: Croom Helm, 1986.

Dewandre, Nicole, and Jacques Lenoble, eds. *Projekt Europa: Postnationale Identität: Grundlage für eine europäische Demokratie?* [Project Europe: Postnational Identity: Basis for a European Democracy.] Berlin: Schelzky and Jeep, 1994.

Dubiel, Helmut. "Über moralische Souveränität, Erinnerung und Nation." [On Moral Sovereignty, Memory and Nation.] *Merkur. Deutsche Zeitschrift für Europäisches Denken* 48.9/10 (1994): 884–897.

Fink, Gonthier-Louis. "Das Bild des Nachbarvolkes im Spiegel der deutschen und der französischen Hochaufklärung (1750–1789)." [The Image of a Neighboring People in the Mirror of German and French Enlightenment (1750–1789).] *Nationale und kulturelle Identität: Studien zur Entwicklung des kollektiven Bewusstseins in der Neuzeit*. Ed. Bernhard Giesen. Frankfurt: Suhrkamp, 1991. 453–492.

Geertz, Clifford. *Negara: The Theatre State in Nineteenth-Century Bali*. Princeton: Princeton UP, 1980.

Gellner, Ernest. *Nations and Nationalism*. Oxford, UK: Blackwell, 1983.

——. *Encounters with Nationalism*. Oxford, UK: Blackwell, 1994.

Giesen, Bernhard. *Nationale und kulturelle Identität: Studien zur Entwicklung des kollektiven Bewusstseins in der Neuzeit*. Frankfurt: Suhrkamp, 1991.

Handler, Richard. "Is 'Identity' a Useful Cross-Cultural Concept?" *Commemorations: The Politics of National Identity*. Ed. John R. Gillis. Princeton: Princeton UP, 1994. 27–40.

Hastings, Adrian. *The Construction of Nationhood: Ethnicity, Religion and Nationalism*. Cambridge, UK: Cambridge UP, 1997.

Havel, Vaclav. "The New Measure of Man." *New York Times*, 8 July 1994.

Hobsbawm, E. J. *Nations and Nationalism since 1780: Programme, Myth, Reality*. Cambridge, UK: Cambridge UP, 1990.

Hofstede, Geert. *Cultures and Organizations*. Hammersmith, London: HarperCollins, 1994. (Originally published in 1991)

Huntington, Samuel P. *The Clash of Civilizations and the Remaking of World Order*. New York: Touchstone, 1997

Hutchinson, John, and Anthony D. Smith, eds. *Nationalism*. New York: Oxford University Press, 1994.

Jepperson, Ronald L., and Ann Swidler. "What Properties of Culture Should We Measure?" *Poetics* 22 (1994): 359–371.

Lechner, Frank J., and John Boli, eds. *The Globalization Reader*. Malden, Mass. and Oxford, UK: Blackwell, 2000.

Luhmann, Niklas. *Soziale Systeme: Grundriss einer allgemeinen Theorie*. [Social Systems: Basics of a General Theory.] Frankfurt: Suhrkamp, 1988.

Ohmae, Kenichi. *The End of the Nation State: The Rise of Regional Economies*. New York: Free Press, 1995.

Organisation for Economic Co-operation and Development (OECD). *Multicultural Education*. Paris: Organisation for Economic Co-operation and Development, Centre for Educational Research and Innovation, 1987.

————. *One School, Many Cultures*. Paris: Organisation for Economic Co-operation and Development, Centre for Educational Research and Innovation, 1989.

————. *Trends in International Migration*. Paris: Organisation for Economic Co-operation and Development, Centre for Educational Research and Innovation, 1992.

Parker, Andrew, Mary Ruso, Doris Sommer, and Patricia Yaeger. *Nationalisms and Sexualities*. New York and London: Routledge, 1992.

Picht, Robert. "Europa—aber was versteht man darunter? Aufforderung zur Überprüfung der Denkmuster." [Europe—But What Is Meant by That Concept? An Invitation to Check Paradigms of Thinking.] *Merkur. Deutsche Zeitschrift für europäisches Denken* 48.9/10 (1994): 850–866.

Radhakrishnan, R. "Nationalism, Gender, and the Narrative of Identity." *Nationalisms and Sexualities*. Eds. Andrew Parker, Mary Ruso, Doris Sommer and Patricia Yaeger. New York and London: Routledge, 1992. 77–95.

Rusch, Gebhard. "Zur Systemtheorie und Phänomenologie von Literatur. Eine holistische Perspektive." [Systems Theory and Phenomenology of Literature: A Holistic Perspective.] *SPIEL. Siegener Periodikum zur Internationalen Empirischen Literaturwissenschaft* 10 (1991): 305–339.

Schein, Edgar H. *Organizational Culture and Leadership*. San Francisco: Jossey-Bass, 1992.

Schlesinger, Philip. "Europeanness: A New Cultural Battlefield?" *Nationalism*. Eds. John Hutchinson and Anthony D. Smith. New York: Oxford UP, 1994. 316–325.

Segers, Rien T. "Research into Cultural Identity: A New Empirical Object. The Case of Japanese 'Uniqueness' Between East and West." *SPIEL. Siegener Periodikum zur Internationalen Empirischen Literaturwissenschaft* 11 (1992): 149–162.

————. *Sleutelboek Japan*. Amsterdam: Balans, 1996.

————& Reinhold Viehoff, eds. *Kultur Identität Europa: Über die Schwierigkeiten und Möglichkeiten einer Konstruktion*. [Culture, Identity Europe: Difficulties and Possibilities of a Construction.] Frankfurt: Suhrkamp, 1999.

Sevänen, Erkki. "Art as an Autopoietic Sub-System of Modern Society." *Theory, Culture & Society* 18.1 (2001): 75–103.

Sinclair, John, Elizabeth Jacka, and Stuart Cunningham. "Peripheral Vision." *The Globalization Reader*. Eds. Frank J. Lechner and John Boli. Malden, Mass. and Oxford, UK: Blackwell, 2000. 301–306.

Soyinka, Wole. "Culture, Democracy and Renewal." *1999 World Bank/International Monetary Fund Seminars*. 27 Mar. 2003. <http://www.worldbank.org/html/extdr/pos99/wssp092799.htm>

Sparks, Allister. *The Mind of South Africa: The Story of the Rise and Fall of Apartheid*. London: Mandarin, 1991.

Tötösy de Zepetnek, Steven. "Systemic Approaches to Literature: An Introduction with Selected Bibliographies." *Canadian Review of Comparative Literature/Revue Canadienne de Littérature Comparée* 19 (1992): 21–93.

Yoshino, Kosaku. *Cultural Nationalism in Contemporary Japan: A Sociological Enquiry*. London and New York: Routledge, 1992.

Notes on Contributors

Willie Burger is professor of literature and chair of the Afrikaans Department at the Rand Afrikaans University, Johannesburg. He completed his Ph.D. on postmodernist fiction in 1995. He has published articles on various topics and has co-edited the standard work on South African writer Karel Schoeman, *Sluiswagter by die dam van stemme* (Sluice-Keeper at the Dam of Voices) (2002).

Annette L. Combrink is dean of arts at the Potchefstroom University for Christian Higher Education. For her D.Litt. at the same university, she did a study of British comedy in the 1970s, focusing on a number of plays by Harold Pinter. She has published on South African drama and on translation studies and is very active in community work.

Marianne Dircksen obtained her D.Litt. et Phil. at the Rand Afrikaans University in 1996 with a narratological analysis of Tacitus' *Historiae I*. She is currently head of Latin and Ancient Culture in the School of Languages at the Potchefstroom University for Christian Higher Education. She is the author of five articles on questions of mythology in accredited journals.

Heilna du Plooy received a D.Litt. from the Potchefstroom University for Christian Higher Education in 1985. Her thesis was an overview of the development of narrative theory in the twentieth century and was published in 1986. She has published widely in accredited academic journals and in books (which includes nine international publications). She has also published two books of poetry. At present she is professor and chair of Afrikaans and Dutch at the Potchefstroom University for Christian Higher Education.

Minnie Lewis is a Ph.D. student in Afrikaans and Netherlandic Studies at the University of Cape Town, working on the in-between space of "colored" writers in Afrikaans. She is employed part-time as a researcher at the Centre for Socio-Legal Research of the University of Cape Town. Her M.A. dissertation was on the work of the Afrikaans writer Elise Muller.

Rien T. Segers is professor of Organizational Culture at the University of Groningen in the Netherlands. He is also director of the Center for Contemporary Japanese Studies at the same university. He did his graduate work at Yale University and received his Ph.D. from the University of Utrecht. He is well known for his publications on comparative literature and on reception studies. Recently, he has been working on cultural identity, on which he has published a number of articles in addition to the book *Europa, Kultur, Identität* (with R. Viehoff) (1999). He also published a Dutch introduction to contemporary Japanese culture, *Sleutelboek Japan*. He was a visiting professor at several universities abroad—in South Africa at the universities of Cape Town, Potchefstroom and Pretoria.

Chris N. van der Merwe is associate professor of Afrikaans and Dutch Literature at the University of Cape Town and a well-known Afrikaans literary critic. He passed his doctoral examination cum laude at the University of Utrecht (Netherlands) and obtained his Ph.D. at the Rand Afrikaans University (Johannesburg) with a dissertation on the Flemish poet and playwright Hugo Claus. He has published widely on Afrikaans literature. Noteworthy in particular are *Breaking Barriers: Stereotypes and the Changing of Values in Afrikaans Writing, 1875–1990 (1994)* and *Strangely Familiar: South African Narratives on Town and Countryside (2001)*, which he edited.

Hein Viljoen is professor of Afrikaans and Dutch literature at the Potchefstroom University for Christian Higher Education. He received his D.Litt. from the same university in 1985 on a comparative study of three South African novels using a systems approach. He has published widely on Afrikaans literature and literary theory since then. His previous publications include a joint volume on methodology and representation and an Afrikaans introduction to literary theory (with Chris N. van der Merwe), entitled *Alkant olifant* (1998). He also writes poetry.

Louise Viljoen received her D.Litt. at the University of Stellenbosch in 1988 with a thesis on Breyten Breytenbach's poetry. She is currently professor in the department of Afrikaans and Dutch at the University of Stellenbosch. She compiled (with Ronel Foster) an anthology of Afrikaans poetry written after 1960, *Poskaarte: Beelde van die Afrikaanse poësie sedert 1960 (1997)*. She works in the field of Afrikaans literature and literary theory with a special focus on postcolonialism, gender as well as space and identity.

Marita Wenzel received her Ph.D. in English literature from the Potchefstroom University for Christian Higher Education in 1995. At present, she is associate professor of English at the same university. Her main field of interest relates to comparative literature in postcolonial, feminist and translation studies. She has already published eleven articles on these topics with particular focus on Latin American and South African novels.